W9-CXT-201

DAVID HUME

DAVID HUME

Prophet of the Counter-revolution

by

Laurence L. Bongie

CLARENDON PRESS · OXFORD
1965

Oxford University Press, Amen House, London E.C.4

GLASGOW NEW YORK TORONTO MELBOURNE WELLINGTON
BOMBAY CALCUTTA MADRAS KARACHI LAHORE DACCA
CAPE TOWN SALISBURY NAIROBI IBADAN ACCRA
KUALA LUMPUR HONG KONG

Printed in Great Britain by
The Camelot Press Ltd., London and Southampton

CONTENTS

ACKNOWLEDGEMENTS vi

INTRODUCTION vii

I. BEFORE 1789

1. Royal panegyrics 1
2. The science and art of English history 2
3. Jehovah among the Hebrews 8
4. Papist or Pyrrhonian? 13
5. The Scottish Bossuet 30
6. Debate with Turgot 47
7. Early hostility: Mirabeau, Mably and Brissot 52
8. Defence and defiance 56
9. Anticipating the storm 64

II. THE REVOLUTION AND THE RÔLE OF HISTORY

1. History as a weapon of counter-revolution 68
2. History as the superstition of slaves 80

III. FROM 1789 TO THE TRIAL OF LOUIS XVI

1. Prophetic parallels and the counter-revolutionary lessons of Hume 88
2. The Long Parliament: Brissot versus Clermont-Tonnerre 105
3. A Republican antidote: Catherine Macaulay-Graham 113

IV. THE TRIAL OF 'LE STUART FRANÇAIS'

1. Louis XVI and Charles I: a condemned king's meditations 120
2. David Hume and Stuart history for the defence 126
3. Cromwell in the Convention: the judgement of posterity 133
4. The parallel rejected: Brutus to the rescue 140
5. Principles versus precedents 145

V. THE AFTERMATH

1. Republican qualms 151
2. Waiting for General Monk 158
3. Conclusion 167

INDEX OF NAMES AND TITLES 173

ACKNOWLEDGEMENTS

MY THANKS are due: to the late Daniel Mornet for graciously allowing me, some fifteen years ago, to intrude upon the quiet of his Sunday mornings with various problems of pre-revolutionary bibliography; to Professor Charles Dédéyan of the University of Paris who offered much help and encouragement during the early stages of my research; to several of my colleagues at the University of British Columbia who have read my work in typescript or in proofs; and not least to my wife who performed several times over the wearisome tasks of typing, reading proofs, and preparing the index.

Lastly, I must record my very special indebtedness to the Canada Council and to the University of British Columbia whose help in the form of a Senior Research Fellowship and a year of study leave made the completion of this work possible.

Vancouver
May 1965

L. L. B.

INTRODUCTION

I

DAVID HUME was undoubtedly the eighteenth-century British writer whose works were most widely known and acclaimed on the continent during the later Enlightenment period. Two fairly recent doctoral theses[1] have given ample proof of the great reputation he acquired in France as an historian and philosopher at this time. Contrary to various expectations, however, evidence of a profound influence as opposed to the mere reputation of his purely philosophical writings has proved to be disappointingly meagre. Occasionally even, Hume's most telling impact in this respect appears, not in the works of his brother *philosophes*, who largely misunderstood or wilfully ignored his highly original epistemological doctrine, but—usually through the device of *rétorsion*—in the writings of their greatest enemies, the religious traditionalists.[2]

Less surprising, perhaps, is the fact that these same traditionalists in formulating their political principles found it possible to profit to an even greater extent from Hume's historical writings. His unrivalled history of the Stuarts had not only enjoyed spectacular success in eighteenth-century France; it had related as well what many viewed as the most significant, or at least the most horrifying, series of political events in the annals of modern Europe, namely the seventeenth-century English revolution. The particular manner in which Hume had narrated the hapless career of Charles I and had presented the short-lived English republican experiment was to seem to many French conservatives, both before and after 1789, of great practical applicability in their defence of the *ancien régime*. It will be seen, I think, that Hume's impact here was of undeniable importance, greater even for a time than the related influence of Burke, although it represents a contribution to French counter-revolutionary thought which, unlike that

[1] My own, 'Hume en France au dix-huitième siècle', University of Paris, 1952, and Paul H. Meyer's 'Hume in Eighteenth-Century France', Columbia University, 1954.

[2] See my 'Hume "Philosophe" and Philosopher in Eighteenth-Century France', *French Studies*, 1961, XV. 213–27.

of Burke, has been almost totally ignored by historians to this day.

It is perhaps necessary to indicate at this point certain limitations which I have felt it wise to impose on this study. I have attempted—admittedly not always with complete success—to disregard the question of Hume's 'true' intentions or the real nature of his political thought. Such considerations, however important they may be in themselves, seem largely irrelevant to an investigation of the kind I have undertaken. Similarly, I have not tried to make any general assessment of the merits of David Hume as an historian.[1] Whether Hume interpreted well or badly the events of Stuart history, whether he was more of a Tory than Burke was a Whig, is of little consequence to my purpose. My chief concern has not been with what really happened in England between 1603 and 1660 nor even primarily with what Hume really said about the Great Rebellion although, with regard to this last point, I have provided in the second part of my introduction a brief survey of his general views concerning the activities of that period. I have done this because Hume's *History* is neither widely read nor readily available today. My hope is that even so cursory an account of it will prove to be, for the general reader, preferable to none at all.

What has been my major concern in the present study is rather the manner in which the French, from the *ancien régime* to the counter-revolutionary period, interpreted Hume's very popular history of those crucial English events. That the French *misinterpreted* the Scottish historian in many instances is, of course, entirely possible, but I have not insisted on this point. Influence thrives on illusion as easily as on truth. It is the image—whether faithful or distorted—that transmits influence. It will be seen that Hume's version of English history projected at first against the background of pre-revolutionary politics a number of blurred and even contradictory images. Later, however, the continental focus

[1] A short critical bibliography of some important works on this subject may be found in a note at the beginning of E. C. Mossner's comprehensive article 'An Apology for David Hume, Historian', *PMLA* September 1941, LVI. 657–90. See also the extensive study by Giuseppe Giarizzo, *David Hume politico e storico,* Turin, 1962, and the brief but illuminating remarks in Hugh Trevor-Roper's essay 'David Hume as a Historian', *The Listener*, December 1961. In general, I have throughout this work relinquished the use of secondary source materials, since it would seem especially important in a study of image and influence to allow the original documents to speak as much as possible for themselves. Spelling in the quotations has been standardized.

of interpretation sharpened acutely as the urgency of contemporary events compelled the Scottish historian's various French readers to unify more militantly their political views.

II

When, in his *History of the Stuarts*, Hume came to consider the scholarly merits of his predecessor Clarendon, he gave expression to a sentiment which he might easily have allowed, I think, to be quite properly applied to himself. The 'entertaining' Clarendon in his most 'candid' history of the Great Rebellion is, Hume tells us, 'more partial in appearance than in reality'; for though he seems perpetually anxious to apologize for the King, his apologies 'are often well grounded'.[1]

In the seventeen-fifties when Hume composed his *History of the Stuarts* it was clearly neither fashionable nor profitable to apologize for King Charles. The whig party, Hume tells us, had, for a course of nearly seventy years, enjoyed the whole authority of government. In some particulars the state had not suffered as a result. But history, certainly, had suffered and truth had suffered. The biased writings of such apologists as Rapin-Thoyras, Locke and Sidney were praised and propagated as if they equalled the most celebrated compositions of antiquity. 'And forgetting', Hume complains, 'that a regard to liberty, though a laudable passion, ought commonly to be subordinate to a reverence for established government, the prevailing faction has celebrated only the partisans of the former, who pursued as their object the perfection of civil society, and has extolled them at the expense of their antagonists, who maintained those maxims that are essential to its very existence' (IX. 524). Liberty is a good and noble principle but it has its dangers and if one has to choose, it is surely much better for human society 'to be deprived of liberty than to be destitute of government' (VII. 125–6). Hume also observes that extremes of all kinds in these matters are to be avoided; truth and certainty are most likely to be met with on middle ground. There is little doubt that Hume hoped his own history would be seen as brilliantly impartial. In fact, he may even have believed that he would, by some miracle, please all factions with his 'moderate opinions'.

[1] David Hume, *The History of England*, London, 1808–10, VIII. 414. Further references in this section to *The History of England* will be placed within parentheses in the text itself.

As he set about his attack on the fortress of whig dogma, Hume made persistent, almost obsessive use of one favourite weapon: his contrary—and many thought, perverse—view of what the English constitution was like before the accession of the Stuart kings. The partisans of liberty were in the habit of affirming that the English constitution, long before the settlement of 1688, was 'a regular plan of liberty'. They heaped abuse on James I and Charles I as usurpers and innovators in the hated arts of despotism. But what a paradox in human affairs it is, Hume objected, that Henry VIII should have been almost adored in his lifetime, and his memory be respected, 'while Charles I should, by the same people, at no greater distance than a century, have been led to a public and ignominious execution, and his name be ever after pursued by falsehood and by obloquy!' (X. 205, note F to vol. VIII). Hume found a similar paradox in whig estimates of Elizabeth's reign. However different it may have been in other particulars, the government of England under Elizabeth bore, with respect to the question of liberty, a distinct resemblance to that of the eighteenth-century Turks (VI. 414). Under Elizabeth the legislative power of Parliament was a mere illusion, the liberty of the subject non-existent. And yet, Hume adds, the whigs have long indulged their prejudices against the Stuarts 'by bestowing unbounded panegyrics' on the virtue and wisdom of that Queen. They have even been so extremely ignorant of her reign as to praise her for a quality 'which, of all others, she was the least possessed of; a tender regard for the constitution, and a concern for the liberties and privileges of her people' (VI. 403).

The popular party, on the other hand, exclaimed constantly against the arbitrary principles of Charles I. This was yet another paradox, to be sure, for 'one may venture to assert', Hume tells us, 'that the greatest enemies of this Prince will not find, in the long line of his predecessors, from the conquest to his time, any one king, except perhaps his father, whose administration was not more arbitrary and less legal, or whose conduct could have been recommended to him by the popular party themselves, as a model, in this particular, for his government' (X. 205, note F to vol. VIII).

We are not to believe, however, that Hume looked back with fond regret to the days of the Tudors or Stuarts. This would be missing the entire point he attempted to make. No, the eighteenth-century English had no reason, following the example of their ancestors, to be in love with the picture of absolute monarchy 'or to prefer the unlimited authority of the prince and his unbounded prerogatives to that noble liberty, that sweet equality, and that happy security, by which they are at present distinguished above all nations in the universe' (VI. 429–30). But the eighteenth-century English did have one obligation at least as they looked back on their own political history: this was the duty to approach past events with a proper sense of perspective. The activities of the Stuart kings, though they might appear arbitrary and illegal to Englishmen in the seventeen-fifties, could, if judged according to the principles and practices of the times in which they were carried out, 'admit of some apology'. After all, most of the modern liberties were, in the days of the Stuarts, and to an even greater extent during the Tudor period, totally unknown and deemed everywhere to be incompatible with all good government. 'It seems unreasonable', Hume maintained, 'to judge of the measures embraced during one period, by the maxims which prevail in another' (VII. 204).

Hume clearly felt that he had achieved this just sense of perspective and the result is that he made every effort while dealing with the civil-war period to understand and forgive the policies of James I and Charles I. Whether he also understood and forgave with equal sympathy and justice the policies of their opponents has remained, however, a matter of much heated debate ever since the first volume of his *Stuarts* appeared in 1754.

For Hume the moral issues of the case are not simplified, moreover, by the fact that what were traditionally described as the major vices of these early Stuarts could equally well be viewed as ill-timed but honest virtues. These were not the grander virtues, to be sure, but the every-day virtues of sincerity, integrity and conviction. These kings were not 'great' men but they were 'good' men. In all history, for example, it would be difficult to find a reign 'less illustrious, yet more unspotted and unblemished, than that of James' (VI. 662). Perhaps James erred occasionally in forgetting to ask himself the question *What is best?* This is because he believed in all piety that the question *What is established?* was more important. Hume has no doubts about what was established when James came to the English throne. Everyone accepted in those times the doctrine of blind and unlimited passive obedience to the prince. Under no pretence had it ever been seen as lawful for subjects to depart from or infringe that doctrine. So completely had these principles prevailed that, during the reigns of Elizabeth and her predecessors, opposition to them was regarded as the most flagrant sedition not only by the monarch but by the people as well. James I had thus inherited an absolute throne. His predecessor was, for example, allowed to have a *divine* right; was not James I's title quite plainly the same as that of his predecessor? Was it not natural for him to take the government as he found it and to pursue the long-applauded measures of the popular Elizabeth? Perhaps, Hume adds, but it is something of an afterthought, James should have realized that his character and his circumstances could not support so extensive an authority. In fact his major difficulties arose chiefly from these circumstances which had suffered during his reign a radical transformation. Partly as a result of the changing economic situation, partly as a result of the increase in knowledge, a new spirit of liberty was born at this time and spread rapidly under the shelter of 'puritanical absurdities'—that theological plague which had so suddenly and inexplicably infested the people. The results were disastrous to all hopes for stable government, since the religious spirit, when it mingles with faction, contains in it, our sceptical historian believed, 'something supernatural and unaccountable' (VI. 569). Ordinary human prudence, the usual trust in cause and effect is baffled by it and the operation of every motive which normally influences human society fails (VII. 171).

Now this spirit of religion or rather of *enthusiasm*, uncontrolled, obstinate and dangerous, violently inclined the Puritans to adopt republican principles and to form a strong attachment to civil liberty. The two principles are 'nearly allied' (VI. 473), and by this prevalence of fanaticism a gloomy and sullenly independent disposition established itself among the people who became animated with a contempt for authority and a hatred for all other religions and especially for Catholicism. James, of course, helped matters not at all when, for essentially worthy reasons, he attempted to civilize the barbaric austerity of the sects by infusing a small tincture of ceremony and cheerfulness into this 'dark spirit of devotion'. Nor, alas, was Charles subsequently more fortunate in the consequences of his efforts to abate the people's extreme rage against popery. And yet, it must be confessed, Laud's innovations deserve our praise, for pious ceremonies, however ridiculous they may seem to a philosophical mind, can be very advantageous to the rude multitude and tend to mollify that fierce and gloomy spirit of devotion to which the rude multitude is subject. Even the English Church 'may justly be thought too naked and unadorned, and still to approach too near the abstract and spiritual religion of the Puritans' (VII. 589). Laud and his associates by reviving a few primitive institutions of this nature had corrected the error of the first reformers. It is true that Laud had attempted to introduce the fine arts into religion 'not with the enlarged sentiments and cool reflection of a legislator, but with the intemperate zeal of a sectary' (VII. 590). The net result of his action was to inflame that religious fury which he meant to repress. It is, however, 'sufficient for his vindication to observe, that his errors were the most excusable of all those which prevailed during that zealous period' (loc. cit.). Indeed, whereas the crude political advantages derived by the parliamentary party from the judicial murder of the 'magnanimous' Strafford, 'one of the most eminent personages that has appeared in England' (VII. 330, 356), could perhaps in some degree palliate the iniquity of the sentence pronounced against him, the execution of England's old infirm prelate, on the other hand, 'can be ascribed to nothing but vengeance and bigotry in those severe religionists, by whom the Parliament was entirely governed' (VII. 587).

Mainly as a result of his worldly distaste for 'enthusiasm', Hume, we see, held a rather low opinion of the various parliamentary heroes. Was not Parliament after all the aggressor during this unhappy period of civil discord? The Stuart kings had fought only a defensive campaign forced on them by the fact that Parliament had unilaterally seen fit to change the rules of the game and had innovated violently in constitutional matters. All things considered, Hume readily admitted that many constitutions in the history of human affairs and 'none more than the British' have in fact been improved by such violent innovations. He felt compelled to insist, nevertheless, that 'the praise bestowed on those patriots to whom the nation has been indebted for its privileges, ought to be given with some reserve, and surely without the least rancour against those who adhered to the ancient constitution' (VI. 404). The motivation of these patriots is suspect. Hume notes, for example, that the untimely end of Hampden leaves doubtful and uncertain whether his conduct was founded in a love of power or a zeal for liberty. With Cromwell, of course, there is no such doubt and uncertainty. Hume sees him as a fanatical, ambitious hypocrite; an artful and audacious conspirator who from the beginning engaged in his crimes 'from the prospect of sovereign power', a temptation, Hume adds, which is, in general, 'irresistible to human nature' (VII. 572). Hume admits, however, that Cromwell, by making some good use of the authority he had attained by fraud and violence, 'has lessened, if not overpowered, our detestation of his enormities, by our admiration of his success and of his genius' (loc. cit.).

More repelled than amused by the 'cant', 'mystical jargon', 'hypocrisy', 'fury' and 'fanaticism' of the Parliamentarians, Hume found himself unable to take too seriously patriotic attempts to dignify the Civil War with causes more considerable or noble than bigotry and theological zeal. Of course the Royalists too were zealots 'but as they were at the same time maintaining the established constitution, in state as well as church, they had an object which was natural, and which might produce the greatest passion, even without any considerable mixture of theological fervour' (X. 183, note DD to vol. VII). The opponents of Charles did not fight for liberty; they fought for ignorant and fanatical trivialities. 'The generality of the nation', Hume writes, 'could never have flown out into such fury in order to obtain new privileges and acquire greater liberty than they and their ancestors had ever been acquainted with. Their fathers had been entirely satisfied with the government of Elizabeth: why should they have been thrown into such extreme rage against Charles, who, from the beginning of his reign, wished only to maintain such a government? And why not, at least, compound matters with him, when by all his laws, it appeared that he had agreed to depart from it? Especially, as he had put it entirely out of his power to retract that resolution' (loc. cit.).

Perhaps the revolution, up to a certain point and despite its trivial origins, did achieve some positive good. During the first period of the Long Parliament's operations, if we except the cruel iniquity of Strafford's attainder, the merits of its transactions may be judged to outweigh its mistakes and even entitle those measures which remedied abuses and redressed grievances to the praise of 'all lovers of liberty' (VII. 361). Hume even confesses a willingness at one point to admit that a few old eggs had to be broken to make the new omelette. Such is the price of progress and if the means used to obtain these salutary results savour often of artifice and violence 'it is to be considered, that revolutions of government cannot be effected by the mere force of argument and reasoning; and that factions, being once excited, men can neither so firmly regulate the tempers of others, nor their own, as to ensure themselves against all exorbitances' (VII. 362). But, while exalting their own authority and diminishing the king's, the patriots went too far and totally subverted the constitution. They forgot that authority as well as liberty is requisite to government and is even requisite to the support of liberty itself, by maintaining the laws which can alone regulate and protect it (VII. 406). Soon, not a limitation but a total abolition of monarchical authority appeared as the true aim of these 'sanctified hypocrites'. Their violence disgraced the cause of liberty and was injurious to the nation: 'It is seldom', Hume concluded, 'that the people gain any thing by revolutions in government; because the new settlement, jealous and insecure, must commonly be supported with more expense and severity than the old: but on no occasion was the truth of this maxim more sensibly felt, than in the present situation of England. Complaints against the oppression of ship-money, against the tyranny of the Star-Chamber, had roused the people to arms: and having gained a complete victory over the crown, they found themselves loaded with a multiplicity of taxes, formerly unknown; and scarcely an appearance of law and liberty remained in the administration' (VIII. 102).

So great were the alterations imposed forcibly on the constitution in this later period that Hume feels Charles I was essentially right in saying, 'that he had been more an enemy to his people by these concessions, could he have prevented them, than by any other action of his life' (VIII. 110). Having violently pulled the government to pieces, the patriots of course thought up schemes for establishing a perfect republic in its place, parts of which, Hume observes, were plausible but other parts were 'too perfect for human nature' (VIII. 122, 412). Such schemes when held by men in power are dangerous. Dangerous also was the current doctrine of popular sovereignty. That the people are the origin of all just power is a principle which, Hume asserts, 'is noble in itself, and seems specious, but is belied by all history and experience' (VIII. 124).

Finally, 'the height of all iniquity and fanatical extravagance' (VIII. 123), the public trial and execution of England's legal sovereign, remained to be added to the list of parliamentary crimes. It is clear from the *History* that the King's behaviour during the last scenes of his life commanded Hume's greatest admiration. Our historian notes that Charles in all appearances before his judges never forgot his part 'either as a prince or as a man' (VIII. 131). The people too, though under the rod of lawless unlimited power, could not forbear, with the most ardent prayers, pouring forth their wishes for his preservation (VIII. 132). How they regretted the blind fury with which they had earlier rejected their king! The enormity of the trial 'was exclaimed against by the general voice of reason and humanity; and all men, under whatever form of government they were born, rejected this example, as the utmost effort of undisguised usurpation, and the most heinous insult on law and justice' (VIII. 133).

I shall not dwell further on Hume's account of the grief, indignation and astonishment which struck the whole nation as soon as the news of Charles I's execution, or rather his 'murder', reached the nation. Hume's version of these events will be encountered with perhaps more than sufficient frequency in the various French counter-revolutionary writings dealt with later in this study.

The English soon realized that they had murdered an honourable and honest king, who was, moreover, innocent of the crimes with which he was charged. 'And though', Hume adds, 'some violations of the Petition of Right may perhaps be imputed to him; these are more to be ascribed to the necessity of his situation, and to the lofty ideas of royal prerogative, which, from former established precedents, he had imbibed, than to any failure in the integrity of his principles' (VIII. 142). Nor is it even possible to say that with a little more tact here, a little more imagination there, Charles could have perhaps avoided this fatal clash with Parliament. Even long after the event, when it is commonly a simple matter to sort out the errors of bygone quarrels, one is at a loss to determine what course Charles, in his circumstances, could have followed to maintain the authority of the Crown and preserve the peace of the nation. Had Charles been born an absolute prince, 'his humanity and good sense' would have rendered his reign happy and his memory precious. If the English constitution and the extent of prerogative had been in his day quite fixed and certain, his integrity would have made him regard as sacred the boundaries of that constitution. 'Unhappily,' Hume concludes, 'his fate threw him into a period when the precedents of many former reigns savoured strongly of arbitrary power, and the genius of the people ran violently towards liberty' (VIII. 141).

Hume drew—or at least seemed to draw—various lessons from the great events of this period and these too we shall leave until they are pointed out again by the French traditionalists who opposed, almost a century and a half later, what they considered to be extraordinarily similar tendencies and events in their own country. One of these lessons which was to strike with especially great force a good many disillusioned Frenchmen not long after 1789 nevertheless deserves mention here. It is, in effect, that the English revolution had been a pernicious act of folly, a wasted venture, and that perhaps all similar revolutions are condemned to a like fate. The King once out of the way, the English revolutionary factions set about eliminating one another in an endless striving for greater and greater 'sanctity'. In the end, from the too eager pursuit of liberty, the nation fell into the most abject servitude. To emphasize the point, Hume concluded his chapter immediately preceding that which is devoted to Cromwell with the following warning: 'By recent, as well as all ancient, example, it was become evident that illegal violence, with whatever pretences it may be covered, and whatever object it may pursue, must inevitably end at last in the arbitrary and despotic government of a single person' (VIII. 240).

I

BEFORE 1789

1. Royal panegyrics

IN 1763 David Hume arrived in Paris to take up duties with Lord Hertford, Britain's first peacetime Ambassador to France since the outbreak of the Seven Years War. Author of a famous *History of the Stuarts*, David Hume, frequently hailed as the *Tacite des Anglais*, was given an official and personal welcome such as few foreign authors have ever received in the French capital.

The story of France's adulation is too well known to need retelling here[1] although one example of it is particularly relevant to our purpose. Let us read Hume's own account of his presentation at Versailles in 1763 to the children of the Dauphin, three future kings of France:

The scene which passed today really pleased me without embarrassing me. I attended Lord Hertford to Versailles in order to be presented to the Dauphiness and the young Princes, the only part of the royal family whom we had not yet seen. When I was presented to the Duc de Berry, a child of ten years of age, he said to me, 'Monsieur, vous avez beaucoup de réputation dans ce pays-ci; votre nom est très bien connu; et c'est avec beaucoup de plaisir que je vous vois.' Immediately upon which his brother the Comte de Provence, who is two years younger, advanced to me and said with great presence of mind, 'Monsieur, il y a longtemps que vous êtes attendu dans ce pays-ci avec beaucoup d'impatience: je compte avoir bien du plaisir quand je pourrai lire votre belle histoire.' But what is more remarkable, when we were carried to make our bows to the Comte d'Artois, who is about five years of age, and to a young Madame of between two and three, the infant prince likewise advanced to me in order to make me his harangue, in which, though it was not very distinct, I heard him mumble the word *Histoire*, and some other terms of panegyric. With him ended the civilities of the royal family of France towards me; and I may say it did not end till their power of

[1] See R. Metz, 'Les amitiés françaises de Hume et le mouvement des idées', *Revue de littérature comparée*, 1929, pp. 644–713; E. C. Mossner, *The Life of David Hume* (Nelson), 1954, pp. 441–506.

speech failed them: for the Princess was too young to be able to articulate a compliment.[1]

David Hume, we see, was merely flattered. At the time, he could not have known the extent to which events described so skilfully in his *History* would one day assume a new and urgent meaning in the political life of the French nation. Nor could he have known that, not quite thirty years later, the eldest of these charming children, condemned to die by the will of that same nation, would once more take up the famous Monsieur Hume's great work as part of his last searching meditations.

2. *The science and art of English history*

The quite unusual popularity of Hume's *History of England* in eighteenth-century France requires perhaps some preliminary general explanation. His *Political Discourses* and *Philosophical Essays* introduced on the continent several years earlier had won him little more than the unflatteringly mild contempt of the devout and the intense but largely uncomprehending praise of a number of *philosophes* and *salonnières*. Originality in epistemological writings has rarely given any philosopher a great popular audience. The story is complicated too by the fact that the *philosophes* did not wish originality in a field which they believed had been definitively treated by Locke.

But history was a very different matter. As a genre it represented to the eighteenth century the most digestible form of narrative and was contrasted frequently with the novel which, though equally appealing to the mass of readers, was rarely considered to be a serious or worthy vehicle of truth. Such was the reputed superiority of history as a vantage point from which to view the human passions that many good and bad novels of the day conventionally attempted to pass themselves off as personal histories, memoirs, or collections of letters.[2]

[1] David Hume to Alexander Wedderburn, from Paris, 23 November 1763, in *The Letters of David Hume*, ed. J. Y. T. Greig, Oxford, 1932, I. 414–15.

[2] Note on this point the common eighteenth-century antithesis of the words *roman* and *histoire*, as in Voltaire's *Lettres philosophiques* (13e Lettre), where we find the terms contrasted in a parallel of Locke (who wrote *l'histoire de l'âme*) and Descartes (*le roman de l'âme*). For a defence of the truth of the novel, see Choderlos de Laclos' review of Fanny Burney's novel, *Cecilia*, in the *Mercure de France*, 17 April 1784, pp. 103ff. See also P.-A.-F. Choderlos de Laclos, *Œuvres complètes* (Pléiade), Paris, 1943, pp. 523–5.

Voltaire, Hume, and Gibbon, the three greatest historians of the century, were in agreement that history represented the most popular species of writing. History was an art the models of which were best found in antiquity. To be called, as Hume often was, the Tacitus of the English was to receive, even in that 'modern' period, the highest possible tribute. Seen not only as an art, history was viewed too as perhaps the most valuable of the human sciences—a unique storehouse of empirical facts without which no generalizations about man's nature, his motivations and passions, were possible. Speculation on almost any subject other than the physical sciences was considered worthless unless Clio had first been heard. Grimm, pointing out in 1767 that not a single 'trait d'histoire' was cited in a work by Le Mercier de La Rivière, concluded: 'cela seul prouve ce qu'il faut penser de son ouvrage.'[1] Similarly, Louis de Bonald singled out Rousseau's *Contrat social* for attack 'parce que son auteur . . . sacrifie sans cesse la société à l'homme, l'histoire à ses opinions'.[2] De Bonald adds that 'les propositions générales ou *abstraites*, qui ont rapport à la société, c'est à dire à l'homme, ne peuvent recevoir d'application que de l'histoire, ou des actions de l'homme en société.'[3]

Joseph de Maistre, Louis de Bonald's spiritual ally in the counter-revolution, agreed: 'L'histoire est la politique expérimentale, c'est à dire la seule bonne; et comme dans la physique, cent volumes de théories spéculatives disparaissent devant une seule expérience, de même, dans la science politique, nul système ne peut être admis s'il n'est pas le corollaire plus ou moins probable de faits bien attestés.'[4]

The *idéologue* Volney speaks of history as 'la science physiologique des gouvernements' and as a 'cours d'expériences que le genre humain subit sur lui-même', the purpose of which is to find 'un ordre généalogique de causes et d'effets, pour en déduire une théorie de règles et de principes propres à diriger les particuliers et les peuples vers le but de leur conservation ou de leur perfection'.[5]

[1] *Correspondance littéraire, philosophique et critique*, ed. Tourneux, Paris, 1877–82, 15 October 1767, VII. 449.

[2] *Théorie du pouvoir politique et religieux dans la société civile, démontrée par le raisonnement et par l'histoire* (1796); in *Œuvres de M. de Bonald*, Paris, 1843, XIII. 14.

[3] Ibid., XIII. 17.

[4] *Etude sur la souveraineté* (1794–6); in *Œuvres complètes de J. de Maistre*, Lyon, 1884, I. 426.

[5] *Séances des écoles normales*, Paris, 1800, I. 78; II. 219, 441.

History at its best was thus a pleasantly disguised form of social science long before Cambacérès triumphantly proclaimed to the Institut National on 25 February 1798 the advent of that new saviour: 'Législateurs, philosophes, jurisconsultes, voici le moment de la science sociale, et nous pouvons ajouter, de la véritable philosophie.'[1] I shall have occasion to come back to this view as well as to an important body of eighteenth-century thought which violently disagreed with it. For the moment it might be worth while to quote Hume's own similar view of history's purpose as expressed in the *Enquiry concerning Human Understanding* (1748):

Its chief use is only to discover the constant and universal principles of human nature, by showing men in all varieties of circumstances and situations, and furnishing us with materials, from which we may form our observations, and become acquainted with the regular springs of human action and behaviour. These records of wars, intrigues, factions, and revolutions, are so many collections of experiments, by which the politician or moral philosopher fixes the principles of his science; in the same manner as the physician or natural philosopher becomes acquainted with the nature of plants, minerals, and other external objects, by the experiments, which he forms concerning them. Nor are the earth, water, and other elements, examined by Aristotle, and Hippocrates, more like to those, which at present lie under our observation, than the men, described by Polybius and Tacitus, are to those, who now govern the world.[2]

It should also be noted that Hume's earlier writings in philosophy and economics could only add to his potential success and stature as an historian in the eyes of the eighteenth-century reader. History, as we know, had to be 'philosophical'—*l'histoire raisonnée* as opposed to *l'histoire simple*. Only the profound thinker was judged worthy of attempting it and such non-professionals as Smollett did little more than anger the French with their amateurish and pretentious imitations. 'De quoi s'avise M. Smollett,' indignantly writes Chastellux in 1766, 'd'écrire son *Histoire* en même temps que M. Hume fait la sienne! La partie n'est pas égale. . . .'[3] That history ought to be written only by men 'profonds dans la science de la politique' is the corresponding

[1] 'Discours sur la science sociale' in *Mémoires de l'Institut National des Sciences et Arts*, III. 13.

[2] *Essays Moral, Political and Literary by David Hume*, ed. T. H. Green and T. H. Grose, London, 1875, II. 68.

[3] *Gazette littéraire de l'Europe*, February 1766, p. 382.

sentiment expressed in the fashionable *Mercure de France* of 1763.[1]

To recapitulate, then, history in the eighteenth century was a very popular literary genre, vested also with an almost sacred function; and Hume was judged to be of a sufficiently reflective turn of mind to put a soul into its otherwise dead bones.

Another explanation of Hume's great success in this field lies undoubtedly in the fact that he had chosen to write a history of the English nation at a time when a strange anglomania was at its height on the continent. French interest in all things English from *jurys* to *jokais*, from fist-fights to glorious naval battles, despite the frequently inane sacrifice of national pride involved, hardly subsided even during the Seven Years War. Gibbon tells of his welcome in Paris in 1763 and speaks of how English opinions, fashions, even games were adopted in France at this time, and of how every Englishman was viewed as a born patriot and philosopher.[2] Garat gives an account of this anglomania which conveys perhaps a special meaning to readers of our own space age:

> Depuis que Voltaire et Montesquieu avaient publié sur les Anglais, l'un ses lettres, l'autre les deux chapitres de l'Esprit des Lois, on était singulièrement avide, en France, de tout ce qui pouvait se penser, se passer, se faire, se dire, se rêver en Angleterre. Si un télescope comme ceux d'Herschel et un cornet acoustique de la même portée avaient existé à cette époque, ils auraient été dirigés sur l'Angleterre plus souvent encore que sur la lune et les autres corps célestes. L'enthousiasme était à la fois une admiration profondément raisonnée, et une manie.[3]

British national history naturally reaped the benefits of the current mania and Hume is but the first in rank of many authors on the subject who were read widely in France at this time. In 1765 the *Bibliothèque des Sciences et des Beaux-Arts*, seeking an appropriate metaphor to describe the great number of publications in the field of English history, felt compelled to exclaim: 'Les Histoires d'Angleterre pleuvent!'[4]

Anglomania, however, is not a sufficient explanation of this torrent. One must also bear in mind the fact that English history,

[1] June issue, p. 54.

[2] Edward Gibbon, *Autobiography*, Everyman's Library, p. 114.

[3] D.-J. Garat, *Mémoires historiques sur le 18e siècle et sur M. Suard*, Paris, 1821, I. 72.

[4] January–March 1765, p. 232.

per se, was judged to be peculiarly superior to all other modern national histories, both as an artistic theme-source and as a scientific repository. Hume himself had written to the Abbé Le Blanc in 1754 that he esteemed the Stuart period 'both for signal events and extraordinary characters to be the most interesting in modern history'.[1] Voltaire, who frequently complained of the *insipidité* of French history and wondered even if it were worth writing,[2] agreed that the superiority of English events gave Hume an advantage in the field. Writing in 1769 to Gabriel-Henri Gaillard, he expressed the following bitter sentiments on the subject:

Enfin, depuis Saint Louis jusqu'à Henri IV, je ne vois rien. Aussi les recueils de l'histoire de France ennuient-ils toutes les nations ainsi que moi. David Hume a un grand avantage sur l'abbé Velly et consorts, c'est qu'il a écrit l'histoire des Anglais, et qu'en France on n'a jamais écrit l'histoire des Français. Il n'y a point de gros laboureur en Angleterre qui n'ait la grande charte chez lui et qui ne connaisse très bien la constitution de l'état. Pour notre histoire, elle est composée de tracasseries de cour, de grandes batailles perdues, de petits combats gagnés, et de Lettres de cachet. Sans cinq ou six assassinats célèbres, et surtout sans la Saint-Barthélemy, il n'y aurait rien de si insipide. Remarquez encore s'il vous plaît, que nous n'avons jamais rien inventé; et qu'enfin, à dire la vérité, nous n'existons aux yeux de l'Europe que dans le siècle de Louis XIV. J'en suis fâché, mais la chose est ainsi.[3]

Later on in the century, Soulavie, commenting on a similar view of the dullness of French history—this time expressed by Rousseau—showed to what extent the question of whether their subject truly 'existed' or not had become a matter of serious concern to French historians. His conclusions were, however, rather hopeful: 'Les situations du peuple français ont . . . été assez variées jusqu'à ce jour, et les passions humaines ont agi parmi nous avec assez d'énergie et d'effet pour intéresser et instruire tous les âges et toutes les nations. Cependant nous n'avons point encore une histoire qui puisse honorer la France, quoique nous ayons tant de chefs-d'œuvre littéraires dans tous les genres.'[4]

We see that a nation's history, to be interesting and significant,

[1] Greig, op. cit., I. 193.

[2] See, for example, his letter to the Marquise Du Deffand, 20 June 1764, in *Voltaire's Correspondence*, ed. Besterman, LV. 114, Letter 11,103.

[3] Ibid., LXXI. 267, Letter 14,638.

[4] J.-L. Soulavie, *Traité de la composition et de l'étude de l'histoire*, 1792, p. 64.

had to present the greatest possible variety of human social situations; first, because such variety was aesthetically necessary in a literary composition and secondly, because the greater the number of events permutated and combined, the greater the resulting information about man's moral nature. English history best fulfilled both of these requirements according to an anonymous counter-revolutionary work of 1793: 'L'histoire des nations, et particulièrement celle de la Grande-Bretagne, instruit et intéresse par la variété des tableaux et des événements; c'est dans ce miroir fidèle où l'on voit le jeu de toutes les passions qui agitent le cœur humain.'[1] The *Journal Encyclopédique* thirty years earlier had made the same point: '. . . il n'y a point de nation qui offre des scènes plus variées, des caractères plus divers et plus illustres; nulle histoire qui fournisse un fond plus vaste et plus riche, d'instruction, d'étonnement et de plaisir, que l'histoire de la Grande-Bretagne . . .; quel peuple dans l'Europe a vu plus fréquemment changer ses mœurs, ses lois et son gouvernement?'[2]

Perhaps the only serious competitor to English history was, as could well be expected in this neo-classical age, that of the ancients. Sénac de Meilhan in 1787 expressed his opinion on the problem in the following manner: 'Il est peu d'historiens parmi les modernes, qui puissent être mis en parallèle avec Thucydide, Xénophon, Salluste, Tite-Live, et Tacite surtout: Hume et Robertson paraissent être ceux qui suivent de plus près leurs traces; peut-être les auraient-ils atteints, s'ils avaient écrit dans leur langue, s'ils avaient eu des tableaux aussi intéressants à peindre.'[3] Mme de Staël, writing some years later, agreed and also explained the superiority of the ancients in history by the superiority of their subject matter: 'Les historiens de l'antiquité sont les premiers de tous, parce qu'il n'est point d'époque où les hommes supérieurs aient exercé plus d'ascendant sur leur patrie.' She added, however, that English historians were next in rank: 'C'est la nation en Angleterre, plus encore que tel ou tel homme qui a de la grandeur; aussi les historiens y sont-ils moins dramatiques mais plus philosophiques que les anciens.'[4]

[1] *L'Angleterre instruisant la France*, Londres, 1793, p. 70.

[2] August 1764, V. 8–10. See also ibid., June 1760, IV. 3–4.

[3] *Considérations sur l'esprit et les mœurs*, Londres, 1787, pp. 364–5.

[4] *De l'Allemagne*; in *Œuvres complètes de Mme La Baronne de Staël*, publiées par son fils, Paris, 1820–1, XI. 113.

Other opinions expressed during the first decades of the nineteenth century suggest that this view of English national history still widely prevailed. We read the following observation, for example, in *La Quotidienne* of 1826: 'De toutes les histoires des nations modernes, celle d'Angleterre est sans contredit la plus attachante: l'intérêt y va toujours croissant comme dans un drame, et les péripéties ainsi que les catastrophes y renaissent à chaque instant.'[1]

We see how important this largely eighteenth-century concept of the *art* of history still was in 1826—not just the art of the individual historian, but the dramatic art, as it were, of a nation's own past in its unfolding. The great variety of events in English history and the order in which these had occurred seemed to permit a perfect fusion of both artistic and scientific elements in one literary genre. The modern world had, quite plainly, no greater or more significant story to tell. This view was to change only after a somewhat delayed realization came to Europe that the events of the French revolution had suddenly presented historians with an even greater story.

We shall in the course of this study see that there are many additional reasons which explain why David Hume succeeded so well in eighteenth-century France as an historian. These are of a more particular nature and more complex to analyse. Generally, and perhaps truistically speaking, however, we might initially conclude that his great success was to a large extent founded on the fact that he could have chosen no other topic more suited to satisfy at the same time both the political curiosity and the artistic interests of most French readers of his day.

3. Jehovah among the Hebrews

Already in 1754, even before the English publication of his *Stuarts*, Hume had intimated to the Abbé Le Blanc, translator of his moderately successful *Political Discourses*, that the *History* would succeed well in France.[2] Hume proposed at this same time that Le Blanc should also translate the *History* and Le Blanc accepted, although he later found it necessary to give up the translation, which was continued by the Abbé Prévost and published in

[1] *La Quotidienne*, No. 39, 8 February 1826.
[2] Greig, op. cit., I. 193.

1760.[1] There is a good deal of evidence to show that, even before the long-delayed appearance of Prévost's translation, impatient readers in France had turned to the original English version. Morellet tells us how, imprisoned in the Bastille in 1760, he had asked Malesherbes to bring him a copy of Tacitus and Hume's *History* in English.[2] Chastellux the social historian declared to friends that he had learned English only to read Hume;[3] and Turgot at this time felt the *Stuarts* important enough to justify a personal translation.[4] Several hundred pages of *extraits* from the *Stuarts* also appeared in various French journals before 1760. Additional proof of such pre-translation success is provided by the results of a survey which I carried out some years ago in the 'Delta' series at the Bibliothèque Nationale in Paris. Out of 240 private library catalogues chosen completely at random in the pre-revolutionary period, 109 listed Hume's historical writings. Of these 109, 12 included versions of the *Stuarts* in English as well as in French. This work, in fact, was already well enough known in France by 1759 for Hume to convey to his fellow-historian Robertson in March of that year the facetious warning that the latter would find it more difficult to thrust him out of his place in Paris than he had in London.[5]

Once Prévost's translation was published in 1760, page after page of acclamatory notices appeared in the leading French journals. Similar editorial attention was generously accorded in 1763 and 1765 to Mme Belot's translations of the *Tudors* and the *Plantagenets*. During this time too Hume received in his correspondence a great many tributes from distinguished continental readers. A letter in 1761 from the Comtesse de Boufflers is extreme in its praise but quite sincere; parts of it are worth quoting here as fairly typical of the reactions to Hume's *Stuarts* among the fashionable Parisian nobility:

Je ne sais point de termes qui puissent vous rendre ce que j'éprouve en lisant cet ouvrage. Je me sens attendrie, transportée, et l'émotion qu'il

[1] For further details on Hume's French translations see my 'David Hume and the Official Censorship of the "Ancien Régime"', *French Studies*, 1958, XII. 234–46.

[2] *Mémoires de l'Abbé Morellet*, Paris, 1821, I. 92.

[3] Greig, op. cit., II. 348.

[4] See *Œuvres de Turgot et documents le concernant*, ed. G. Schelle, Paris, 1913, I. 27. Turgot's translation was not published.

[5] Greig, op. cit., I. 302–3.

me cause est en quelque façon pénible par sa continuité. Il élève l'âme, il remplit le cœur de sentiments d'humanité et de bienfaisance. . . .

Vous êtes, Monsieur, un peintre admirable. Vos tableaux ont une grâce, un naturel, une énergie qui surpasse ce que l'imagination même peut atteindre.

Mais quelles expressions emploierais-je, pour vous faire connaître l'effet que produit sur moi votre divine impartialité? J'aurais besoin en cette occasion de votre propre éloquence pour bien rendre ma pensée. En vérité je crois avoir devant les yeux l'ouvrage de quelque substance céleste dégagée des passions, qui pour l'utilité des hommes a daigné écrire les événements de ces derniers temps. . . .[1]

Similar references to David Hume as the 'angel of truth', the 'voice of pure reason', the 'voice of posterity', are not uncommon at this time. Rousseau, who was soon to write of Hume in a different tone, made equally laudatory statements in a letter of February 1763 to the Scottish philosopher: 'Vos grandes vues,' he wrote, 'votre étonnante impartialité, votre génie, vous élèveraient trop au-dessus des hommes, si votre bon cœur ne vous en rapprochait. . . .'[2] Also in 1763 Helvétius wrote bursting with enthusiasm for Hume's 'esprit philosophique et impartial'[3] and a year later the Président de Brosses, who judged that Hume had surpassed even Tacitus, repeated the same sentiment: 'Vous avez dépeint au vrai et avec une impartialité sans exemple votre nation, ses mœurs, ses esprits, son gouvernement.'[4] In another letter Chastellux told Hume that his name had become 'aussi respectable dans la république des lettres que celui de Jéhovah l'était parmi les Hébreux'.[5]

The words *impartial* and *impartialité* seem to occur also in nearly every press review of Hume's *History* at this time, whether of traditionalist or *philosophe* inspiration. Fréron, one of Voltaire's greatest enemies, after making the usual comparison with Tacitus, affirmed that Hume was the first 'English' author ever 'qui ait rendu justice à notre nation et aux ministres de notre religion quand il a cru que la vérité leur était favorable'.[6] The *Journal*

[1] Greig, op. cit., II. 366–7. [2] Ibid., II. 382.

[3] *Letters of Eminent Persons addressed to David Hume*, ed. J. H. Burton, Edinburgh, 1849, p. 13.

[4] Ibid., p. 275.

[5] Greig, 'Some Unpublished Letters to David Hume', *Revue de littérature comparée*, 1932, XII. 830.

[6] *Année littéraire*, 1763, III. 39–40; see also ibid., 1760, IV. 313.

Encyclopédique pointed out that no historian of the Stuart period had been impartial before Hume. Most Englishmen had, like Burnet, written as paid propagandists of the usurper William of Orange. Foreign historians of the English revolution had not succeeded either. Some, like the Huguenot Rapin-Thoyras, were blinded by the prejudices of their religion and had interpreted events only in the light of an apology for Protestantism. Others, like le Père d'Orléans, though not unfavourable to the Catholic side, had shown an inadequate knowledge of the English system of government. 'On l'a dit,' the journal goes on, 'et l'expérience n'a que trop vérifié cette sentence, que *les peuples seraient souverainement heureux quand ils seraient gouvernés par des princes philosophes.* Ajoutons que l'histoire ne sera jamais bien écrite que par des historiens philosophes; c'est à dire par ces hommes qui, sans égard pour aucun pays, pour aucune faction, pour aucune secte, ont la seule ambition d'être vrais. Notre auteur approche beaucoup de ce modèle. . . .'[1]

Voltaire, the most important historian of the day, praised Hume on much the same grounds in a long review published in 1764:

On ne peut rien ajouter à la célébrité de cette Histoire, la meilleure peut-être qui soit écrite en aucune langue. . . .

Jamais le public n'a mieux senti qu'il n'appartient qu'aux philosophes d'écrire l'histoire. . . .

Le philosophe n'est d'aucune patrie, d'aucune faction. On aimerait à voir l'histoire des guerres de Rome et de Carthage écrite par un homme qui n'aurait été ni Carthaginois ni Romain. . . .

. . . M. Hume, dans son Histoire, ne paraît ni parlementaire, ni royaliste, ni anglican, ni presbytérien; on ne découvre en lui que l'homme équitable. . . .

La fureur des partis a longtemps privé l'Angleterre d'une bonne histoire comme d'un bon gouvernement. Ce qu'un Tory écrivait était nié par les Whigs, démentis à leur tour par les Torys. Rapin-Thoyras, étranger, semblait seul avoir écrit une histoire impartiale; mais on voit encore la souillure du préjugé jusque dans les vérités que Thoyras raconte; au lieu que dans le nouvel historien on découvre un esprit supérieur à sa matière, qui parle des faiblesses, des erreurs et des barbaries comme un médecin parle des maladies épidémiques.[2]

[1] June 1760, IV. 3–6.

[2] *Gazette littéraire de l'Europe*, 2 May 1764, I. 193–200; see also *Œuvres complètes de Voltaire*, ed. Moland, XXV. 169–73.

The apparent total agreement of such unlike men as Voltaire, Fréron, and Rousseau, on the subject of Hume's impartiality should be enough to indicate in this respect the unanimity of opinion in France. Since, however, many of my later conclusions concerning the influence of the Hume image must stand or fall on the basis of a careful evaluation of that image, and since it is important to show that this view of Hume's history persists in France[1] with a few notable exceptions right up to the time of the Revolution, I may be permitted to labour this point a little longer.

Dom Louis-Mayeul Chaudon in a work of 1772 again reviewed the three most widely-read authors of English history: Hume, Rapin-Thoyras, and le Père d'Orléans. Rapin, as was usual in French Catholic estimates at this time, is accused of Huguenot prejudices: 'Un reproche . . . qu'il mérite c'est de se montrer prévenu contre sa patrie, que les rigueurs de Louis XIV avaient exposée à la haine des protestants, et de favoriser le parti des puritains, de ces dangereux enthousiastes, dont le système de religion n'est propre qu'à rendre les hommes farouches, et le système d'indépendance qu'à faire des factieux et des rebelles.' As for le Père d'Orléans, Abbé Chaudon shows surprising frankness in judging his fellow-ecclesiastic: 'Ce qui concerne les *Stuarts* est écrit avec une partialité trop évidente. Le Jésuite français règle la plupart de ses jugements tantôt sur les intérêts de la Cour romaine, tantôt sur les principes de la monarchie française.' Hume's fairness is seen, on the other hand, as completely unique and without precedent: 'Jamais auteur ne s'est plus élevé au-dessus des préjugés des sectes et des préventions des partis qui divisent le Royaume, toujours impartial, il semble être l'organe des jugements de la postérité. . . .'[2]

Also defending Hume's impartiality, the Reverend Samuel Formey, secretary of the Berlin Academy and formerly hostile editor of the French translation of Hume's *Philosophical Essays* (1758), contrasted in 1777 the anticlericalism of the *philosophes* with Hume's fairness towards the representatives of the church:

[1] Hume's great reputation in history was, of course, by no means restricted to France. In Italy, for example, such men as Beccaria, Algarotti, and Genovesi, were no less flattering in their praise.

[2] *Bibliothèque d'un homme de goût*, Avignon, 1772, II. 178–80. See also similar opinions of Court de Gébelin and de Tressan in *Le guide de l'histoire*, ed. J.-F. Née de la Rochelle, Paris, 1803, I. 161–2, 280.

Rien de si singulier que l'acharnement que témoignent contre eux des gens qui, bien loin d'en avoir reçu aucun sujet de plainte, leur ont de véritables obligations, puisque ce sont eux qui, dans la plupart des états, ont conservé, à travers les siècles de barbarie, des connaissances, un fond d'humanité, de la bénéficence et de la charité; sans quoi le brigandage de ces malheureux temps aurait été porté à de beaucoup plus grands excès. Hume dont on ne récusera pas le témoignage, le reconnaît formellement par rapport à l'Angleterre; et cet aveu fait honneur à son impartialité. On est au contraire indigné de trouver à chaque page des écrits d'Helvétius ces ironies amères, ces sorties non seulement vives, mais presque toujours furieuses, contre un clergé qui méritait certainement ses égards, et qui ne lui déplaisait que parce qu'il cherchait à préserver la France du venin de sa doctrine.[1]

The section *Histoire* of the *Encyclopédie Méthodique* in 1788 gave perhaps the ultimate in praise to the impartiality of Hume's *History of England*: 'Un des plus beaux morceaux d'histoire et de philosophie qu'il y ait dans aucune langue, et l'ouvrage le plus impartial et le plus raisonnable peut-être qui soit sorti de la main d'un homme.'[2] It is obviously impossible to say more!

4. Papist or Pyrrhonian?

It is well known that the English at this time did not agree with the French about Hume's impartiality. The strange combination of two reputations which Hume enjoyed in England, one as a foolish atheist, the other as a perverse Jacobite, was scarcely of a nature to please any large group in that country.

In *My Own Life* Hume speaks of his disappointment at the domestic reception given the *Stuarts*:

I was, I own, sanguine in my expectations of the success of this work. I thought that I was the only historian that had at once neglected present power, interest, and authority, and the cry of popular prejudices; and as the subject was suited to every capacity, I expected proportional applause. But miserable was my disappointment: I was assailed by one cry of reproach, disapprobation, and even detestation; English, Scotch, and Irish; Whig and Tory; churchman and sectary, free-thinker and religionist; patriot and courtier, united in their rage against the man who had presumed to shed a generous tear for the fate of

[1] 'Examen de la question si toutes les vérités sont bonnes à dire?' in *Nouveaux Mémoires de l'Académie Royale des Sciences et Belles-Lettres*, Berlin, 1777, XXXIII. 336.

[2] *Encyclopédie Méthodique: Histoire* (1788), III. 111.

Charles I and the Earl of Strafford; and after the first ebullitions of this fury were over, what was still more mortifying, the book seemed to sink into oblivion. Mr. Millar told me, that in a twelvemonth he sold only forty-five copies of it. I scarcely, indeed, heard of one man in the three Kingdoms, considerable for rank or letters, that could endure the book. I must only except the Primate of England, Dr. Herring, and the Primate of Ireland, Dr. Stone; which seem two odd exceptions. These dignified prelates separately sent me messages not to be discouraged.

Hume was, nevertheless, discouraged and he tells us in this same brief autobiographical sketch that, had not the war at that time been breaking out between France and England, he would have retired for ever from England to some provincial French town. Horace Walpole clearly reflects the typical attitude to the *History* in England, in a letter to Montague from Paris in 1765. Parisians, he affirmed, were totally lacking in literary taste: '. . . could one believe that when they read our authors, Richardson and Mr. Hume should be their favourites? The latter is treated here with perfect veneration. His History, so falsified in many points, so partial in as many, so very unequal in its parts, is thought the standard of writing. . . .'[1]

The French were fully aware of the discrepancy between their own estimates of Hume's worth and those of the English. We read, for example, in the *Journal Etranger* of 1760 the following statement on that subject:

M. Hume a été accusé par ses compatriotes de rechercher trop les opinions singulières; ce n'est pas à nous à discuter ce reproche. Nous remarquerons seulement que M. Hume, quoique Anglais, républicain et protestant, a toujours parlé des Français avec estime, des rois et des catholiques avec modération; et cette singularité a pu blesser une nation trop accoutumée à ne voir dans les monarchies qu'un troupeau d'esclaves, et dans les *papistes* qu'une ligue de fanatiques, et à ne reconnaître ni liberté, ni vertu, ni philosophie dans tout autre gouvernement que le sien.[2]

To show how wrong they feel the English are with respect to Hume, the editors of this very orthodox *ancien-régime* journal do not hesitate to call his work 'la seule bonne histoire que l'on connaisse en anglais, et l'une des meilleures sans doute qu'il y ait dans aucune langue'. Hume is also commended for being 'le

[1] W. S. Lewis and R. S. Brown, *Horace Walpole's Correspondence with George Montague*, New Haven, 1941, II. 176, Letter of 22 September 1765.

[2] See May issue, 1760, pp. 169–70.

premier écrivain anglais qui ait osé écrire que les monarchies sont à peu près aussi favorables aux progrès des arts, de la raison et du commerce que les républiques'.[1]

In a work intended for the instruction of Marie-Antoinette, the future *Historiographe de France*, J.-N. Moreau, implied that Hume had probably carried impartiality to an undesirable extreme: '. . . il ne devrait être qu'impartial, et il se pique de l'indifférence la plus outrée. Les Anglais, qui ont la vertu des Romains, la partialité pour leur Patrie, lui ont eux-mêmes reproché ce défaut, et font de cet auteur moins de cas que nous n'en faisons nous-mêmes.'[2]

It must be noted, however, that Moreau's attempt to understand and forgive England's hostility to Hume the historian is a French attitude rarely encountered at this time. Much more common is the indignant reaction of the former Jesuit and future speech writer for Mirabeau, J.-A.-J. Cerutti, who wrote in 1783: 'L'histoire de M. Hume pourrait s'intituler: L'histoire des passions anglaises, par la raison humaine. Les Anglais lui ont reproché d'avoir fait verser des larmes sur le sort de Marie Stuart et sur celui de Charles Ier. Ils l'ont appelé la bonne femme Hume. Cette bonhomie rend son impartialité plus noble et sa philosophie plus touchante.'[3]

More angry still was the response of one of Hume's French anthologists, Damiens de Gomicourt, who pointed out that the ungrateful English seemed to make more fuss over their race-horses than they did over a Hume. De Gomicourt makes astute conjectures as to the reasons for this neglect: 'Cette façon désintéressée d'écrire sur sa nation et sur ses ennemis . . . est précisément ce qui lui fait plus de tort parmi ses compatriotes; s'ils étaient aussi philosophes que le dit M. de Voltaire, *lorsqu'il appelle l'Angleterre l'île des philosophes*, ils se laisseraient moins emporter au sentiment d'animosité contre la nation française qui les domine; le bien qu'en dit M. Hume lorsqu'il croit qu'elle le mérite, la façon modérée dont il parle de la cour de Rome, ou de la maison

[1] Ibid., p. 171.

[2] *Bibliothèque de Madame la Dauphine:* No. 1, *Histoire*, Paris, 1770, p. 125.

[3] 'L'Aigle et le Hibou' in *Œuvres diverses de M. Cerutti ou recueil de pièces composées avant et depuis la Révolution*, Paris, 1792, II. 47. Hume in fact shed few tears for Mary Stuart: see my article 'The Eighteenth-Century Marian Controversy and an Unpublished Letter by David Hume', *Studies in Scottish Literature*, April 1964, pp. 236–52.

infortunée des Stuarts, ne serait pas une raison pour eux d'accuser cet auteur de *papisme*, de *jacobitisme*, et de *francomanie*, et ses ouvrages auraient à Londres la même célébrité qu'à Paris.'[1]

Papisme, *jacobitisme*, and *francomanie*—three qualities well calculated to enhance an English historian's reputation in France; their effect would, of course, be just the opposite in England. That Hume himself felt his history would hold a special appeal for Catholic, monarchical France is made clear in his original letter to Abbé Le Blanc in 1754 proposing a French translation of the *Stuarts*. 'Considering', Hume wrote, 'some late transactions in France, your Ministry may think themselves obliged to a man, who, by the example of English history, discovers the consequences of puritanical and republican pretensions. You would have remarked in my writings, that my principles are, all along, tolerably monarchical, and that I abhor that low practice, so prevalent in England, of speaking with malignity of France.'[2] One month later, Hume came back to this point, advising Le Blanc to make any necessary attenuations in his translation of the *Stuarts*: 'If there be some strokes of the *L'esprit fort* too strong for your climate, you may soften them at your discretion. That I am a lover of liberty will be expected from my country, though I hope that I carry not that passion to any ridiculous extreme.'[3]

For an example of current French reactions to British historians who did indulge in 'that low practice' of speaking with malignity of France, we have only to see what the French thought of Smollett's *History*. A fairly typical review of it can be found in the *Journal Encyclopédique* of 1764:

M. Smollett se croit entièrement libre de toute jalousie nationale et de tout préjugé; il se croit parfaitement dégagé de ces partialités injustes qui déshonorent les ouvrages de plusieurs historiens anglais; il assure qu'il n'a point pris feu pour aucune controverse de religion, ni aucune faction politique. . . . Cette espèce de déclaration nous paraît d'autant plus surprenante, que nous ne connaissons guère d'historien plus partial que M. Smollett, soit dans les divers parallèles qu'il a faits des monarques français avec les rois de la Grande Bretagne, soit dans les éloges outrés qu'il ne cesse de donner à ses compatriotes. Quelquefois plus circonspect, mais quelquefois aussi plus satirique et plus mordant

[1] *L'Observateur Français à Londres*, Londres, 1769, I. 349–50; IV. 109.
[2] Greig, op. cit., I. 193–4: letter of 12 September 1754.
[3] Ibid., I. 198: letter of 15 October 1754.

que Rapin de Thoyras, il se déchaîne contre le catholicisme, il ramasse tout ce qu'ont inspiré l'irréligion et l'indécence contre les Sts Evêques qui ont illustré l'Angleterre; il ne voit dans leur zèle qu'un fanatisme aveugle, dans leur candeur, qu'hypocrisie, dans leur attachement à l'église romaine, que des vues criminelles, une indépendance outrée, une coupable félonie.[1]

To find the French equivalent of English hostility to Hume's history during this early period, it is necessary to look through the pages of the erudite 'Dutch' journals, edited by the Huguenot refugees. Here the similarity of views seems almost automatic. Maty in the *Journal Britannique*, speaking of the first volume of Hume's *Stuarts*, declared: 'Tant s'en faut que l'ouvrage que j'ai sous les yeux me paraisse un modèle à suivre, que je crois au contraire y découvrir les divers défauts, qu'un auteur, que M. Hume ne désavouerait pas pour maître regarde comme incompatibles avec les obligations de l'historien.' Maty then cites Voltaire's *Défense du Siècle de Louis XIV* on the necessity for the historian to stick to the truth.[2]

The *Bibliothèque des Sciences et des Beaux-Arts*, published at The Hague, spoke unfavourably of the same work in 1756: 'Nous n'avons rien dit de cette *Histoire*, parce que rien ne nous y a paru digne d'éloge que le style, et que nous n'avons pas envie d'être éternellement aux prises avec cet auteur. . . . Nous n'avons jamais vu d'histoire où régnât tant l'art dangereux de rendre les plus mauvais caractères supportables, en cachant certains traits, et en adoucissant les autres par des nuances et des ombres habilement placées. Mais ce n'est pas tout. Ici M. Hume s'est avisé de faire envisager le *fanatisme* comme le caractère distinctif de la Réformation. . . .'[3]

The year following, the same journal reviewed the second volume of the *Stuarts* and warned its readers again concerning Hume's dangerous portraits: '. . . qu'on se défie toujours de ses portraits! Son goût pour les paradoxes et sa partialité n'éclatent que trop souvent dans les caractères qu'il trace de plusieurs grands personnages. . . . Le portrait de Jacques II présente si peu de traits qui ressemblent à l'original, qu'il faut y avoir vu le nom

[1] August 1764, V. 6–7. The probable author of the above is J.-L. Castilhon who repeated his charges six years later in *Le Diogène moderne ou le désapprobateur*, Bouillon, 1770, II. 228. See also E. Joliat, *Smollett et la France*, Paris, 1935.

[2] *Journal Britannique*, May–June 1755, p. 133.

[3] April–June 1756, p. 498.

de ce monarque pour croire que c'est lui que M. Hume a voulu dépeindre comme un prince qui était *ferme* dans ses conseils, *industrieux* dans ses projets, *courageux* dans ses entreprises, *fidèle*, *sincère*, et *plein d'honneur* dans son commerce avec tout le monde.' Obviously, no continental 'whig' could accept such a picture of the monster who had been driven out by the Glorious Revolution of 1688. Quite to the contrary, the Huguenot editor asserts, James II had been, in fact, *cruel*, *vindicatif*, *pusillanime et perfide*.[1]

A fairly similar tone predominates in this same journal's review of the *Tudors* in 1759, although, for obvious reasons, now that the Jacobite question was left behind, the editors found, as had contemporary English readers, that Hume's *History* was somewhat improved in quality:

L'esprit de parti qui gênait l'auteur en décrivant la domination des Stuarts et qui, joint à l'affectation d'impartialité, le jetait si souvent dans des contradictions révoltantes, l'embarrasse moins à mesure qu'il s'éloigne des temps modernes. . . . Mais de l'autre côté, on souhaiterait bien trouver ces mêmes qualités dans ce qu'il dit de l'origine et des progrès de la Réformation et de l'esprit qui a animé tous les Réformateurs. Il y a des endroits où on serait tenté de croire M. Hume *Papiste*. si on ne le connaissait pas déjà pour *Pyrrhonien*.[2]

Hume points out in *My Own Life* that the English accorded at last 'tolerable' success to the *Plantagenets*, the third and last part of the *History*. The *Bibliothèque des Sciences et des Beaux-Arts*, reviewing that work in 1761, naïvely confessed to a similar change of heart: 'Cette histoire devient meilleure à mesure que l'auteur s'éloigne de notre temps. Le bon esprit historique qui écarte ou ne touche que légèrement les objets peu essentiels, qui combine avec choix et présente avec netteté les événements intéressants, se fait sentir partout dans ces deux nouveaux volumes.'[3] It is perhaps unnecessary to point out that any attacks Hume made against religious fanaticism in this part of the *History*, which deals with the Middle Ages, would not normally be interpreted as immoderately hostile by the Protestant editors.

If we now compare these 'Dutch' accounts with opinions expressed in the Catholic French journals, we find that the progression of ideas on the subject of Hume's *History of England* is

[1] January–March 1757, pp. 245–6.
[2] January–March 1759, pp. 211–12.
[3] October–December 1761, p. 460.

neatly reversed. The pious *Mémoires de Trévoux* enthusiastically devoted many pages to reviewing Hume's *Stuarts* and commended Hume as an author who had written 'sans prévention'.[1] The manner in which Hume had dealt with the civil war period seemed especially appealing:

Les suites horribles n'en sont que trop connues: toute l'Europe en fut frappée et indignée: ce juste sentiment se renouvelle tout entier en lisant cette histoire. Avec toutes les vertus du meilleur roi, Charles Ier y reparaît, poursuivi, saisi, captif, prisonnier. Ce monarque, accusé sans forme de procès, jugé sans autorité, condamné sans crime, attendrit ici tous les lecteurs, qui le retrouvent encore plus grand, plus ferme, plus généreux et plus vertueux sur l'échafaud qu'il ne l'avait paru dans les succès et dans les revers qui ont fait la gloire comme le malheur de son règne.[2]

Every passage in which Hume rehabilitates the names of English Catholics is underlined by the Jesuit editors. Concerning the London fire, attributed by certain historians to the malevolence of Catholics, they are especially pleased to note that Hume 'n'en accuse pas plus les catholiques que les presbytériens: il convient que cette imputation ne fut qu'une calomnie accréditée par les préjugés populaires'.[3] As for the Popish plot, Hume 'en reconnaît l'évidente fausseté, sans disconvenir de l'impression fâcheuse que fit sur les Anglais une fable si mal ourdie. . . .'[4] On one occasion only do the Jesuit editors find Hume biased—when he is seen as 'aussi animé contre l'enthousiasme des puritains que partial contre les catholiques'.[5]

More significant still were the 'lessons' the *Mémoires de Trévoux* editors derived from their reading of Hume's *Stuarts*. These lessons are quite explicit and anticipate very similar interpretations of the work by counter-revolutionary thinkers after 1789:

Il ne faut que comparer cette histoire du règne de Charles Ier avec les autres qui ont été également écrites selon les préjugés propres aux protestants, pour sentir la supériorité de M. Hume, du côté du génie, du style, de l'exactitude et de l'impartialité. De cette comparaison, sans y comprendre aucun écrivain catholique, il résulte 1. Que, depuis leur séparation de l'Eglise Romaine, les protestants, livrés à leur propre esprit, ne peuvent avoir qu'une doctrine flottante et incertaine qui les

[1] *Mémoires de Trévoux*, February 1759, p. 468. [2] Ibid., p. 471.
[3] Ibid., March 1759, p. 184. [4] Ibid., p. 188.
[5] Ibid., January 1759, p. 217.

expose aux plus affreux égarements, sans avoir aucune ressource solide pour régler leur créance, et la rappeler à une vraie uniformité. 2. Que l'influence de leur doctrine a causé les troubles les plus horribles en Angleterre, et les attentats les plus abominables contre les souverains. 3. Qu'à la faveur des divisions dogmatiques entre les Réformés, le fanatisme se glissant d'abord sourdement, s'élevant ensuite avec éclat, a mis le comble aux désordres de la nation. 4. Que ce fanatisme hérétique n'est pas seulement prompt et rapide dans ses progrès, mais fécond et intarissable en monstres dangereux; puisque les *Indépendants*, si Cromwel leur chef n'eût pas prévenu le danger, furent à la veille d'être subjugués par les *Agitateurs* ou les *Aplanisseurs*, secte dont l'enthousiasme, enté sur le fanatisme des mêmes *Indépendants*, aspirait à mettre parmi les citoyens la plus parfaite égalité, et par conséquent la confusion et l'anarchie la plus monstrueuse dans le gouvernement. 5. Que, *comme l'insinue M. Hume*, les questions, même spéculatives, sur l'étendue ou les bornes de la puissance royale, ne doivent jamais être portées au tribunal du peuple; que sur ces matières on doit imposer le plus rigoureux silence, même aux philosophes *raisonneurs*; et qu'en général il y a moins de danger à laisser ignorer au peuple les limites de son obéissance, qu'à l'instruire de celles où ses souverains devraient se renfermer.[1]

As I have already pointed out, the question of whether Hume really implies all this, or whether the Jesuits made a correct or distorted interpretation of his intentions, is somewhat irrelevant to my purpose. The essential fact is that this interpretation *was made* and made frequently by a great variety of readers in eighteenth-century France. Of course, the *Mémoires de Trévoux* editors are forced to dodge about rather awkwardly when they encounter passages inspired by Hume's more frankly irreligious moods. Still, this side of the *History* was not seen as an insuperable problem. The *Stuarts* was after all by a 'Protestant' and even a Hume must be expected to wander from the truth from time to time. The Protestant *Bibliothèque des Sciences et des Beaux-Arts*, we remember, had found Hume's portrait of James II totally false. The *Mémoires de Trévoux*, on the other hand, did not find it sufficiently 'false', that is to say, sufficiently 'true': 'Il ne faut pas s'attendre que M. Hume, en écrivant l'histoire de ce règne, garde une exacte impartialité: il est trop prévenu d'une part contre la personne, la cour, la religion de Jacques II, de l'autre, contre la France, Louis XIV et toute espèce de zèle pour que sa plume ne répande

[1] Ibid., February 1759, pp. 475–6.

pas dans cette histoire des traces de ses préventions.'[1] Hume's occasional lapses were seen as faults only in some absolute sense; on this question the journal concluded: 'Quoi qu'il en soit, parmi les historiens protestants qui ont écrit l'histoire d'Angleterre du dernier siècle, M. Hume est encore le moins partial contre l'Eglise de Rome, et pour les sectes de la Réforme; c'est un mérite dont on doit lui tenir compte.'[2]

The same aspects of the *Stuarts* pleased Voltaire's enemy Fréron in the *Année littéraire*. He points out first of all that Hume has none of that 'prévention odieuse qu'on reproche aux écrivains anglais et dont nos historiens français eux-mêmes ne sont pas toujours exempts'.[3] He notes with particular approval Hume's treatment of Charles I's trial and execution: 'Il faudrait copier plusieurs pages entières pour présenter à votre humanité et à votre indignation cette scène horrible où ce roi fut jugé, condamné et conduit au supplice par ses propres sujets.'[4] All the horrors surrounding the monster republican Cromwell, the regicide fanaticism of the hated Puritans, are evoked in this *ancien-régime* Frenchman's review. Later, while examining the *Tudors*, Fréron shows the same highly favourable attitude to the Scottish historian's impartiality. He underlines the fact that Hume, for example, 'prend hautement la défense du Cardinal Wolsey . . . contre les écrivains protestants qui ont flétri sa mémoire.'[5] On the question of Henry VIII's divorce he is happy to point out also that Hume 'justifie conséquemment la résistance inflexible du pape aux sollicitations impérieuses et menaçantes du roi d'Angleterre.'[6] Along the same lines Hume's impartiality is contrasted with Burnet's bias on the question of the suppression of monasteries:

> . . . le Docteur Burnet raconte avec complaisance toutes les infamies dont les moines étaient accusés par les procès-verbaux des commissaires que Henri VIII avaient envoyés dans tous les couvents pour informer des moeurs et de la conduite des religieux et des religieuses. M. Hume, plus sage et plus circonspect dans ses jugements, ne compte pas beaucoup sur la vérité de ces procès-verbaux; toujours en garde contre l'esprit de parti qui les avait dictés, il avoue que dans ces temps de factions, et particulièrement de factions fomentées par un intérêt de religion, l'on ne doit pas s'attendre à trouver beaucoup de fidélité dans

[1] Ibid., March 1759, p. 197.
[2] Ibid., p. 198.
[3] *Année littéraire*, 1760, IV. 313.
[4] Ibid., IV. 323.
[5] Ibid., 1763, II. 297.
[6] Ibid., II. 301.

les témoignages qui paraissent les plus authentiques. . . . Il ne veut pas non plus que l'on impute à la religion catholique des abus qu'elle condamne, tels que l'exposition des fausses reliques et les pieuses impostures dont les moines se servaient en quelques endroits pour *accroître la dévotion et par conséquent la libéralité du peuple. De semblables bagatelles*, dit-il, *qui sont accréditées dans tous les temps et chez toutes les nations du monde, même pendant les siècles les plus éclairés de l'antiquité, ne portent aucune atteinte essentielle à la religion catholique.* Il faut avouer, Monsieur, que rien ne ressemble moins aux déclamations ordinaires des écrivains protestants qu'un pareil langage.[1]

Fréron too admits that Hume experienced difficulty occasionally in stripping himself entirely of 'English' ideas when speaking about religion; he states, however, that it would be ridiculous and unjust to judge the Scot 'selon les principes reçus parmi nous'.[2] Hume is occasionally wrong, but he is wrong with sincerity: 'On voit qu'il cherche sincèrement la vérité, et, s'il s'en écarte quelquefois, c'est moins par un dessein prémédité de la déguiser ou de la corrompre, que parce qu'il n'est pas donné à l'esprit humain de la trouver toujours.'[3]

It would be difficult to find any other subject on which Voltaire and Fréron seem to have been in such complete agreement. But even here we must make a distinction. Fréron's praise so far has been for the *Stuarts* and the *Tudors*. Voltaire, when he extolled Hume's virtues in the long review of 1764 already referred to, was judging the English edition of the *History* in its completed form—after, that is to say, the publication of the *Plantagenets*. It was especially this last section which permitted the French historian to praise the work as a more geographically restricted version of his own *Essai sur les Mœurs*. Conversely, when Fréron considered the *Plantagenets* in 1766, his admiration suddenly became considerably less warm: 'La moitié du premier volume de cette Histoire', he writes, 'n'a qu'un rapport fort éloigné avec ce qu'elle doit traiter. Si vous retranchez, de ce qui compose le reste, les fréquentes sorties de l'auteur contre l'Eglise et le clergé . . . ses déclamations contre l'ancienne religion catholique, vous trouverez l'Histoire de tous les princes de la maison de Plantagenet fort succincte.'[4] There is no doubt that Fréron was genuinely surprised to find what appeared to be a wealth of insulting epithets and vulgar abuse directed

[1] Ibid., II. 302–3.
[2] Ibid., 1760, IV. 313.
[3] Ibid., 1763, III. 35.
[4] Ibid., 1766, II. 4.

against religion in this work. Hume no longer seemed to be the divinely impartial historian, that rare angel of truth. He is now accused of having failed in the first duty of an historian, and Fréron notes that it was not with works like the *Plantagenets* that Hume had built up his great reputation in the literary world.[1]

Just as many traditionalists in France had been disappointed in 1758 to see the free-thinking *Philosophical Essays* appear only a few years after the fairly orthodox *Political Discourses* of 1754, a number of conservative French admirers of the *Stuarts* and *Tudors* withdrew their support for the historian after the appearance of the *Plantagenets*. As in the case with the *Philosophical Essays*, however, a much smaller group, the *philosophes*, greeted Hume's apparent return to sanity with a sigh of relief.

To say that the *philosophes* liked the last part of Hume's *History* with its *à la Voltaire* treatment of the Middle Ages, and disliked the *Stuarts* and the *Tudors*, would be to propose a rather neatly symmetrical but not entirely true simplification. One can note, however, among members of this group, a distinct preference for the more 'philosophical' Hume who had angered the Frérons with his essay 'Of Miracles', his *Natural History of Religion*, and his *Plantagenets*. The *philosophes* too spoke admiringly of impartiality but felt, certainly, that it should never be allowed to develop to the point where it might become a source of comfort to the enemy. Lockian in their political outlook—one is very tempted to see in them a close French equivalent of the English Whigs—they were chary of the Tory flavour of Hume's *Stuarts*. Grimm, perhaps the most critically astute and alertly orthodox of the 'frères', accused Hume as early as 1754, while reviewing the *Political Discourses*, of having slightly unsound political views: 'Je n'ai qu'un grief contre M. Hume, c'est d'aimer trop le paradoxe, ce qui le fait déraisonner quelquefois, et d'être jacobite.'[2] In the same year he expressed certain doubts concerning Hume's over-all ability as an enlightened thinker and added: 'Je me trompe, ou ses compatriotes doivent lui reprocher son goût décidé pour les Français, et ceux-ci n'en doivent pas être trop flattés, parce qu'il ne les voit pas par les côtés les plus estimables. . . .'[3] This same author was one of the first to express dissatisfaction several years later with those essays in the *Understanding* which did not attack miracles or Providence.

[1] Ibid., II. 28.
[2] *Correspondance littéraire*, 15 August 1754, II. 393.
[3] Ibid., 1 October 1754, II. 415.

Why, Grimm complained, did Hume feel it necessary to add to the confusion of the philosophic battle by discussing rather sceptically and with an appalling lack of originality the epistemological doctrines Locke had settled once and for all?[1]

Similarly, in the very year that Voltaire praised Hume's *History*, *l'homme aux Calas* confided to the Marquise Du Deffand: 'J'aime bien autant encore la philosophie de M. Hume que ses ouvrages historiques. Le bon de l'affaire c'est qu' Helvétius, qui dans son livre *De l'esprit*, n'a pas dit la vingtième partie des choses sages, utiles et hardies dont on sait gré à M. Hume et à vingt autres Anglais, a été persécuté chez les Welches et que son livre y a été brûlé. Tout cela prouve que les Anglais sont des hommes et les Français des enfants.'[2]

Hume in his *History* perhaps flattered those naughty children too much. The more unified story of how English liberty had emerged from despotism as told in the *Lettres philosophiques* was a much better way to improve *les Welches* than shedding sympathetic tears for a beheaded king or making statements that the *Mémoires de Trévoux* could interpret as great lessons. There is more than a hint of the back-handed compliment in at least one of Voltaire's recorded comments made during the guided tour he sometimes gave visitors through his vast library at Ferney. After pointing to the volumes of Shakespeare, Milton, Congreve, Rochester, Shaftesbury, Bolingbroke, Robertson, and Hume, Voltaire once turned to his guests and added for the last-mentioned author that David Hume had written his history 'to be praised' and that he had attained his goal.[3]

The fact remains that the *philosophes* did identify or did their best to identify the historical efforts of Hume and Voltaire. They, as well as Dr. Sam Johnson and Horace Walpole—though, of course, not with the same cranky and contemptuous hostility these two Englishmen affected—saw Hume as Voltaire's pupil: an accusation which Hume, who held a fairly low opinion of Voltaire's merit as an historian, frequently denied. There is no doubt that it was the occasional Voltairian tone of the *History* which appealed most to the *encyclopédiste* party. Helvétius, for example,

[1] See the *Correspondance littéraire*, 15 January 1759, IV. 70 and my article 'Hume, "Philosophe" and Philosopher in Eighteenth-Century France', *French Studies*, 1961, XV. 216.

[2] See Besterman, op. cit., LV, Letter 11,103 of 20 June 1764.

[3] See *Lettres de Madame de Graffigny*, Paris, 1879, p. 431.

writing to Hume on Prévost's forthcoming translation of the *Stuarts*, characteristically expressed the fear that the Abbé would not dare 'tell all'.[1] In doing so he probably betrayed unwittingly an interpretation of Hume's intentions which scarcely corresponds to the very complacent advice Hume had given Le Blanc to attenuate at will all strokes of *esprit fort* too strong for the French climate. Helvétius speaks of the *hardiesse* of the *Stuarts* but makes no particular mention, on the other hand, of the manner in which Hume had shed a tear for Charles I. Similarly, the *Plantagenets* aroused his greatest admiration, and in a letter to Hume of 1763 he especially commended that work for 'l'esprit philosophique et impartial qui l'a écrit'.[2] Moreover, in his own bold composition, *De l'homme*, Helvétius made good use of the anti-clerical arsenal he was able to find in this part of the *History*.

Perhaps no better evidence exists of this *philosophe* view of Hume as yet another soldier in the Voltairian war of propaganda against *l'infâme* than the numerous, almost urgent, appeals he received from his closest friends among the *encyclopédistes* to write an ecclesiastical history. In the same letter written to congratulate him on his 'esprit philosophique' in the *Plantagenets*, Helvétius also begged the Scottish historian to continue his efforts with 'le plus beau projet du monde'—a history of the Church: 'Pensez donc', he writes, 'que le sujet est digne de vous, comme vous êtes digne du sujet. C'est donc au nom de l'Angleterre, de la France, de l'Allemagne, de l'Italie et de la postérité que je vous conjure de faire cette histoire. Songez qu'il n'y a que vous en état de l'écrire. Qu'il se passera bien des siècles avant qu'il naisse un Monsieur Hume, et que c'est un bienfait que vous devez à l'univers présent et à venir.'[3]

Grimm in 1766 formulated the same wish: 'Nous avons souvent sollicité M. Hume, pendant son séjour en France, d'écrire une Histoire Ecclésiastique. Ce serait en ce moment une des plus belles entreprises de littérature, et un des plus importants services rendus à la philosophie et à l'humanité. . . . M. de Voltaire n'a plus une vigueur de tête assez soutenue pour se charger d'un pareil travail, il tournerait son sujet trop du côté de la plaisanterie et du ridicule. . . .'[4]

[1] *Letters of Eminent Persons*, p. 10: letter of 12 July 1759.
[2] Ibid., p. 13: letter of 2 June 1763. [3] Loc. cit.
[4] *Correspondance littéraire*, 1 April 1766, VII. 13.

Diderot, congratulating Hume for having finally put behind him the *affaire* with Rousseau, added in a letter of 1768 the advice that it was now high time to get on with more serious matters: 'Revenez, revenez vite, mon cher philosophe, à vos livres, à vos occupations. Je vous aime bien mieux le fouet à la main, faisant justice de tous les célèbres brigands qui ont troublé votre contrée. . . .'[1]

After the *Plantagenets*, Hume abandoned English history. Although he had at one time thought of continuing the work, the plan was never realized. D'Alembert, writing to Hume in 1766, urged him on in this project and showed in his letter that he too saw Hume's chief historical merit as a wielder of the philosophic scourge: 'Vous aurez si vous le voulez, de bien bonnes vérités à dire sur toutes les sottises que la France et ses ennemis ont faites pendant la Guerre de la Succession, et sur les causes qui ont produit ces sottises. Quelque intéressante que cette matière puisse être entre vos mains, j'aurais pourtant mieux aimé vous voir entreprendre l'histoire ecclésiastique. Il est, ce me semble, plus curieux de voir les hommes s'égorger pour des impertinences théologiques, que pour des provinces et des royaumes qui en valent un peu plus la peine.'[2]

What the *philosophes* wanted from an ecclesiastical history is not a matter of doubt. D'Alembert himself had given only a year before an example of the best clichés of the genre in his anonymously published work, *Sur la destruction des Jésuites en France* (1765). Ecclesiastical history would show all manner of usurpation of the spiritual powers over the temporal, the hideous crimes and bloody wars caused by religious fanaticism, the persecutions and murders committed in the name of Christ—such were the gifts of Christianity to mankind that would be recorded in a good 'philosophically' inspired ecclesiastical history. In a letter of 1773, d'Alembert once again solicited Hume on the subject and commiserated at the same time on the fate of that 'poor lady' who is called Philosophy: '. . . ceux qui voudraient écrire pour elle ne l'osent—ceux qui le pourraient, comme vous, aiment mieux dormir et digérer, et peut-être prennent le bon parti. Je ne me consolerai, pourtant, jamais d'être privé de cette histoire ecclésiastique, que je vous ai demandée tant de fois, que vous seul peut-être en Europe êtes en

[1] *Letters of Eminent Persons*, p. 284: letter of 22 February 1768.
[2] Ibid., p. 183: letter of 28 February 1766.

état de faire, et qui serait bien aussi intéressante que l'histoire grecque et romaine, si vous vouliez prendre la peine de peindre au naturel notre mère Ste Eglise.'[1]

It is perhaps not strange that the practical implications of the *Stuarts* as interpreted by the *Mémoires de Trévoux* were largely ignored by the *philosophes* rather than overtly attacked or even commented on. Clearly it was the medieval section of the *History* which proved most useful to them. In the work, *De la félicité publique*, which Voltaire perversely judged as at least equal in merit to Montesquieu's *Esprit des Lois*, the *philosophe* Chastellux showed how valuable the *Plantagenets* could be if properly used—used, that is, as a work to supplement Voltaire's more famous catalogue of medieval barbarities. A disciple of progress, Chastellux had no patience with those who rhapsodized (as Burke was to do twenty years later) on the glories of the age of chivalry, the former splendour of the nobility, the stability of feudal law, the exalted courage of the crusaders, &c. Those who superstitiously lamented the departure of those good old days could be cured by reading two authors especially: 'Mais consultez', Chastellux advises, '*l'Essai sur l'histoire générale*, le modèle des ouvrages historico-philosophiques; consultez M. Hume, illustre dans la même carrière. . . .'[2]

Delisle de Sales, another of Voltaire's understudies but fond too

[1] Ibid., p. 218: letter of 1 May 1773. Hume's sceptical lack of anti-clerical or anti-religious militancy was also a source of considerable disappointment to the atheist Naigeon. Writing in 1792 he tells us how, try as he might, and after two careful readings of Hume's posthumously published *Dialogues concerning Natural Religion*, he was unable to find in the work any clear-cut statement that God did not exist. Why, he asks, should a man be timid about the truth once he is dead? 'On est excusable de composer avec les erreurs et les préjugés du vulgaire, lorsqu'en les foulant ouvertement aux pieds, on peut craindre de se commettre avec les fanatiques et les persécuteurs; mais quand on est censé parler aux hommes du fond de son tombeau, il faut alors leur dire la vérité sans détours, sans ménagement. . . .' (See the *Encyclopédie Méthodique: Philosophie ancienne et moderne*, par M. Naigeon, Paris, 1792, II. 748.) It would have been better, Naigeon added, had Hume remained entirely silent on the matter of religion, since his last word on the subject 'n'offre au fond que les mêmes difficultés, les mêmes doutes qu'il avait proposés il y a 40 ans dans ses essais sur l'entendement humain. D'où l'on peut conclure que sur la première des *vérités théologiques*, Hume n'a jamais été plus loin que le scepticisme. . . .' Diderot, Naigeon concluded, had handled the question of God rather more skilfully. (Ibid., II. 750–1).

[2] *De la félicité publique* (1772), nouvelle édition, augmentée de notes inédites de Voltaire, Paris, 1822, II. 48–49; see also II. 10, 13, 24, 31, 43, 91.

of calling Hume 'le Tacite de l'Angleterre',[1] found materials for the good cause not only in the *Plantagenets* but in the *Tudors* and *Stuarts* as well. Particularly useful to his purposes was Hume's account of the religious massacres in Ireland, seen by the French author as having been unequalled even by that of Saint Bartholomew's Day, the event, we remember, which made French history almost worth writing about in the opinion of Voltaire. Delisle de Sales ignored, curiously enough, Hume's own estimate of the number of victims, established in the *History* at the sufficiently horrifying figure of 40,000, and chose instead the more polemically useful figure of 200,000.[2]

As an illustration of how the same passage from Hume's *History* could at times inspire both the *philosophes* and their enemies to reach completely antithetical conclusions, it is amusing to note that the Abbé Bergier, a Roman Catholic apologist to whom we shall refer again, discussed in 1767 this same massacre; and he was delighted to point out that religion was not the only nor even the principal cause of it: 'M. Hume, témoin non suspect, avoue de bonne foi que l'animosité invétérée des Irlandais contre les Anglais, l'amour de la liberté, de la propriété et de leurs anciens usages, la jalousie contre les Anglais nouvellement transplantés en Irlande, la crainte d'en être encore plus maltraités à la suite, en un mot, le mécontentement contre le gouvernement anglais, furent les vraies causes de cette guerre civile. Quand on fait monter le nombre des morts à soixante ou quatre-vingt mille, on exagère de moitié.'[3]

Quite obviously there were possibilities for distortion, in this and in other instances, by all sides, including Hume's no doubt. The major conclusion that emerges from an examination of the evidence is, however, that the *History*, valuable as it may have seemed to the *philosophes*, proved to be infinitely more exploitable by the traditionalists. It is, in fact, quite possible that, as a group,

[1] *De la philosophie de la nature ou Traité de morale pour l'espèce humaine tiré de la philosophie et fondé sur la nature*, troisième édition, Londres, 1777, II. 274; VI. 412.

[2] Ibid., VI. 317–18. Hume's text is as follows: 'By some computations, those who perished by all these cruelties are supposed to be a hundred and fifty, or two hundred thousand: by the most moderate, and probably the most reasonable account, they are made to amount to forty thousand; if this estimation itself be not, as is usual in such cases, somewhat exaggerated.' (*The History of England*, VII. 388.)

[3] *Œuvres complètes de Bergier*, publiées par M. l'Abbé Migne, Paris, 1855, VIII. 228.

the *philosophes* seriously misjudged Hume's capacity to further their cause. An anonymous eighteenth-century commentator of the Hume-Rousseau quarrel astutely suggested that this was the case:

Vous n'ignorez vraisemblablement pas que nos philosophes étaient tombés dans un grand décri, lorsqu'ils jugèrent que David Hume était propre à entrer dans leur secte, et à la relever. Il était étranger, flegmatique, hardi dans ses systèmes et assez sage dans ses actions. Il avait fait l'Histoire de son pays pour l'Angleterre, et quatre volumes de philosophie pour la France. Son histoire qui n'avait pas eu beaucoup de succès à Londres, réussit très bien à Paris, parmi nos philosophes et leurs sectateurs, à cause des quatre volumes de philosophie qui étayaient leurs principes. Ils en parlèrent avec enthousiasme: on l'acheta, on ne la lut guère, on la loua beaucoup.[1]

That Hume was more praised than read by the *philosophe* party is entirely possible. With the exception of the Turgot–Hume correspondence which we shall examine later and in which are clearly apparent the genuine differences which separated the Scottish philosopher's rather pessimistic, perhaps complacent, acceptance of the *status quo* and the young Intendant's eagerly optimistic hopes for change, the many letters Hume received from his *philosophe* friends seem strangely misdirected. Helvétius flatters himself, at the beginning of a letter to Hume in 1759, that he is in almost total agreement with his correspondent concerning ethical motivation. A few lines farther along in his letter, however, he shows that nothing could be more distant from the truth and displays an almost wilful tendency to ignore the fact that Hume's *Enquiry* specifically combats such simplistic 'self-interest' theories as his own. D'Holbach, in a letter of August 1763, calls Hume one of the greatest philosophers of any age. There is evidence to show too that he had read, or at least that he owned, all of Hume's works and yet, again on the question of ethics, he maintained in several of his own compositions that only ignorant theologians deny self-interest as the basis of morality.[2]

[1] *Réflexions posthumes sur le grand procès de Jean-Jacques avec David* (1767), p. 12.

[2] G.-J. Holland, in the most valuable of the many contemporary refutations of d'Holbach's *Système de la Nature*, pointed out on this question that Hume—who did defend ethical motivation as involving more than self-interest—could hardly be classed as an ignorant theologian. See *Réflexions philosophiques sur le Système de la Nature*, Paris, 1773, p. 129. Also in this work, in an analysis quite unusual before Kant, Holland uses Hume's causality doctrine to combat d'Holbach's determinism. (See ibid., pp. 5–6, 16–17.)

We have perhaps another example of this basic lack of comprehension, I think, in Helvétius' rather earnest reaction to Hume's fairly ironically-titled essay on the 'perfect' commonwealth. Hume warns in his preliminary remarks that all plans of government which pre-suppose a great change in man's nature are 'imaginary'. He seems to intend, as he does so often in his epistemological inquiries also, nothing more than a good intellectual exercise; but it is a game which we suspect Helvétius takes perhaps too seriously when he solemnly speculates in *De l'homme* on the practical applicability of the means Hume proposes.[1] D'Alembert, though perhaps Hume's closest friend in Paris, seems to labour under a somewhat similar misconception in a letter to the Scot introducing his neighbour and friend, the latitudinarian Abbé de Vauxcelles: 'Il va en Angleterre', d'Alembert writes without any excessive appearance of irony, 'pour avoir le plaisir de crier avec vous "Wilkes and Liberty!". . . .'[2] David Hume, it need hardly be said, never waved a *mouchoir à la Wilkes*!

5. The Scottish Bossuet

Ideally for the *philosophes*, Hume's presentation of England in the *History* should have confirmed most of the polemical doctrine of Voltaire's famous *Lettres philosophiques*, holding up the English to the French as an enlightened, tolerant, politically and religiously emancipated nation. There is very little in the pages of Voltaire's *Letters* which was calculated to give comfort to the French except perhaps the general statement that Corneille and Racine wrote better tragedies than Shakespeare.

But, quite to the contrary, there is much evidence to suggest that Hume's *History* was often used to show how wrong Voltaire actually was and to illustrate to the French how lucky they were not to be English. Gallic *amour-propre*, in the thirty years following the first appearance of the *Lettres philosophiques*, had taken some very hard knocks from France's intellectual leaders. Reaction was inevitable.

[1] See *Œuvres complettes de M. Helvétius*, Londres, 1781, IV. 268. This same essay was commented on at great length in the revolutionary period by J.-M.-A. Servan, *Correspondance entre quelques hommes honnêtes*, Lausanne 1795, III. 136–78. See also Joseph de Maistre, *Considérations sur la France* (1796) in *Œuvres complètes*, I. 72–73.

[2] *Letters of Eminent Persons*, p. 214.

An example of how Hume's *History* was used by traditionalists to combat the *philosophe's* exploitation of England as a propaganda symbol can be found in the *Dictionnaire social et patriotique* of the French lawyer Claude-Rigobert Lefebvre de Beauvray. Published in 1770, his work, bearing the epigraph 'Soyez Anglais à Londres et Français à Paris', was intended as a remedy to the disease of *philosophisme anglais*, seen thirty years later by some extreme commentators of the Right as one of the chief causes of the Revolution.

Voltaire had spoken of the English as tolerant in religion, moderate and free in politics and, most important of all, profound in their philosophical thinking. If only, Voltaire seemed to be saying, France took England for its model, then all would be well.

Lefebvre de Beauvray disagreed violently. Quoting as evidence Hume's sentiments on England's lack of an equivalent of the French Academy, he stated that the city of Paris by itself had more to offer the intellectual than the whole of Great Britain.[1]

As for England's hideous 'republican' liberty, so often praised by the *encyclopédistes*, de Beauvray proposed the following counter-arguments in his article 'Frondeurs':

> On déclame tous les jours contre le peu de liberté dont on jouit sous un gouvernement monarchique. . . .
>
> Pour fermer la bouche à tous ces frondeurs, nous les prierons seulement de peser un peu les réflexions suivantes, exposées de bonne foi par M. Hume lui-même, dans son *Histoire de la Maison de Stuart*, tome 3e, page 429: 'Le gouvernement est institué pour restreindre la furie et l'injustice du Peuple. Son fondement étant toujours l'opinion, non la force, il est dangereux d'affaiblir par de téméraires spéculations, le respect que le Peuple doit à l'autorité. . . . Ou, s'il est réellement impossible de mettre un frein à la license des recherches humaines, on doit reconnaître que la doctrine de l'obéissance est la seule qui doive être recommandée, et que ses exceptions, qui sont extrêmement rares, ne doivent jamais être remarquées dans les discours, et dans les écrits publics. Il n'y aurait même aucun danger que cette sage réserve fît tomber le Genre Humain dans une abjecte servitude.'[2]

The bloody revolutions of England's history strongly suggest to de Beauvray that liberty is not a worth-while political goal.

[1] *Dictionnaire social et patriotique ou précis raisonné des connaissances relatives à l'économie morale, civile et politique,* Par M.C.R.L.F.D.B.A.A.P.D.P., Amsterdam, 1770, p. 141.

[2] Ibid., pp. 176–8.

Hume's opinion of the British parliamentary leaders during the Civil War is seen as sufficient proof of this point:

'Si l'on ne peut contester à la gloire des premiers (des partisans outrés de la liberté anglaise) que leurs fins ont été plus nobles et leurs vues plus avantageuses à la race humaine, il faut avouer aussi que leurs moyens sont plus difficiles à justifier. . . . Dans la nécessité de faire leur cour à la Populace, ils se voyaient obligés d'applaudir à sa folie, ou de suivre les mouvements de sa rage. . . .' (*Hist. de la Maison de Stuart*, t. 1 et 6.)[1]

Hume is especially commended as an 'écrivain judicieux' for having analysed with great truth and force the character of the usurper Cromwell. Cromwell was not just the worst of these parliamentary leaders; no man since Mohammed, de Beauvray affirms, had exhibited to the same degree such a harmful mixture of genius and low cunning.[2]

Voltaire had painted a very rosy picture of religious toleration in England; each Englishman, we remember, is seen as going to heaven by the road of his choice. Hume, in his descriptions of the Civil War period, gives us a rather different version of things and, still according to Lefebvre de Beauvray, his picture is one which deprives the British people of any right to accuse other nations of religious persecution:

Jamais Inquisition ne fut pareille à celle qu'exercèrent les Puritains d'Angleterre et les Covenantaires d'Ecosse. Cette confédération, prétendue religieuse, connue sous le nom de Covenant, porta le fer et la flamme dans toutes les parties des Trois Royaumes. Ce fut elle qui prépara en quelque sorte cette affreuse tragédie dont le dénouement fut si funeste à la famille royale, et qui fait encore verser aux fils des larmes sur le crime de leurs pères.

Jamais peut-être écrivain ne sut, comme l'auteur de l'Emile, prêcher l'Humanité du ton le plus dur, et la liberté de l'air le plus despotique. C'est ainsi que ceux qui affichent davantage la tolérance, laissent souvent percer le caractère le plus intolérant. En un mot, ils veulent que tout le monde les tolère, sans daigner eux-mêmes tolérer personne.

On est confirmé dans cette opinion par l'aveu singulier d'un historien anglais: 'Il faut, dit-il, l'avouer, à la honte de ce siècle et de l'Ile Britannique, tous les désordres de l'Ecosse, sans exception, et la plupart de ceux de l'Angleterre, tirent leur source d'une si vile et si méprisable origine, telle que l'aversion pour le surplis, les balustrades placées

[1] Ibid., pp. 179–80. [2] Ibid., pp. 225–6.

autour de l'autel, la liturgie, les châpes brodées, l'usage de la bague nuptiale et du signe de la croix dans le Baptême.' (Voyez *l'Histoire de la Maison de Stuart sur le trône d'Angleterre*, t. 2, p. 327.)[1]

De Beauvray also cites Hume on the advantages of the monarchical form of government as compared with the English 'republican' system.[2] In support of such anti-liberal views, the article 'Liberté' of the *Dictionnaire* reproduces a long quotation from Hume which de Beauvray interprets as a lesson to the French on the worthlessness of England's much-vaunted Magna Carta.[3]

Intellectually backward, intolerant in religion and bloody in politics, the English are seen by de Beauvray as perversely wrong even in the way that they treat their only good historian, the judicious David Hume: 'Il s'en faut de beaucoup que l'ouvrage de M. Hume ait reçu un accueil également favorable de la part de tous les Anglais. Plusieurs d'entr'eux lui reprochent sa naissance en Ecosse, et sa prédilection pour le parti de la Cour. Ils refusent en conséquence à cet auteur les éloges, que son travail et ses recherches méritent. Si l'on s'obstine à dire que M. Hume n'est point un bon historien, l'Angleterre n'a point encore d'histoire nationale, et n'en peut jamais avoir.'[4] Not only is Hume a great historian, he is, 'de tous les philosophes politiques, celui qui connaît le mieux les intérêts et les ressources de sa nation'.[5]

We see that it was only too easy, albeit with a certain measure of misrepresentation, for *anti-philosophes* like de Beauvray to interpret much of Hume as supporting the cause of the *ancien régime* against the lessons of Voltaire's *Lettres philosophiques*. Voltaire had praised the English too for their civic virtues. He had especially applauded the English nobility for its modern commercial spirit, and contrasted their efforts at honest capitalism with the non-existent contributions of the foppishly ornamental French *petits-maîtres* who refused to engage in trade and commerce because of feudal prejudices. Voltaire, to show his feelings in this respect, had

[1] Ibid., pp. 257–8. [2] Ibid., pp. 356, 365, 469, 514–15.
[3] Ibid., pp. 275–8. [4] Ibid., p. 284.
[5] Ibid., p. 446. Readers of de Beauvray's *Dictionnaire* may be somewhat surprised after such praise to discover that in a parallel of English and French thinkers matching Hobbes and Gassendi, Shaftesbury and Montaigne, and in which no English equivalent of Montesquieu can be found, Hume is labelled the English equivalent of Buffier (ibid., p. 26). The mystery is solved, however, when we encounter, buried away in another part of the *Dictionnaire*, proof that de Beauvray considered Buffier to be 'le plus judicieux et le plus profond peut-être de tous nos philosophes' (p. 329).

even set a precedent in French theatre by dedicating his tragedy *Zaïre* to an English businessman.

But was England really such a model island of patriots and philosophers? Another French lawyer, Basset de la Marelle, asked the question in a speech delivered in 1762 to the Académie de Lyon. His answer, given while the Seven Years War was still in progress, was, of course, vehemently negative. What is significant for us is that he too found proofs of his arguments in the impartial M. Hume. Hume frankly admitted, for example, that the English at the time of the Norman Conquest showed very little of that patriotism which they liked to boast of as almost hereditary in their nation.[1] Moreover, there was little to admire in Britain's modern commercial conquests. The British attitude to trade formed the basis of a vicious imperialism and was a constant cause of England's unjust wars. The British Cabinet had always known that its unruly subjects had either to be amused or to be feared.

> ... pour n'être pas réduit à cette dernière extrémité, il occupe ce peuple inquiet, chez lequel un état de paix est toujours un présage d'orages ou de révolutions; il lui fait prendre part dans le continent à des intérêts étrangers, qu'il lui fait envisager comme les siens propres; il lui présente l'empire des mers comme son patrimoine naturel, exclusivement à tous les peuples; il offre à son avidité le projet d'envahir, au préjudice de toutes les nations, par le commerce des deux mondes, les richesses de l'univers entier; . . . S'agit-il d'entreprises ruineuses pour la nation, il l'enivre de la gloire des succès qui l'épuisent; c'est ce qui fait dire à un des plus habiles politiques anglais (M. Hume, *De la balance du pouvoir*) que la moitié de leurs guerres avec la France, et toutes leurs dettes publiques, sont plutôt provenues de leur imprudente véhémence, que de l'ambition de leurs voisins. . . .[2]

Let us proceed now to examine the writings of a number of French traditionalists who exploited Hume's impartiality as they defended not only the *ancien régime*'s national *amour-propre* and its politics but its religion as well. Here too the *faux-frère* David Hume made valuable contributions. Immediately after the French publication of his philosophical essays, for example, he was

[1] *La différence du patriotisme national chez les François et chez les Anglois*, Lyon, 1762, pp. 16–17. The author was executed during the Terror.

[2] Ibid., pp. 60–62. French *anglophobes* of the Napoleonic era seized upon similar passages from Hume's writings. See, for example, the anonymous pamphlet, *Le peuple anglais bouffi d'orgueil, de bière et de thé, jugé au tribunal de la raison,* Paris, An IX–1803, pp. 67–87.

recognized by yet another enemy of Voltaire, the Abbé Trublet, as a useful source of ideas against the current irreligion. Voltaire and the *philosophes* had made a great man of John Locke and had praised especially Locke's rejection of innate ideas. In the *Journal Chrétien* of 1758 Abbé Trublet applauded the 'judicious' Hume for having shown at last that Locke's ideas on this subject, as well as on many other subjects, were totally confused.[1]

It is strange irony that the *philosophes*, who at this time praised Hume so much as a kindred spirit, had failed to recognize his originality in epistemology even as Christian apologists, however insincerely, were using Hume's theory of knowledge to attack the very basis of Enlightenment philosophy. Hume's scepticism, perhaps even charitably viewed as an unavoidable first step toward fideism, seemed particularly useful to Trublet against the dogmatic conclusions of rationalism. In the same way, the French Abbé had earlier defended Berkeley against the charge made by some Catholic apologists that the Irish bishop's strange idealism was impious. British philosophers, it had to be admitted, could be rather eccentric but they were 'inégalement faux' and proper distinctions had to be made if one rejected them.[2] With such distinctions in mind, Trublet and other eighteenth-century apologists occasionally attempted to revive the old technique of *rétorsion*, the *machine de guerre* which had earlier been used with success against the Protestants and rationalists of the Renaissance.

David Hume's scepticism with its dialectic based on the maximum multiplication of view-points was particularly vulnerable to exploitation by this technique. The *philosophes* were not to be allowed the satisfaction of thinking that all of modern philosophy supported their cause. They prided themselves on having recourse to reason alone, but if a sceptic could show, as David Hume, for example, had shown, that many of their arguments were based on Lockian 'acts of faith', then that sceptic, though not a religious man, could be useful in the defence of religion. Hume was not really an angel of truth, but he could be spirited away from his evil brothers and put to work against their incredulity. 'L'objet de M. Trublet', writes the Abbé Joannet, editor of the *Journal Chrétien*, '. . . dans la plupart des morceaux répandus dans ce

[1] August 1758, IV. 59–63. The same debate is repeated in Abbé Chaudon's *Dictionnaire anti-philosophique*, Avignon, 1767, pp. 375–7.

[2] See ibid., May 1759, III. 91–92; March 1760, II. 36–38.

journal a toujours été d'enlever à l'impiété et à l'irréligion, les hommes de lettres, que la vanité de nos philosophes prétendus range sous les drapeaux du matérialisme et de l'incrédulité.'[1]

In 1768, although all of Hume's works were by then on the *Index*, the future cardinal, Gerdil, showed that even some of the higher church officials were on occasion able to view David Hume in this same friendly light. In his *Discours sur la divinité de la religion chrétienne*, for example, Gerdil attacked the *philosophes* for their irreverent views on the lives of the Christian saints. Happily, he maintained, there was a remedy for their blindness:

. . . des auteurs plus judicieux ont remédié à ce défaut par des ouvrages plus exacts, fondés sur des monuments authentiques. Si parmi ceux que de malheureux préjugés éloignent de la religion il est des esprits droits et équitables, des coeurs portés à la vertu, quoi de plus propre pour les guérir de leurs préventions, et les réconcilier avec le Christianisme, que la lecture de la vie de Jésus-Christ et de celles des saints, qui, remplis de l'esprit de Jésus-Christ ont représenté dans toute leur conduite la grandeur et la simplicité de l'Evangile? Ils y verront la nature humaine ennoblie par les plus hautes vertus, pratiquées avec éclat et sans ostentation.[2]

Apparently a perusal of Hume could be added profitably to that of the gospels; Gerdil continues: 'Le portrait que M. Hume a tracé du célèbre Chancelier Thomas Morus, peut servir à justifier l'idée que nous donnons de la justice chrétienne dans tous les états et dans toutes les situations de la vie'—Gerdil then quotes Hume's portrait of the English saint at length.[3]

In a much more significant work of 1769, the *Discours philosophiques sur l'homme considéré relativement à l'état de nature et à l'état social*, Gerdil returned to Hume for inspiration, and anticipated in his use of the Scot's political ideas the almost identical lines of reasoning proposed later by such counter-revolutionary ideologists as Maury, Ferrand, de Bonald, and de Maistre. Already author of an anti-*Emile* and an anti-*Contrat social*, Gerdil set out again to attack the artificiality of contract theory. Society, he asserted, is a moral and political fact of man's nature. Quoting Hume's own analysis of the subject, Gerdil agreed that man is not

[1] Ibid., September 1762, p. 5.

[2] *Œuvres du Cardinal Gerdil de l'ordre des Barnabites*, publiées par M. L'Abbé Migne, Paris, 1863, p. 989.

[3] Loc. cit.

solely motivated by self-interest. Man is born for society; the contracts of Hobbes, Locke, and Rousseau are false, the concept of natural equality is a harmful myth; ultimately the organization of man in society is a reflection of the government of God.[1]

One is not surprised to find this learned ecclesiastic defending theocracy as the true basis of government. What is mildly astonishing, however, is the way he transforms David Hume's social naturalism into a specific defence of this divine-right view attacked by Hume in the same essay in which he assails contract theory. Little more than a clever transition is required to perform this textual miracle. Society, it is agreed, is not based on an arbitrary contract but on the natural fact of man's sociability. The origin of public authority does not rest, then, in the free consent of individuals who have given up for this purpose part of their natural rights. Public authority takes all its force from the right that nature implicitly gives every society to see to its well-being and survival:

La puissance souveraine dans la société est donc établie sur la loi de la nature, et comme la loi naturelle a Dieu pour auteur, il faut convenir que la puissance souveraine est fondée sur l'ordre même établi de Dieu pour la conservation et le bien-être du genre humain: *Qui potestati resistit, ordinationi Dei resistit:* tel est l'oracle de l'Apôtre.

M. Hume rend hommage à cette vérité dans son vingt-cinquième essai moral et politique: 'Dès lors, dit-il, qu'on admet une providence universelle qui préside sur l'univers, qui suit un plan uniforme dans la direction des événements et qui les conduit à des fins dignes de sa sagesse, on ne saurait nier que Dieu ne soit le premier instituteur du gouvernement. Le genre humain ne peut subsister sans gouvernement: au moins n'y a-t-il point de sécurité où il n'y a point de protection. Il est donc indubitable que la souveraine bonté qui veut le bien de toutes ses créatures, a voulu que les hommes fussent gouvernés: aussi le sont-ils, et l'ont-ils été dans tous les temps et dans tous les pays du monde, ce qui fait encore une preuve plus certaine des intentions de l'Etre tout sage à qui rien ne saurait faire illusion.'[2]

Gerdil applauds this argument as entirely solid. Unfortunately, Hume spoils his line of reasoning somewhat by his subsequent conclusions. Gerdil then quotes the passage in Hume's essay 'Of the Original Contract' which his friend, the Abbé Maury, another Hume-inspired future Cardinal of the Church,

[1] Ibid., pp. 1326–30. Gerdil, incidentally, also quotes a fragment of Hume's *Natural History of Religion* as evidence against deism (p. 1393).

[2] Ibid., pp. 1414–15.

did not dare cite later while debating the concept of sovereignty with Mirabeau on the floor of the Assemblée Nationale.[1] If the nature of things and providential arrangement are equated, the authority exercised by a pirate or a common robber is, Hume contends, as inviolable as that of any lawful prince. Gerdil gives the obviously confused but no doubt well-intentioned Monsieur Hume a kindly correction on this point:

'Dieu qui veut le bien de ses créatures, veut que les hommes soient gouvernés': c'est le principe de M. Hume. L'établissement du gouvernement est conforme aux *intentions de l'Etre tout sage*, et le souverain tient une place dans la société, marquée par l'ordre même de la Providence; mais l'abus que fait un brigand de ses forces physiques pour dépouiller les passants est un attentat contre les lois de Dieu, qui, en permettant ce mal, le réprouve, le condamne et le punit. Comment donc M. Hume a-t-il pu avancer que l'autorité du prince le plus légitime n'est pas plus sacrée, ni plus inviolable que celle d'un brigand?[2]

After thus disposing of this minor lapse in what is otherwise seen as a brilliant argument, Gerdil returns to base his conclusion on Hume's authority:

Nous ne devons donc pas regarder l'établissement du gouvernement comme un simple effet de *cette influence secrète qui anime toute la nature*, mais, de plus comme une institution que Dieu veut, qui est conforme aux intentions de l'Etre tout sage et à sa souveraine bonté. Cette conformité que la droite raison nous découvre de l'aveu de M. Hume, nous fait connaître, par une conséquence claire et immédiate, qu'on ne peut outrager l'autorité souveraine du gouvernement, sans résister aux intentions, aux lois, à la volonté de l'Etre tout sage. Ce qui suffit pour rendre cette autorité sacrée et inviolable. Ce que la raison démontre sur ce sujet est pleinement confirmé par l'autorité même des livres saints, qui nous découvrent d'une manière plus distincte et plus authentique les volontés de l'Etre suprême. Pour s'en convaincre, on n'a qu'à consulter le troisième livre de la *Politique tirée de l'Ecriture Sainte* de Bossuet.[3]

It can be easily imagined how Hume's alleged testimony in favour of what is in fact a full-blown system of theocracy was seen as all the more valuable by religious conservatives precisely because it did not come from Bossuet but rather from the sceptical and therefore 'impartial' Hume. Joseph de Maistre, who was later

[1] See below, chapter III. pp. 91–92.
[2] Ibid., p. 1416.
[3] Ibid., p. 1417.

probably even more thoroughly influenced by Hume in this direction, expressed the belief that one could trust such a man to speak the truth because, as he tells us, 'Hume, . . . ne croyant rien, ne se gênait pour rien. . . .'[1]

On another matter, the Jesuit Claude-François Nonnotte, remembered today especially as an adversary of Voltaire's *Essai sur les Mœurs* and *Dictionnaire philosophique*, also occasionally invoked the testimony of David Hume. In the article 'Christianisme' of his own antidotal *Dictionnaire philosophique de la religion*, Nonnotte set out to disprove the common *philosophe's* contention that Christ's kingdom has been the scene of mankind's bloodiest wars. Christianity, he maintained to the contrary, has been a civilizing and beneficial factor in good government throughout the ages:

> . . . le christianisme a adouci les mœurs, arrêté l'esprit de sédition, déraciné et détruit le germe des guerres civiles. Il est donc incontestable qu'il a fait un véritable bien à l'univers.
>
> Ces mêmes déclamateurs furieux qui ne cessent de représenter le christianisme comme une religion de troubles et de discordes, et qui bouleverse les états, les royaumes et les empires, la veulent faire passer encore pour une religion meurtrière, et la plus dangereuse pour les têtes couronnées.
>
> Il ne sont point en cela de l'avis d'un des plus célèbres docteurs de ce siècle, qui tout protestant qu'il est, avoue que, de toutes les religions, la catholique est celle qui est la plus favorable aux souverains. (Hume, *Hist. de la Maison de Stuart.*)[2]

Nonnotte also attacks Voltaire for what he considers to be the French historian's too favourable attitude to that hypocritical assassin Cromwell and, for that matter, to the entire Puritan rebellion.[3] Voltaire, moreover, Nonnotte informs us, lies in his teeth when he praises Elizabeth as tolerant and attacks Mary as a persecutor: the 'sage écrivain, Monsieur Hume' in his 'excellente *Histoire*' easily proves how wrong the great infidel is in both cases.[4]

[1] *Du Pape* (1817) in *Œuvres complètes*, II. 413.

[2] *Dictionnaire philosophique de la religion, où l'on établit les points de la religion attaqués par les incrédules, et où l'on répond à toutes leurs objections.* Nouvelle édition, Besançon, 1774, I. 368–9.

[3] An example of Voltaire's opinion of the Protector may be found in the article 'Cromwell' of the *Dictionnaire philosophique* in *Œuvres complètes de Voltaire*, XVIII. 294–9; see also *Essai sur les Mœurs*, ibid., XIII. 74–82.

[4] Nonnotte, op. cit., I. 370; III. 328–9. See also his *Erreurs de Monsieur de Voltaire*, Paris, 1770, I. 273–7; II. 407–10.

In an article attacking d'Alembert's eulogy of George Keith, Hereditary Earl Marischal of Scotland and Governor of Neuchâtel, the future counter-revolutionary journalist, Abbé Royou, also illustrated how it was possible to appeal to Hume for aid in protecting the ideological inertia of the *ancien régime*.[1]

D'Alembert in his *Eloge* had spoken disparagingly of the Stuart kings and had referred specifically to James II as Jesuit-inspired and intolerant. As we have already noted, eighteenth-century French Catholics seemed to find it particularly important to defend James II's memory: '. . . le jésuitisme du roi Jacques', Abbé Royou insists, 'est une de ces opinions populaires enfantée par la haine, adoptée par la malignité crédule, mais qui ne fut jamais constatée par aucun témoin digne de foi. *Hume* n'en parle pas. . . .'[2] As for the alleged intolerance of James II, that too, Royou affirms, is a malicious lie. Quite to the contrary, James was forced to leave the English throne because he was excessively tolerant. 'S'il avait favorisé les lois atroces et sanguinaires de la secte *Anglicane*, il eût joui et sa famille jouirait encore de tout l'amour que ses vertus lui méritèrent d'abord de la part de ses sujets. Mais il voulut *accorder à toutes les sectes de son royaume une entière liberté de conscience*, et adoucir la rigueur des lois pénales, portées contre les Catholiques, sans cependant, comme il protesta jusqu'à la mort (Hume, t.6, p. 536), toucher *aux privilèges et prérogatives des Protestants*. Voilà la source de ses malheurs!'[3]

D'Alembert's radical view of Stuart intolerance inspired this brother-in-law of Fréron and future editor of *l'Ami du Roi* to attack the *philosophes* generally for endlessly speaking of tolerance and, at the same time, for being highly intolerant toward Catholics. Coming back to d'Alembert's portrait of James II, he proposed to show what that monarch was really like: 'Opposons à ce portrait vraiment *odieux* et *coupable* de la conduite du roi Jacques celui qu'en a tracé M. Hume: Protestant d'origine, incrédule de

[1] Abbé Royou's publication appeared in the *Année littéraire*, June 1779, IV. 73–113 and was reprinted in S.-N.-H. Linguet's *Annales politiques, civiles et littéraires du dix-huitième siècle*, 1779, VI. 15–48. Linguet, himself an enemy of d'Alembert, also lauded Hume's impartiality and quoted his authority in 1774 to prove that so-called English liberty was nothing more than the muddle-headed delusion of those who wished to foment political disorder. (*Œuvres de M. Linguet*, Londres, 1774, II. 139, 244.) It is well known that Linguet, following a two-year imprisonment in the Bastille, was destined to revise his opinion on this last point.

[2] Linguet, *Annales*, VI. 21; *Année littéraire*, 1779, IV. 77.

[3] Linguet, VI. 21–23; *Année littéraire*, IV. 79–80.

profession, sujet et partisan de la maison d'Hanovre: son autorité ne doit pas être suspecte au panégyriste. Voici comme il termine l'histoire de Jacques II. . . .'[1] Royou's attack concludes with a triumphant confrontation of the impartial Hume and his vanquished *philosophe* friend d'Alembert.

The last example we will consider with regard to the influence of Hume's conservative image in the pre-revolutionary period is much along the same lines. It cannot be ignored, however, because of the sheer quantity of references to Hume's works involved and because of the importance of the Abbé Nicolas-Sylvestre Bergier, the apologist in question.

Abbé Bergier saw himself as something like a new Samson sent by God to destroy the Philistines of eighteenth-century French philosophy. Some idea of the stature of his attacks may be had, perhaps, from the fact that, for a time, he frequented the d'Holbach *côterie* and that rival apologists occasionally complained of his treating *philosophe* opponents with more respect and temperance than he accorded the Jansenists.[2]

The extent of Hume's philosophical influence on Bergier, following in the tradition already established by Trublet, is a question which need not detain us here.[3] More important to our purpose is an examination of the religious, social, and political image of David Hume that emerges from the mass of references found in the Abbé's works published between 1765 and the Revolution.

Any statement made by Hume that could be construed or, to be quite frank, half-construed and even misconstrued as testifying in favour of religion or of the Catholic Church is laboriously noted

[1] Linguet, VI. 23–24; *Année littéraire*, IV. 81.

[2] See the correspondence of Bergier published by Léonce Pingaud in the proceedings of the *Académie des sciences, belles-lettres et arts de Besançon* (1891). Bergier, whose dates are 1718–90, spent his last days editing the massive three-volume *Théologie* section of the *Encyclopédie Méthodique* (Paris, 1788–90).

[3] Bergier, unlike the *philosophes*, gives ample proof of having recognized the originality of Hume's contributions to epistemology. Like Holland (see *supra* p. 29, no.2), he makes clever polemical use of Hume's analysis of causation against the determinism of such materialist philosophers as d'Holbach. See in *Œuvres complètes de Bergier* the following references: I. 38–42, 61–72, 624–30, 691–3; II. 40–44, 713; III. 749–50; IV. 786–7; V. 385–7; VI. 340–2, 358, 561–2, 602–15, 696–7, 941–2, 1002–3, 1031–2, 1346–7; VII. 813; VIII. 412–13, 527. It is fairly evident, however, that Bergier merely exploits Hume's scepticism against the philosophical dogmatists. He makes it clear, at the same time, that he wholeheartedly disapproves of the Scottish philosopher's irreligion.

down in Bergier's works. The Abbé records emphatically, for example, that Hume 's'est exprimé d'une manière très forte sur les effets salutaires de la religion: "Ceux qui s'efforcent, dit-il, de désabuser le genre humain de ces sortes de préjugés (de religion) sont peut-être de bons raisonneurs; mais je ne saurais les reconnaître pour bons citoyens, ni pour bons politiques, puisqu'ils affranchissent les hommes d'un des freins de leurs passions, et qu'ils rendent l'infraction des lois de l'équité et de la société plus aisée et plus sûre à cet égard".'[1] Like Voltaire quoting the Bible, Bergier does not hesitate to repeat his favourite Hume passages and he used this particular one in at least four different works.

The *philosophes* maintain that religion is unnecessary in a well-run society. But, objects Bergier, 'depuis le commencement du monde l'on n'a vu, chez aucune nation, de bonnes lois civiles, une sage police, un gouvernement sans religion. Aucun législateur n'a essayé de soumettre les peuples aux lois sans la croyance d'un Dieu et d'une autre vie. Il y a de la folie à regarder comme possible une entreprise qu'aucun sage n'a jamais osé tenter. "Cherchez, dit M. Hume, un peuple qui n'ait point de religion; si vous le trouvez, soyez sûr qu'il ne diffère pas beaucoup des bêtes brutes." (*Hist. nat. de la relig.*, p. 133). . . . De ce fait incontestable, nous concluons que la religion est incorporée, pour ainsi dire, à la constitution de l'homme. . . .'[2]

Hume is also cited against those who maintain that religion takes its origins in the duplicity of priests and the credulity of the masses: 'Il serait inutile de répondre aux clameurs de ceux qui prétendent que ce sont les prêtres qui ont forgé la religion pour leur intérêt. C'est d'abord une absurdité de supposer qu'il y a eu des prêtres avant qu'il y eût une religion. M. Hume, qui n'est rien moins que prévenu en leur faveur, avoue de bonne foi qu'ils ne sont point les premiers auteurs de la religion ou de la superstition; qu'ils peuvent tout au plus avoir contribué à l'entretenir. (*Hist. nat. de la relig.*, n. 14, p. 127.)'[3]

Bergier defends religious belief as a normal part of man's nature. Is it sensible, then, he asks, to spend one's lifetime questioning a duty which is born with us, which makes for the happiness of virtuous people and determines our eternal fate? Even Hume—for the moment a Hume *pascalisant*—was forced to admit

[1] Ibid., VI. 137, 451; III. 1357; VIII. 195.
[2] Ibid., VI. 156–7, 1347. [3] Ibid., VI. 105.

that no good can come of religious scepticism: 'David Hume, zélé partisan du scepticisme philosophique, après avoir étalé tous les sophismes qu'il a pu forger pour l'établir, est forcé d'avouer qu'il n'en peut résulter aucun bien, qu'il est ridicule de vouloir détruire la raison par le raisonnement; que la nature, plus forte que l'orgueil philosophique, maintiendra toujours ses droits contre toutes les spéculations abstraites. Disons hardiment qu'il en sera de même de la religion, puisqu'elle est entée sur la nature. . . .'[1]

Even a certain fanaticism in a nation is preferable to the total absence of religion: 'Le fanatisme n'a lieu que lorsque les esprits sont d'ailleurs en fermentation et que la religion paraît être en péril; c'est une fièvre passagère dont les accès ne sauraient être fréquents, et qui s'affaiblit par ses propres efforts. "Sa fureur, dit M. Hume, ressemble à celle du tonnerre et de la tempête qui s'épuise en peu de temps, et laisse ensuite l'air plus calme et plus serein." L'athéisme est un poison lent, qui détruit le principe de l'être social, et dont les effets sont incurables. . . .'[2]

With Hume defending religious fanaticism in small doses and even proving to the Abbé's satisfaction that the ancients were very much in need of Christ's mission,[3] let us now turn to hear what he has to say, still according to Bergier, specifically in defence of Christianity and the Catholic Church.

Bergier quotes from Hume's *Tudors* to show the important rôle played by the Church during the Dark Ages: 'Les nations féroces, qui ravagèrent l'Europe au Ve siècle et dans les âges suivants, auraient étouffé jusqu'au dernier germe des connaissances humaines, si la religion n'avait opposé des barrières à leur fureur. . . . Si donc il s'est trouvé quelques vestiges d'humanité, de mœurs, de police, de lumières, parmi les hommes au XVe siècle, c'est incontestablement au Christianisme que l'on en est redevable.'[4] We remember that the Protestant minister Formey had cited Hume to the same effect. The clergy, Hume is quoted as maintaining, also served during this time as a barrier against political despotism.[5]

Attacking the Reformation, Bergier finds himself able to quote profitably page after page of Hume's work. Not only did the clergy of the pre-Reformation Church stand as a barrier against despotism, but the union of the Western Churches under one sovereign pontiff facilitated commerce and was a highly desirable politically

[1] Ibid., V. 385–7. [2] Ibid., VI. 149. [3] Ibid., VI. 269, 289.
[4] Ibid., II. 34–35. [5] Ibid., VIII. 571.

unifying principle. The wealth and splendour of the Church had the effect of encouraging the arts. Though some corruption in the Church indeed existed, it was not the main cause of the Reformation, nor was the issue of religion the main cause of the massacres which took place in England, Scotland, and Ireland at that time.[1] After giving consecutively five 'impartial' Hume quotations to support this view, Bergier adds: 'Voilà ce me semble, la confirmation de tout ce que nous avons dit jusqu'ici au sujet de la prétendue réforme; et c'est un protestant qui nous la fournit.'[2] Were the Protestants right, Bergier asks, to attack the Church for depriving the faithful of scripture in the vernacular? 'David Hume nous apprend qu'en Angleterre, après la naissance de la prétendue réforme, on fut obligé d'ôter au peuple les traductions vulgaires de l'Ecriture Sainte à cause des conséquences qui en résultaient et du fanatisme que cette lecture entretenait. (*Tudor*, II. p. 426.)'[3] Hume also states that the destruction of the monasteries at the time of the Reformation in England did no possible good to the country: 'Belle leçon', Bergier adds, 'pour les réformateurs des richesses du clergé!'[4] For his defence of the utility of convents and for his denial that the celibacy of priests has base political motives, Hume receives once again the French Abbé's benediction. The Scot had shown on these matters 'plus de discernement que nos philosophes'.[5] Like Louis de Bonald later on, Bergier also cites Hume's authority to support his arguments against divorce.[6]

One last example of Bergier's use of Hume must suffice although it by no means exhausts the list of references scattered throughout the Abbé's voluminous works. After stating on the great historian's authority that the *philosophes* were wrong to attach intolerance exclusively to religious opinions, that, in fact, any opinions men hold dear, whether out of vanity or self-interest, can occasion intolerance and that, consequently, atheists can be found who are just as intolerant as believers,[7] Bergier approached the problem of toleration in seventeenth-century France:

La question est de savoir si la demande des calvinistes était légitime, si le gouvernement était obligé, de droit naturel, à l'accorder, s'il le pouvait en bonne politique: nous prions qu'on pèse sans partialité les réflexions suivantes.

[1] Ibid., V. 82; VII. 896, 902; VIII. 228.
[2] Ibid., VIII. 228.
[3] Ibid., VII. 925–6.
[4] Ibid., VIII. 584.
[5] Ibid., VIII. 538–9.
[6] Ibid., III. 237–8; IV. 571; VIII. 1302.
[7] Ibid., I. 329.

1° L'on sait quels furent les premiers prédicants du calvinisme, et quelle était leur doctrine; ils enseignaient que le catholicisme est une religion abominable, dans laquelle il n'est pas possible de faire son salut . . . que l'Eglise romaine est la prostituée de Babylone, et le pape l'antéchrist; qu'il fallait abjurer, proscrire, exterminer cette religion par toutes les voies possibles. . . . David Hume convient qu'en Ecosse, l'an 1542, la tolérance des nouveaux prédicants, et le dessein formé de détruire la religion nationale, auraient eu à peu près le même effet; il le prouve par la conduite fanatique de ces sectaires, *Histoire de la Maison de Tudor*, t. III, p. 9; t. IV, p. 59 et 104; t. V, p. 213, etc. Il en était de même en France. Partout où les calvinistes ont pu se rendre les maîtres, ils n'ont souffert aucun exercice de la religion catholique: de quel droit voulaient-ils que l'on permît la leur?[1]

We see, then, how Hume's impartiality, far from supporting the *philosophes*, often served the cause of their enemies. Apologists like Bergier and Gerdil quote Hume as naturally, almost, as they quote Bossuet. In fact, they both sometimes quote Hume and Bossuet together on the same point. Moreover, since Bossuet's authority meant much less to the eighteenth-century *philosophes* than Hume's, there was all the more reason to prefer Hume. Here was a Protestant Bossuet, nay even an atheist Bossuet, saying all the right things apparently and yet he was a member of the enemy camp, and highly praised by Voltaire and d'Holbach. Bergier's sincerity in many of these quotations can certainly be questioned but it is equally evident that he felt, at least some of the time, that he and Hume were in real agreement. Even during the Hume–Rousseau quarrel his sympathies were not with the Christian (admittedly of the independent variety) Rousseau, but totally with the unbeliever Hume.[2] It is significant too that the *philosophes* themselves found it impossible after a while to ignore Bergier's tricks. After he had quoted Hume for about the fourth time to the effect that those who disabuse the human race of its religious prejudices may be good reasoners but are certainly not good citizens or legislators,[3] the d'Holbach *côterie* decided to mount a

[1] Ibid., IV. 286–7; VII. 890–6.

[2] See Bergier's letter to the lawyer Jacquin, from Besançon, 28 April 1767 (ibid., VIII. 1490).

[3] See *supra*, p. 42. The future counter-revolutionary theoretician, Abbé Duvoisin, also quotes the passage in 1780 adding that 'l'utilité politique du dogme d'une autre vie est si évidente, que l'impiété elle-même s'est vue forcée de la reconnaître' (*Essai polémique sur la religion naturelle* in *Œuvres complètes de Duvoisin, évèque de Nantes*, publiées par M. l'Abbé Migne, Montrouge, 1856, p. 146).

protest in their anonymously published *Recueil Philosophique ou Mélange de Pièces sur la Religion & la Morale.*[1] The work attacks Bergier on this very point:

M. Bergier, suivant l'usage des théologiens, finit par déférer ses adversaires comme des perturbateurs du repos public, comme de mauvais citoyens; il s'appuie de l'autorité d'un philosophe célèbre (M. Hume) qui reconnaît que ceux qui attaquent la religion établie dans un pays peuvent être de bons raisonneurs, mais sont à coup sûr de mauvais citoyens. Nous répondrons à M. Bergier qu'il ne paraît pas qu'il appartienne aux théologiens et aux prêtres d'accuser les philosophes de troubler l'état. Nous lui dirons que c'est la théologie par l'abus honteux qu'elle a fait de son pouvoir qui est depuis près de 18 siècles en possession de troubler le repos des nations; . . . Nous lui dirons que . . . nous ne sommes plus au douzième siècle . . . et que les hommes, fatigués de l'autorité, paraissent enfin vouloir recourir au bon sens et à la raison.

A l'égard de l'opinion de M. Hume, qui semble fournir un grand triomphe à M. Bergier, nous répondrons à celui-ci que l'autorité d'un philosophe n'est pas pour d'autres philosophes du même poids que l'autorité d'un père de l'Eglise ou d'un concile peut être pour un théologien; nous dirons donc que M. Hume a pu se tromper dans son jugement sur les adversaires des opinions reçues, et que s'il eût fait attention aux maux sans nombre que le Christianisme a produits sur la terre, il eût été forcé de reconnaître que c'est être un très bon citoyen que d'attaquer avec force les préjugés et la superstition. M. Hume lui-même s'en est acquitté d'une façon qui lui mérite la réputation dont il jouit si justement dans toute l'Europe, où son histoire et ses écrits philosophiques sont répandus et admirés par tous ceux qui ne pensent pas comme M. L'Abbé Bergier.[2]

[1] . . . *par différents auteurs*, Londres, 1770; possibly edited by Naigeon and containing works by d'Holbach and others as well as Hume's essays 'Of Suicide' and 'Of the Immortality of the Soul'.

[2] *Recueil philosophique*, II. 204–6. Bergier answered by pointing out that he was puzzled as to why Hume's testimony should not be used if he indeed had the great reputation his *philosophe* admirers attributed to him (Bergier, op. cit., VIII. 259). Ironically, the *Recueil philosophique* published at the same time, but anonymously, two of Hume's strongest dissertations 'Sur l'immortalité de l'âme' and 'Sur le suicide', both probably translated by d'Holbach. It also included in its pages some rather different comments by Hume on the clergy—chosen this time by the *philosophes* (*Recueil philosophique*, II. 237). All this was perhaps to show Bergier whose ally Hume really was. For the French Abbé's reactions to the two anonymous dissertations, see Bergier, op. cit., VIII. 262.

6. Debate with Turgot

As their answer to Bergier indicates, the *philosophes* were fairly confident that Hume belonged, despite occasional appearances to the contrary, heart and soul to the camp of the d'Alemberts and d'Holbachs. Moreover, even though this first generation of *philosophes* saw the success of their cause as largely dependent on a victory over traditionalists in the religious controversy, they were probably quite willing to forgive not only David Hume's laziness or lack of militancy in not writing an ecclesiastical history, but also the general ignorance of the harsher 'religious' facts of life he at times displayed as when, for example, he confided naïvely to the astonished baron d'Holbach that he had never seen an atheist and that he did not believe such creatures existed.[1] Such errors were amusing or at least pardonable in a man who had already written so cleverly on miracles, divine providence, and the immortality of the soul. As for Hume's apparent lack of a liberally orientated political philosophy, the *philosophes* of this generation from about 1750 to 1770 could have no insurmountable objections on this point either. Revolution, if not reform, was as far from their aims as it was from Hume's. Few *philosophes* showed any real objections to living under a political despot provided he, like Frederick the Great, for example, was witty and a good priest-hater as well.

As is well known, the intellectual mood in France was soon to change. A second generation of *philosophes* begins to emerge in the 1770's and 1780's, still anti-clerical—although this question was by now rather old hat—but more interested in investigating and pointing out the sins of kings than of priests. These last very definitely do not claim David Hume as an ally. There is even some apprehension on their part that he might be just what Trublet, Bergier, Nonnotte, Royou, Gerdil, Lefebvre de Beauvray and others in their use of him had suggested he was—a treacherous enemy in disguise.

It is in the correspondence of Turgot and Hume exchanged between the years 1766 and 1768 that we catch perhaps our first real glimpse—and it is still only a glimpse—of what was to be a consciously acknowledged fundamental disagreement between Hume and the politically idealistic French intellectuals of this later period. Turgot was with d'Alembert one of Hume's closest

[1] See Diderot, *Lettres à Sophie Volland*, ed. Babelon, Paris, 1938, II. 77.

friends on the continent. Unlike the other *philosophes*, however, he showed on the occasion of the Hume-Rousseau quarrel a certain unflattering if sincere reserve in judging the wrongs of the affair which left unsatisfied the wounded feelings of the Scottish historian. After receiving letters from Turgot in which Rousseau's ingratitude is called real but unpremeditated, more the result of madness than of villainy,[1] Hume could not help accusing the French physiocrat of 'partiality' for the black-hearted *citoyen de Genève*.[2] This aspect of the correspondence will not concern us further here, but what is especially significant for us is the fact that it led finally to an open discussion between Hume and one of his liberal French admirers of their genuine political differences—differences which the earlier uncritical praise of Hume by the *philosophes* had all but totally obscured.

Hume opened the controversy by pointing out that Rousseau's writings, however eloquent, were extravagant and sophistical. Their tendency, moreover, was surely rather to do hurt than service to mankind.

In his reply the distinguished Intendant de Limoges who was soon to attempt his great reforms, and was already aware of the difficulties presented by ill-will and the routine immobility of privilege, defended Rousseau, and at the same time defended his own political involvement in the Enlightenment's hopes to improve the world. Speaking in the new political tones to be heard more and more frequently in France as 1789 approached, he warmly praised Rousseau's works:

> Il s'en faut bien que je les juge, comme vous, nuisibles à l'intérêt du genre humain; je crois, au contraire, que c'est un des auteurs qui a le mieux servi les moeurs et l'humanité. Bien loin de lui reprocher de s'être, sur cet article, trop écarté des idées communes, je crois, au contraire, qu'il a encore respecté trop de préjugés. Je crois qu'il n'a pas marché assez avant dans la route; mais c'est en suivant sa route que l'on arrivera au but qui est de rapprocher les hommes de l'égalité, de la justice et du bonheur.[3]

Turgot adds that of course Hume will not think he is defending Rousseau's early writings against the arts and sciences. These, he

[1] See *Letters of Eminent Persons*, pp. 139, 144–5: letters of 27 July and 7 September 1766.

[2] Greig, op. cit., II. 91.

[3] *Letters of Eminent Persons*, pp. 150–1: letter of 25 March 1767.

says, were the products of a beginning writer's vain desire to make his mark; Rousseau was consciously paradoxical here to avoid being trite. The *Contrat social*, however, is a different matter:

A la vérité, ce livre se réduit à la distinction précise du souverain et du gouvernement; mais cette distinction présente une vérité bien lumineuse, et qui me paraît fixer à jamais les idées sur l'inaliénabilité de la souveraineté du peuple dans quelque gouvernement que ce soit. *Emile* me paraît partout respirer la morale la plus pure qu'on ait encore donnée en leçons, quoiqu'on puisse, selon moi, aller encore plus loin; mais je me garderai bien de vous dire sur cela mes idées, car vous me jugerez peut-être encore plus fou que Rousseau. . . .[1]

We have here, at last, the beginnings of an honest recognition of the vast distance between Hume's political views and those of the French reformers. Hume's *History* had been before the French reading public for several years already without eliciting anything approaching a similar response. Only the extreme right had taken grateful notice of his conservatism. Moreover, to the 'lessons' of the *History* remarked upon by the *Journal de Trévoux*, Bergier, and others, had to be added the fairly explicit anti-liberal doctrine available in Hume's political essays. In these as well the French had been able to read Hume's opinion that the world was still too young and human experience too short to allow much in the way of scientifically valid political speculation. Hume had also declared that the contract theory and the corollary doctrine of the people's inalienable sovereignty were totally without foundation. Opinion, not contract, was at the basis of human government and most governments had, in fact, been founded on conquest or usurpation.[2] Hume implies too that those who reject the lessons of history in favour of *a priori* natural rights are to be condemned. Few changes in government can ever be wisely carried out on such 'philosophical' grounds. Established government bears a sacred authority by the very fact that it is established. Resistance to it is always unwise and must be considered only as a last resort since nothing is more terrible to contemplate than the anarchy that would result from a complete dissolution of government:

[1] Ibid., p. 152.

[2] It is interesting to note that the future *monarchien*, Pierre-Victor Malouet, quoted Hume's authority in rejecting the contract theory in 1777. See J.-B.-A. Suard, *Mélanges de littérature*, Paris, 1803–4, I. 277.

Did one generation of men go off the stage at once, and another succeed, as is the case with silk-worms and butterflies, the new race, if they had sense enough to choose their government, which surely is never the case with men, might voluntarily, and by general consent, establish their own form of civil polity, without any regard to the laws or precedents, which prevailed among their ancestors. But as human society is in perpetual flux, one man every hour going out of the world, another coming into it, it is necessary, in order to preserve stability in government, that the new brood should conform themselves to the established constitution, and nearly follow the path which their fathers, treading in the footsteps of theirs, had marked out to them. Some innovations must necessarily have place in every human institution, and it is happy where the enlightened genius of the age gives these a direction to the side of reason, liberty, and justice: but violent innovations no individual is entitled to make: they are even dangerous to be attempted by the legislature: more ill than good is ever to be expected from them: and if history affords examples to the contrary, they are not to be drawn into precedent, and are only to be regarded as proofs, that the science of politics affords few rules, which will not admit of some exceptions. . . .[1]

Hume may not have been entirely sure that the old gods existed but, in the best sceptical tradition, he held that they ought to be worshipped. An acquiescence in the *status quo*, a shrinking from change, a pessimistic desire to retrench, to set up comforting barriers against the 'frenzy of liberty' permeates many of his personal comments on political events at this time. The course of history is cyclical; the new ideals of liberty and progress represent recurrent political delusions. In his answer to Turgot, Hume expressed a weary unwillingness to believe in man's ability to improve his lot by seeking such lofty goals:

I know you are one of those, who entertain the agreeable and laudable, if not too sanguine hope, that human society is capable of perpetual progress towards perfection, that the increase of knowledge will still prove favourable to good government, and that since the discovery of printing we need no longer dread the usual returns of barbarism and

[1] 'Of the Original Contract' in Green and Grose, op. cit., I. 452–3. The passage just quoted, which first appeared in the 1777 edition of Hume's essays, corresponds with the increasing conservatism he expressed in the later revisions of his *History*. Hume found that the first editions of that work were still too full of 'those foolish English prejudices' and he tells us in *My Own Life* that in 'above a hundred alterations, which farther study, reading, or reflection, engaged me to make in the reigns of the two first Stuarts, I have made all of them invariably to the Tory side.' (See Greig, op. cit., I. 5.)

ignorance. Pray, do not the late events in this country[1] appear a little contrary to your system? Here is a people thrown into disorders (not dangerous ones, I hope) merely from the abuse of liberty, chiefly the liberty of the press; without any grievance, I do not only say, real, but even imaginary; and without any of them being able to tell one circumstance of government which they wish to have corrected: They roar liberty, though they have apparently more liberty than any people in the world; a great deal more than they deserve; and perhaps more than any men ought to have. . . . You see, I give you freely my views of things, in which I wish earnestly to be refuted: The contrary opinion is much more consolatory, and is an incitement to every virtue and laudable pursuit.[2]

With all the idealism and moderate optimism which he shared with the Enlightenment's better political prophets, Turgot returned Hume a frank rebuttal:

Si mon départ me laissait quelques moments, je vous dirais quelque chose pour défendre mes idées sur la perfectibilité et le perfectionnement de notre pauvre espèce. Car les petits désordres qui se passent sous nos yeux ne m'ébranlent point du tout; et je dis avec plus de fondement que le Général des Jésuites—*alios ventos alias tempestates vidimus*. . . . Ce bon gouvernement ne s'établira pas sans crise, et ces crises seront accompagnées de désordre. Faudrait-il accuser la lumière et la liberté, qui nous feront passer par ces désordres pour amener un état plus heureux? Non sans doute. Elles feront du mal en passant; à la bonne heure; mais en feront-elles plus que la tyrannie et la superstition qui voudraient les étouffer, et qui s'y efforcent vainement par des voies qui, quand les choses sont à un certain point, sont ou totalement inutiles ou atroces, et souvent l'un et l'autre? Vous ne le pensez, sans doute, pas plus que moi. Le peuple occupé de ses besoins, les grands occupés de leur plaisirs, n'ont pas le temps d'être savants, et de sortir d'eux-mêmes de leurs préjugés; mais l'effet du progrès des connaissances est de faire qu'on n'ait pas besoin d'être savant pour avoir du bon sens, et de rendre populaires les vérités qui exigent aujourd'hui du travail pour s'en convaincre. Adieu, Monsieur—car le temps me presse. . . .[3]

In fact time was running short; there were many important reforms to carry out; perhaps even, for others if not for Turgot, there was a revolution to prepare. Not long after, the unsuccessful

[1] The 'Wilkes and Liberty!' riots.

[2] Greig, op. cit., II. 180: letter of 16 June 1768.

[3] *Letters of Eminent Persons*, p. 163: letter of 3 July 1768.

minister Turgot would warn in fateful words his young King, Louis XVI, about the dangers of ineffective political leadership: 'N'oubliez jamais, Sire, que c'est la faiblesse qui a mis la tête de Charles Ier sur un billot; . . .'[1]

7. *Early hostility: Mirabeau, Mably and Brissot*

Perhaps the earliest work by a future revolutionary expressing open dissatisfaction with Hume's political conservatism is Mirabeau's *Des lettres de cachet et des prisons d'état*. Himself a victim of the *lettre de cachet*, Mirabeau, composing this work in prison in 1778,[2] protested against all forms of ministerial despotism. Both natural and positive law, he affirmed, condemned arbitrary imprisonment.

Although, especially when dealing with the medieval period, Mirabeau occasionally cites Hume's authority and even refers to him as 'ce philosophe, qui, le premier d'entre les modernes, a disputé la palme de l'histoire aux anciens',[3] he cannot accept the timid reservations Hume seems to have concerning the protection of *habeas corpus*. Like Montesquieu in the *Esprit des Lois* (Book XII, ch. 19), Hume believed that there were times of crisis in the affairs of men when certain civil liberties should be suspended. There is even much to suggest that, had he been alive, he would have heartily approved the suspension of *habeas corpus* in England during the period when Mirabeau was actually composing his work.

'Le célèbre Hume', Mirabeau writes, 'en rendant compte de l'acte d'*habeas corpus*, dit: "Qu'il est *assez difficile* de concilier avec cette extrême liberté la police régulière d'un Etat, et surtout celle des grandes villes". . . .'[4] Hume, Mirabeau adds, is guilty of excessive circumspection in the defence of liberty: 'Cette manière de parler ambiguë, à laquelle ce célèbre écrivain est un peu trop sujet dans toutes les matières qui intéressent le gouvernement,

[1] Letter to Louis XVI, 30 April 1776, quoted in *Journal de l'Abbé de Véri*, publié par le baron Jehan de Witte, Paris, 1928–30, I. 455. See also J.-L. Soulavie, *Mémoires historiques et politiques du règne de Louis XVI*, Paris, 1801, II. 55; III. 165; VI. 518–19.

[2] I have found no serious evidence to support the once-current opinion that this work is not by Mirabeau.

[3] *Des prisons d'état* in *Œuvres de Mirabeau*, Paris, 1835, VII. 443.

[4] *Des lettres de cachet*, op. cit., VII. 184.

laisse presque douter s'il approuve ou n'approuve pas sans restriction cette fameuse loi. Ce grand philosophe s'est étrangement oublié s'il est vrai qu'il ait balancé de bonne foi dans cette occasion.'[1]

Mirabeau admits that Hume in a preceding passage had seemed to call this law necessary for the protection of liberty in a mixed monarchy and had seemed to say that, since it existed nowhere but in England, it alone could induce the English to prefer their constitution to all others. To this Mirabeau adds the following comment:

Si la loi qui rend impossible tout emprisonnement arbitraire *est essentiellement nécessaire pour le maintien de la liberté* (essentially requisite for the protection of liberty), elle est à jamais sacrée et irréfragable; car à quoi est bon le gouvernement, si ce n'est à maintenir la liberté? Et qu'est-ce qui peut l'autoriser à commettre le mal qu'il doit prévenir? Les prétendus inconvénients que cette liberté tant calomniée entraînera pour la police seront apparemment et ne pourront être que l'effet de la maladresse des administrateurs, de leur défaut de vigilance, de fermeté ou d'intégrité. Quoi qu'il en soit, si l'objet unique du gouvernement n'est pas de garantir notre liberté et nos propriétés, peu nous importe sa belle police; peu nous importe l'avantage de la société qui sert de prétexte à toutes les injustices particulières, s'il nous faut perdre les avantages et les droits, pour la conservation et l'accroissement desquels nous nous sommes réunis à nos semblables.[2]

Habeas corpus, contrary to Hume's fears, has not produced great disorders. The lesson, Mirabeau concludes, is obvious: France could do away with its system of *lettres de cachet* and its complicated apparatus of despotism which induced foreigners to laugh at Frenchmen as poor, down-trodden slaves. The *raison d'état*, moreover, can never be legitimately invoked to suspend such measures of legal protection:

Qu'on n'abuse donc point de ce mot *nécessité*, qui peut autoriser tout autre acte de tyrannie, aussi bien que les emprisonnements arbitraires. Qu'on ne l'introduise jamais dans une cause légale, ou dans une circonstance que les lois ont prévue. Lorsque cette nécessité funeste existe en effet, elle ne demande aucune explication: personne ne la révoque en doute. . . . Cette supposition d'un cas urgent est donc tout à fait inapplicable à la question présente; nous examinons si l'usage des lettres de cachet est juste, s'il est bon. On nous répond qu'il est des circonstances

[1] Ibid., VII. 184–5. [2] Loc. cit.

où elles sont nécessaires. Pourquoi cette ridicule évasion? Ces circonstances existent-elles? Non, elles n'existent pas, et, dans une pareille occasion, il est fort douteux qu'on leur obéît; car des ordres si arbitraires ne peuvent avoir de force que dans les temps de l'obéissance la plus paisible et la plus complète. . . .[1]

Mirabeau, who like Turgot, shows unbounded admiration for Rousseau's political writings, goes on for an entire chapter defending *habeas corpus* against Hume's objection. He hints that practical observers like Hume are guilty, through their pride in being 'empiriques politiques', of a certain scholarly charlatanism. Mirabeau does in fact condescend to cite facts to support his arguments but, in the typical radical tradition of many later revolutionists, he prefers to talk of principles rather than precedents. History is somehow irrelevant in a question of right:

. . . les détails polémiques ne doivent jamais tenir que le second rang dans les écrits politico-philosophiques, si je puis me servir de cette expression, et les principes de la loi naturelle sont au premier . . . car la loi naturelle est la seule loi qu'il ne soit pas au pouvoir des hommes d'abroger. En général, les arguments de la raison l'emportent infiniment sur toute autre autorité, et rendent assez inutiles, en matière de politique ou de philosophie, les dissertations historiques sujettes à des disputes interminables. On conviendra qu'il serait fort triste que la liberté et les privilèges d'une nation dépendissent de discussions grammaticales. . . .[2]

Besides rejecting history altogether, another possibility open to the revolutionary who finds the evidence of history in apparent contradiction with his principles is, of course, to rewrite history or at least to find historians whose ideas are more in keeping with those principles. We shall see that Mirabeau attempted this last solution as well when he set out later, partially, no doubt, because of dissatisfaction with Hume, to translate and publish the 'republican'-inspired *History of England* by Catherine Macaulay-Graham as well as some of the political doctrine of Milton. But more on that later. Let us now examine the work of another radical theoretician who found it necessary at this time to attack the historian Hume.

Although Mably in 1757 had called Hume the economist 'un homme de génie',[3] he was unable, later, to find any words of

[1] Ibid., VII. 205. [2] Ibid., VII. 388.
[3] *Collection complète des œuvres de l'Abbé de Mably*, Paris, An III, V. 197.

praise for Hume the historian. In the work, *Des droits et des devoirs du citoyen*, this disciple of Rousseau, who tended in his own writings to defend a primitive form of idealistic communism, gives us a fairly good idea why. History, first of all, must be a source-book of liberalism: 'Qu'elle étale les droits des peuples; que jamais elle ne s'écarte de cette première vérité d'où découlent toutes les autres.' Pre-requisite to the writing of history is the study of natural law or of just political theory which is based on 'les lois que la nature a établies pour procurer aux hommes le bonheur dont elle les rend susceptibles'. These laws, Mably tells us, are invariable and 'le monde eût été heureux s'il les eût suivies.'[1] History then has an explicit propaganda purpose: '. . . l'objet de l'histoire n'est pas d'éclairer simplement l'esprit, elle se propose encore de diriger le cœur et le disposer à aimer le bien.'[2] Thus it is that Mably judges Rapin-Thoyras, the Huguenot historian of England, who was generally seen as biased against France and in every way inferior to Hume, as in fact superior to the Scottish historian: '. . . ses vues sont droites, il aime la justice, et sa politique tient aux principes du droit naturel.'[3]

Unusual too in France at this time is Mably's emphasis on the love of liberty rather than on the fanaticism shown by the seventeenth-century Puritans.[4] Beginning as he did with these revolutionary premises, it is perhaps only to be expected that Mably found Hume wanting: 'Quand ses réflexions sont à lui, elles sont communes, et trop souvent d'une fausse politique que la morale ne peut approuver.'[5] In some parts of the *History* Hume is even judged to be 'unintelligible' and Mably, contemptuous of the great praise given Hume in France only twenty years earlier, asks: '. . . et comment pourrai-je approuver un ouvrage que, soit par ignorance de son art, soit par paresse ou lenteur d'esprit, l'historien n'a qu'ébauché? Tous ces faits décousus échappent à ma mémoire, j'ai perdu mon temps. . . .'[6]

During this same period we find the future revolutionary leader Brissot de Warville largely agreeing that history should be, first and foremost, a school of liberalism. Discussing the duties of an historian in 1783, Brissot takes up a position similar to that of Mirabeau and Mably: '. . . il a pour but d'instruire son siècle, la

[1] *De la manière d'écrire l'histoire* (1783) in *Œuvres*, XII. 379.
[2] Ibid., p. 397. [3] Ibid., p. 430. [4] Ibid., pp. 111, 226.
[5] Ibid., pp. 430–1. [6] Ibid., p. 520.

postérité, les princes surtout et les ministres; car c'est à eux que l'histoire peut être utile. Qui d'entr'eux ne se corrigera pas du penchant pour le gouvernement arbitraire, en contemplant Charles Ier et Jacques II? . . . Le premier devoir de l'historien est donc d'être courageux, intrépide, s'il veut être utile. . . .'[1]

Impartiality is seen by Brissot as a rather secondary virtue in the historian. In fact, Brissot makes it something of a sin for the historian to be impartial in the wrong way. Speaking of Catherine Macaulay's *History* which was later to influence the revolutionary Brissot and several other Girondins to a surprising extent, he writes:

On a reproché à cette historienne une partialité trop marquée pour le républicanisme. Mais pouvait-elle s'en défendre, quand elle avait à peindre les excès tyranniques qui signalèrent les ministères des Buckingham, des Laud, des Strafford? La partialité pour ce système fait l'éloge de son âme et de sa tête. La partialité pour les personnages déshonore seule l'historien. . . . C'est le respect pour le droit sacré que l'homme tient de la nature, qui caractérise cette Histoire, qui la met bien au-dessus de l'élégant tableau de Hume, chez qui l'esprit courtisan a souvent altéré ou effacé les couleurs de la vérité. . . . Madame Macaulay a eu le courage . . . de s'écarter de la route des autres historiens, de s'en frayer une nouvelle, de censurer les principes serviles de Hume, de braver l'opinion publique qu'il avait su captiver. . . . Je n'ai plus qu'un souhait à former, c'est que son Histoire soit traduite en français.[2]

8. Defence and defiance

The change in political climate which took place between the 1760's and the 1780's is well illustrated by earlier French reactions to republican interpretations of the English revolution. The *Journal Encyclopédique*, not the least liberal of *ancien-régime* literary reviews, refused in 1760 to go into any details in its account of the guilty activities of Cromwell and his hot-brained parliamentarians: 'Nos lecteurs frémiraient, si les bornes de ce journal permettaient de mettre sous leurs yeux quelques traits de ces tyrans.'[3] Nor is it easy to find at this time in France a very

[1] *Correspondance universelle sur ce qui intéresse le bonheur de l'homme et de la société*, Neuchâtel, 1783, II. 54.

[2] *Journal du Licée de Londres ou Tableau de l'état présent des sciences et des arts en Angleterre*, Paris, No. 1, January 1784, pp. 33–34.

[3] June 1760, IV. 25.

much more favourable opinion of the English Protector and his Puritan supporters. The hostility expressed by Bossuet in the seventeenth century toward these fiendish regicides is still very much alive a century later. Rousseau speaks of Cromwell as irredeemably vile and perhaps best sums up the general view: 'Ce que personne n'a jamais vu', he wrote in 1751, 'c'est un hypocrite devenir homme de bien: on aurait pu raisonnablement tenter la conversion de Cartouche, jamais un homme sage n'eût entrepris celle de Cromwell.'[1] Some further idea of the Protector's reputation in France as the most evil of men may be had from the fact that Crébillon found himself able to use parts of the first two acts of an abandoned tragedy on Cromwell in his *Catilina*.[2] An unsuccessful tragedy, *Cromwel*, by Antoine Maillet-Duclairon, was in fact performed by the Comédiens Français in June 1764, and depicts the prevailing view of the Protector as a murderer and usurper. The last two lines of the play, significantly, are spoken by the heroic General Monk:

> Et montrons aux Sujets que les premières Loix
> Sont d'aimer la Patrie & de servir les Rois.[3]

The youthful poet François de Neufchâteau in a work of 1766 also displays this classic reaction to the leading figures in Stuart history. Charles I is seen as a prince 'malheureux et innocent'.[4] Cromwell, on the other hand, is looked upon as the supreme hypocrite:

> Personne mieux que lui sous l'air de la candeur
> N'a de ses grands desseins voilé la profondeur
> Il a reçu du Ciel des talens en partage,
> La valeur, l'éloquence, et même des vertus;
> Mais ces présens des Dieux, il les a corrompus,
> Il les a dégradés par un coupable usage:
> Il déguise le crime et la rébellion
> Sous le masque sacré de la religion:

[1] *Réponse de J.-J. Rousseau au Roi de Pologne, Duc de Lorraine*, in *Œuvres complètes de J.-J. Rousseau*, Paris, 1852, I. 492.

[2] See *Œuvres complètes de Voltaire*, XXIV. 359.

[3] *Cromwel, tragédie en cinq actes et en vers*. Par M. Du Clairon. Représentée pour la première fois par les Comédiens Français Ordinaires du Roi, le 7 juin 1764, Paris, 1764. The play closed after the fifth performance.

[4] *Lettre de Charles Ier, Roi d'Angleterre, de la Maison de Stuart à son fils le prince de Galles retiré en France*, par M. François de Neufchâteau en Lorraine. Neufchâteau, 1766. See the *Avertissement*.

Il veut être Tyran, sans jamais le paraître;
Ennemi sans retour, Juge sans équité,
Politique subtil, et Guerrier redouté;
Voilà quel est *Cromwel*, voilà cet heureux Traître,
Qui proscrit des Anglais le véritable Maître. . . .[1]

In 1764 the *Journal Encyclopédique* reviewing Catherine Macaulay's work in the English edition illustrates much the same attitude. It begins by translating the horrifying introduction of this female patriot whom Burke was later to number among the *poissardes anglaises*:

Dès ma plus tendre enfance, j'ai nourri mon esprit de toutes les histoires où l'on a peint la liberté de ses plus brillantes couleurs; au seul nom de République, je sens mon cœur s'épanouir, et mon âme s'élève toutes les fois que je songe à l'indépendance des Grecs, à cette fierté noble et libre des Romains. C'est la lecture et l'étude des écrivains de ces deux nations qui ont développé le germe de cet amour extrême que j'ai pour la liberté; passion forte, irrésistible, présent de la nature, que tout être raisonnable a reçu avec la vie. . . . Telle doit être à mon avis, la manière de penser d'un historien, s'il désire de voir les choses qu'il a à raconter tout autrement que ne les voient la plupart de nos écrivains politiques, adulateurs outrés et méprisables, dont les talents se bornent à donner un voile séduisant aux vices les plus monstrueux. . . . Insipides auteurs qui n'ont pas même assez de discernement pour distinguer ces âmes vertueuses et vraiment patriotiques avec ces hommes sans honneur, ces intrigants subalternes, qui ont sacrifié les intérêts les plus essentiels du public à leurs viles passions, et à leur propre intérêt. Dans l'histoire que je me suis proposé d'écrire, je ne donnerai des éloges qu'à la véritable vertu, quelque rang qu'ils aient eu, et quelque illustre qu'ait pu être le nom qu'ils ont déshonoré etc., etc. . . .

The *Journal Encyclopédique* editors, choking with indignation, seem scarcely able to believe that such a writer exists. Still commenting on Catherine Macaulay's introduction, they warn their French readers of her seditious purposes:

Le but de Mlle Macaulay dans ce discours en forme d'introduction à son ouvrage, a été de prévenir ses lecteurs en faveur de l'histoire, ou plutôt du libelle qu'elle va donner et dont elle fait par avance l'apologie. . . . Elle proteste qu'elle ne dira rien d'indécent, ni qui respire la licence et la sédition: mais est-ce parler le langage des bons citoyens? Est-ce aimer la tranquillité publique que d'avancer: *quiconque entreprend de*

[1] Ibid., p. 6.

concilier la monarchie avec la liberté, est un rebelle dans le sens le plus noir et le plus étendu; il est rebelle aux lois de la patrie, aux lois de la nature, aux lois de la raison, comme aussi à celles de la divinité. . . . Nous ne rapporterons de cette histoire que quelques traits isolés; car nos lecteurs seraient trop indignés de l'audace de l'auteur, si nous leur rendions compte des efforts criminels qu'elle fait pour inspirer à ses concitoyens la haine de la royauté, et du mépris pour la mémoire des princes les plus respectables de la Grande-Bretagne.

Significantly, the *Journal Encyclopédique* cites as an example of Catherine Macaulay's bias her portrait of James I and then adds: 'ce que nous avons dit, d'après M. Hume, au sujet de ce monarque, nous dispense de rapporter ici les observations de Mlle Macaulay . . . parce qu'il n'est pas possible de rendre compte à cet égard des récits infidèles et des observations injurieuses.'[1]

The next two decades were to witness a rapid evolution of French political attitudes. This same journal which in 1764 could not even bring itself to reproduce examples of Catherine Macaulay's criminally seditious republicanism for fear of shocking its readers (and, of course, the censors) was able to speak in 1778 of

[1] January 1764, I. 91–100. Brissot (*Mémoires de Brissot*, Paris, 1877, p. 422) was highly indignant on reading the following anecdote reported by Boswell in his *Life of Johnson*:

'He (Johnson) again insisted on the duty of maintaining subordination of rank. "Sir, I would no more deprive a nobleman of his respect, than of his money. I consider myself as acting a part in the great system of society, and I do to others as I would have them to do to me. I would behave to a nobleman as I should expect he would behave to me, were I a nobleman and he Sam. Johnson. Sir, there is one Mrs. Macaulay in this town, a great republican. One day when I was at her house, I put on a very grave countenance, and said to her, 'Madam, I am now become a convert to your way of thinking. I am convinced that all mankind are upon an equal footing; and to give you an unquestionable proof, Madam, that I am in earnest, here is a very sensible, civil, well-behaved fellow-citizen, your footman; I desire that he may be allowed to sit down and dine with us.' I thus, Sir, showed her the absurdity of the levelling doctrine. She has never liked me since. Sir, your levellers wish to level *down* as far as themselves; but they cannot bear levelling *up* to themselves. They would all have some people under them; why not then have some people above them?"'

Dr. Johnson was not alone in criticizing Catherine Macaulay as is evident in the following passage from a letter addressed to her by Hume: 'I grant, that the cause of liberty, which you, Madam, with the Pyms and Hampdens have adopted, is noble and generous; but most of the partizans of that cause, in the last century disgraced it, by their violence, and also by their cant, hypocrisy, and bigotry, which, more than the principles of civil liberty, seem to have been the motive of all their actions . . .'—Letter from Paris, 29 March 1764. (See *New Letters of David Hume*, ed. R. Klibansky and E. C. Mossner, Oxford, 1954, p. 81.)

the 'justesse des idées, la solidité du jugement de Mlle Macaulay, et les profondes connaissances qu'elle a de la nature humaine. . . .'[1]

A similar evolution in political attitudes is reflected to some extent by the opinions of a few pre-revolutionary writers who take a more positive approach to the idea of Cromwell as the central figure in philosophical tragedy. Delisle de Sales, for example, ponders in 1772 the question of a *Cromwel* in which Locke would play an important rôle.[2] Later, the future *conventionnel* Louis-Sébastien Mercier almost begs dramatic authors to treat the subject of Cromwell: 'A quoi songez-vous, poètes tragiques? Vous avez un pareil sujet à traiter et vous allez me parler des Persans et des Grecs; vous me donnez des romans rimés: eh! peignez-moi Cromwel!'[3] Mercier imagines himself at the theatre in the year 2440 just after attending an historical play on the Calas affair. He hears announced that the following day the tragedy *Cromwel ou la mort de Charles premier* is to be performed: '. . . l'assemblée', this visitor to the future informs us, 'parut extrêmement satisfaite de cette annonce. On me dit que la pièce était un chef-d'œuvre, et que jamais la cause des rois et celle des peuples n'avaient été présentées avec cette force, cette éloquence et cette vérité. Cromwel était un vengeur, un héros digne du sceptre qu'il avait fait tomber d'une main perfide et criminelle envers l'état; et les rois dont le cœur était disposé à quelque injustice, n'avaient pu jamais lire ce drame sans que la pâleur ne vînt blanchir leur front orgueilleux.'[4]

Mercier's attitude, unheard of earlier in France, is still extremely rare even at this time. Not only, as we have seen, did the French of the *ancien régime* generally consider Cromwell to be one of the greatest of political criminals, they were also quite certain, and Monsieur Hume had not contradicted their belief in the matter, that the eighteenth-century English fully shared this view. Frequent allusions are made in traditionalist *ancien-régime* literature to the effect that the English nation still felt desperately guilty concerning the crime of regicide committed in its name in

[1] *Journal Encyclopédique*, July 1778, V. 109. In December 1781, however, the editors, albeit more gently than in 1764, again chide her for her anti-royalist bias (ibid., 1 December 1781, VIII. 230–1).

[2] *Essai sur la tragédie:* Par un philosophe, 1772, p. 368.

[3] *L'An deux mille quatre cent quarante*, nouvelle édition, Londres, 1785, I. 162, note A.

[4] Ibid., I. 163.

the seventeenth century—so guilty, in fact, that it annually held a commemorative day of national mourning for the tragic loss of Charles I. A typical expression of this belief is found in Pierre-Jean Grosley's *Londres*:

Le 30 janvier est consacré, dans toute l'église anglicane, à une fête annuelle avec un long office en mémoire du martyre de ce prince. Dans des oraisons qui font partie de cet office, on crie miséricorde, on prie Dieu de ne pas redemander à l'Angleterre le sang du S. martyre, qui a vu d'un oeil serein la mort et tous les outrages dont elle fut accompagnée, et qui, marchant sur les traces de son Sauveur, est mort en priant pour ses assassins et pour ses bourreaux.[1]

So strong indeed were official French feelings on the subject that in 1779 Louis XVI's council, preparing a war manifesto against Great Britain, included among its accusations the charge that the House of Hanover held its power through usurpation and also reproached the English with the assassination of Charles I and Mary Stuart. Louis XVI in marginal comments on the draft manifesto typically pointed out that England was already sufficiently remorseful concerning those crimes and that it would be unwise to include such a reminder: 'Quant à l'assassinat du roi Charles et de Marie Stuart, ce sont là des crimes dont l'Angleterre rougit si bien cent ans après et davantage, que nous ne devons pas lui rappeler ce souvenir par des reproches d'autant plus amers et humiliants, que c'est un roi de France, jouissant de l'amour de son peuple, qui est censé les faire dans une déclaration de guerre. La Maison d'Hanovre est étrangère d'ailleurs à ces attentats.'[2] Where the manifesto pointed out that, since Cromwell, all English treaties had shown revolting and subtle traces of base and envious policy, Louis XVI further observed: 'Je préférerais d'effacer le mot Cromwel, et de substituer la date de son gouvernement; les Anglais nous reprochent aussi d'avoir reconnu le pouvoir de cet homme odieux. J'ôterais toute la phrase: car depuis Cromwel, nous avons acquis bien des provinces et des possessions.'[3]

In total disagreement with such sentiments, Mercier sees the English of the year 2440 as a wiser race and favouring a rather different attitude towards the Protector:

[1] *Londres*, Lausanne, 1770, I. 354–5. In fact the English seem to have had three days commemorating the Stuarts: January 30 in memory of Charles I; May 29 to celebrate the Restoration; and, paradoxically perhaps, November 5 to celebrate the expulsion of James II.

[2] *Œuvres de Louis XVI*, Paris, 1864, II. 49.

[3] Ibid., II. 51.

L'Anglais est toujours le premier peuple de l'Europe: il jouit de l'ancienne gloire d'avoir montré à ses voisins le gouvernement qui convenait à des hommes jaloux de leurs droits et de leur bonheur.

On ne fait plus de processions pour la mémoire de Charles Ier; l'on voit mieux en politique.

On vient d'ériger la nouvelle statue du protecteur Cromwel. . . . Les assemblées du peuple se tiendront dorénavant en présence de cette statue, parce que le grand homme qu'elle représente est le véritable auteur de l'heureuse et immuable constitution.[1]

We will see that not even in the Convention a decade later was such an enthusiastic attitude to Cromwell anywhere to be found. Although during the Revolution his ostensible opinion was to be quite different, the pre-revolutionary Brissot also admired Cromwell if we are to believe his own *après-coup* account of certain cherished youthful dreams:

Cette idée de révolution, que je n'osais avouer, roulait souvent dans ma tête; je m'y donnais un des rôles principaux, comme il est bien naturel de le croire. L'histoire de Charles Ier et de Cromwel m'avait singulièrement frappé; je me rappelais sans cesse ce dernier, déchirant dans son enfance le portrait de son roi, terminant sa carrière par le faire décapiter, et ne devant qu'à son génie le grand rôle qu'il avait joué dans la révolution anglaise. Il ne me paraissait pas impossible de renouveler cette révolution. . . .[2]

Brissot in fact was, perhaps more than any other revolutionary figure, deeply influenced by the events of Stuart history. As in the case of Mirabeau, his favourite historian of those events, several years before the Revolution, was Catherine Macaulay. In May 1784 Brissot expressed the hope that she would also write the history of the American revolution so that Americans might learn how to avoid the faults of the English who had allowed republicanism to die in their own country.[3] Hume, on the other hand, Brissot singles out as the great enemy; only the *capucin*, the Père d'Orléans, had written a worse history[4] but Hume is judged, because of his popularity, to be much more dangerous. Brissot speaks of the need to diminish 'la foi politique implicite qu'on a en lui'.[5]

In September 1784, on the occasion of the English publication of Hume's essays 'Of Suicide' and 'Of the Immortality of the

[1] Mercier, op. cit., I. 382–3.
[2] *Mémoires de Brissot*, p. 19.
[3] *Journal du Licée de Londres*, I. 335–6.
[4] Ibid., July 1784, II. 150–1.
[5] Ibid., p. 151.

Soul', Brissot devoted fourteen pages of his journal to a general review of Hume's reputation. He praises Hume's early philosophical essays and judges that they had been mistakenly neglected by the public since, after all, they contained a good deal of useful material against *les préjugés*.[1] It was because he had failed to please with these, Brissot maintains, that Hume decided to prostitute his pen, vowing to succeed in history at any cost: '. . . et il réussit. Peut-être dut-il une partie de son grand succès au parti qu'il embrassa, c'était le parti de la couronne contre le peuple; il la défendit dans toutes ses entreprises, il se rendit odieux aux partisans du républicanisme; mais les philosophes lui pardonnèrent son attachement, son dévouement à la Couronne d'Angleterre, en faveur des réflexions philosophiques que d'ailleurs il répandit dans son histoire.'[2]

Brissot thus admits that the early *philosophes* had admired Hume for his 'philosophy', meaning his anti-clericalism. This was not in itself bad but French intellectuals had now outgrown that intermediate stage of enlightenment and needed something more. The struggle now had to be more political than religious in emphasis. Now was the time for history to attach itself to a loud and clear defence of the people's liberty; the long-neglected rights of humanity had to be avenged:

> Hume n'a pas, suivant moi, porté assez loin cette espèce de philosophie: on voit qu'il était du temps où l'on criait plus contre l'influence des prêtres qu'en faveur des hommes. C'est le défaut de Voltaire; le pas qu'ils ont fait a mené à celui que nous faisons, et il était plus difficile: il faut les remercier de l'avoir hasardé, car on peut employer ce mot, quand on connaît l'esprit du clergé anglais. On doit plus reprocher à Hume son apologie des Jacques et des Charles, son éloge trop pompeux de la Constitution Anglaise et du Droit Romain; on lui reprochera de confondre trop souvent le peuple avec la populace. . . .[3]

Even Hume's arguments against immortality are cited by Brissot as additional proof of his callous insensibility: 'Hume n'avait donc jamais été tourmenté par l'oppression. Il n'avait jamais donc entendu se fermer sur lui ces verrous dont les sons lugubres déchirent l'âme du captif. . . . Hume n'eut pas ce besoin; il avait l'âme desséchée, il était fait pour la cause qu'il défendait, et dans cette cause le néant est une ressource.'[4] To complete the picture

[1] Ibid., p. 159. [2] Ibid., p. 161. [3] Ibid., p. 164.
[4] Ibid., pp. 171–2.

Brissot adds a note on Hume's *Political Discourses*; it is in these that Hume especially betrays his selfish character: 'Vous trouverez cette aridité, cette insensibilité, cet *unfeeling*, si je puis faire ce mot anglais, dans ses discours sur le commerce, sur le luxe, sur l'argent; il s'y déclare l'apologiste du luxe, et pourquoi? parce que jouissant de pensions et de bons revenus il aimait à boire du champagne, et à jouir en épicurien. . . .'[1] How corrupt, how unclean the *sage Monsieur Hume* seems now! One almost hears in the distance, not the intellectual Brissotins of a decade later, but the morally austere and often frankly obscurantist followers of Robespierre.[2]

9. *Anticipating the storm*

Such bitter attacks on the Scottish historian are still fairly rare before 1789. On the eve of the Revolution, proof of Hume's continuingly great historical reputation can be seen in the appearance of a new edition of the *Stuarts* in 1788—possibly the tenth separate French edition since 1760 of this the most popular part of the *History*. Additional proof of his enduring success is provided by the police records which show that on 20 June 1786 the Paris authorities seized in a book shipment from Marseilles the proof sheets of a counterfeit edition of Hume's *History*.[3] Quite obviously, book pirates do not go to the trouble of printing works whose popularity has run out.

Not only was Hume's *History* still popular on the eve of the Revolution, its authority continued to mould the opinions held by most Frenchmen, whether of traditionalist or liberal persuasion, on the English revolution. If we find, for example, a Mably attacking Hume at this time, we find also a Gudin de La Brenellerie defending him. In fact Gudin de La Brenellerie's important analysis of the British parliamentary system, published

[1] Ibid., p. 172.

[2] Some hint too of the *culte de l'Etre suprême* can be found in Bernardin de Saint-Pierre's virtuous charge of the same year concerning writers like Hume: '. . . leur lecture est si sèche et si rebutante. . . . La postérité préférera Hérodote à David Hume . . . parce qu'on aime encore mieux entendre raconter les fables de la Divinité dans l'histoire des hommes que de voir la raison des hommes dans l'histoire de la Divinité.'—*Etudes de la Nature* (1784), in *Œuvres complètes de Jacques-Henri Bernardin de Saint-Pierre*, Paris, 1830–1, V. 111–12.

[3] See 'Journal des livres suspendus depuis janvier 1788', Bibliothèque Nationale, Fonds Fr. 21,934, p. 67.

in 1789, follows Hume very closely, because, the author tells us, 'il est le moins partial des historiens anglais, et le moins opposé à la prérogative royale.'[1]

Hume, moreover, could still appeal in the 1780's to the fashionable nobility he had pleased so much a quarter of a century earlier. The Comtesse de Boufflers' gracious letter to Hume on his *History*[2] should be contrasted with the following note by the same author to Gustavus III of Sweden concerning, not her great good friend the respectable statesman David Hume, but the rabble-rousing, squalid Raynal: '. . . sans naissance, sans esprit, chassé de France pour avoir attaqué avec impudence et folie les principes qui font le lien de la société et la sûreté des princes, et, par-dessus tout, ennuyeux à l'excès'.[3] Hume, if nothing else, had never been found *ennuyeux à l'excès*. We can especially appreciate the force of the comtesse's words when we learn that this famous *salonnière* on one occasion had lovingly spent an entire day trying to equal in French translation *one* paragraph of Hume's elegant *History*![4]

Our chapter on Hume's pre-revolutionary image can perhaps best be concluded with the quotation of an opinion expressed by Malesherbes late in 1788. At the time he wrote, all of France was waiting for the promised convocation of the Etats-Généraux. Malesherbes, less than one year before the fall of the Bastille, runs over in his mind the intellectual achievements of the century and the titles of important works which, because of censorship restrictions, did not appear in France with the express or sometimes even tacit permission of the authorities and yet which were *necessary*. Montesquieu's *Esprit des Lois* was one such work; another was Hume's *History of England*: 'M. Hume est regardé assez généralement en France comme le modèle des Historiens sages et impartiaux, et depuis que toute la Nation Française parle de la *Constitution*, et a été même invitée par le Roi à s'en occuper, il faut s'instruire dans cet auteur de celle de son pays, soit pour en

[1] *Essai sur l'histoire des comices de Rome, des Etats-Généraux de la France et du Parlement d'Angleterre*, Philadelphie, 1789, III. 111. See also Gudin de La Brenellerie's defence of Hume against Mably in *Supplément à la manière d'écrire l'histoire ou réponse à l'ouvrage de M. l'abbé de Mably*, 1784, pp. 113–14.

[2] See *supra*, pp. 9–10.

[3] *Lettres de Gustave III à la comtesse de Boufflers et de la comtesse au Roi de 1771 à 1791*, Bordeaux, 1900, Letter 62.

[4] See *Nouveaux mélanges extraits des manuscrits de Mme Necker*, Paris, An X, I. 202.

prendre ce qui peut nous être utile, soit pour rejeter ce qui ne s'accorde pas avec nos mœurs et nos lois.'[1]

Someone once said of Malesherbes that he devoted his lifetime to pleading the cause of the people before the tribunal of the king and that he died pleading the cause of the king before the tribunal of the people. We shall see that once more, not long before his death on the revolutionary scaffold, while pleading the cause of his king, he would have occasion to deal with David Hume's *History*. In 1788 his plea is more general; it is for the people as much as for

[1] *Mémoires sur la librairie et sur la liberté de la presse*, par M. de Lamoignon de Malesherbes, Ministre d'Etat, Paris, 1809, p. 306. Additional evidence of Malesherbes' extremely high regard for the wisdom of Hume's *Stuarts* may be found in the following fragment of Abbé de Véri's *Journal*, dated 5 October 1788:

'Après l'éloignement des deux ministres, après la rentrée des Parlements et lorsque la convocation des Etats-Généraux eut été décidée le Roi manda Malesherbes et eut avec lui une conversation de trois quarts d'heure ou d'une heure.

'Malesherbes m'en rapporta quelques traits que je vais rendre en le faisant parler et sans prétendre atteindre à sa touche vive et éloquente.

' "Je ne connais pas, lui dit-il, de position plus fâcheuse que celle d'un Roi dans votre situation présente. . . .

'—Vous lisez beaucoup, Sire, et vous êtes plus instruit qu'on ne croit. Mais la lecture n'est rien sans l'accompagnement de la réflexion. J'ai revu dernièrement, dans l'histoire d'Angleterre de David Hume, le morceau de Charles Ier. Relisez-le avec réflexion. Vos positions se ressemblent. Ce prince était doux, vertueux, attaché aux lois, point dur, point entreprenant, juste et bienfaisant; cependant il a péri sur un échafaud. En voici, je crois la raison. Il arriva dans le moment où la dispute s'élevait entre les prérogatives de la couronne et celles de la nation. S'il eût cédé de ses prérogatives, il eût été vil aux yeux de ceux qui, par habitude de la jeunesse et par les avantages que la noblesse en retirait, les regardaient comme sacrées. Mais d'autre part, il fut le plus faible dans le cours de la dispute pendant laquelle on lui arrachait à chaque instant une nouvelle concession. S'il fût venu cinquante ans plus tôt, ses vertus en auraient fait le modèle d'un roi; s'il fût arrivé cinquante ans plus tard, lorsque les droits mutuels étaient établis sans obstacle, il ne les eût pas transgressés et son règne eût été long et heureux.

'Votre position est la même. La question s'élève entre les usages précédents de l'autorité et les réclamations des citoyens! Heureusement les querelles de religion n'y sont pas mêlées.

'—Oh! pour cela, oui, bien heureusement, me dit le Roi en me prenant par le bras. Ainsi l'atrocité ne sera pas la même.

'—D'ailleurs les mœurs plus adoucies vous rassurent contre les excès de ce temps-là. Mais on vous arrachera par degrés plusieurs de vos prérogatives. C'est à vous à prendre en votre conseil un plan décidé sur les concessions que vous devez faire au bien général et sur ce que vous ne devez jamais céder. Votre seule fermeté peut décider de la réussite d'un tel plan. Sans elle on ne peut rien prévoir d'assuré. Je répondrais pourtant que cela n'ira pas jusqu'au sort de Charles Ier, mais je ne répondrais pas de tout autre excès. Vous devez vous occuper à les prévenir. . . ." ' (See 'L'Abbé de Véri et son journal' par le Duc de Castries, *La Revue de Paris*, November 1953, pp. 84–86.)

the king and he speaks for that peculiarly sane group of moderates who worked actively for reform within the structure of the *ancien régime* and who followed Montesquieu rather than Rousseau. On the whole, it is also to this same group that Hume the historian—despite the extreme reactions of the Bergiers and the Brissots—appealed most during this period. After Montesquieu's death, Hume had been hailed as the only man in Europe capable of replacing the author of the *Esprit des Lois*.[1] With the arrival of the Revolution, the stars of both writers fell considerably. Both were eventually to recover their losses in prestige but at different times and in different ways. Montesquieu would take up his now permanent place as one of the eighteenth century's greatest political theoreticians. Hume, on the other hand, was to be recognized as one of the eighteenth century's most highly original philosophers. But before that, within only a few years, Hume the historian would play his greatest political role ever, as prophet of the French counter-revolution.

[1] Greig, op. cit., I. 259.

II

THE REVOLUTION AND THE RÔLE OF HISTORY

1. History as a weapon of counter-revolution

We have examined at the beginning of Chapter I the prevailing eighteenth-century view of history. Some further general considerations on the subject are necessary at this point, however, since it is especially at the time of the Revolution in France that history's traditional rôle as the scientifically validating factor of all political speculation is seriously questioned.

Of course, with the conservatives, this traditional view of history's function still largely prevails, and, in fact, becomes, if anything, more intense. History shows us the stable facts of human nature. It represents, in a hard physical sense, the unchanging 'nature of things'. It has a certain Newtonian order to its predictably cyclical patterns of unfolding.

True enough, events in one century may differ from events in another: that is because of particular variations which characterize each nation and each century. One does not, therefore, become a helpless prisoner of the 'science' of history; it does not repeat itself exactly. But history's essential aspect is its constant similarity from century to century. Since the human heart and the human passions do not change, the present and the future must resemble the past. If this were not true then history would have no purpose; the past is not studied for its own sake. History has its 'lessons' to teach. It is the science, admittedly imperfect, admittedly based on analogy, of human social behaviour. One must be just as empirically minded, just as anti-*a priori* in dealing with this science as with any other. When one speaks of a 'revolution' in man's form of government, for example, one must understand what can possibly be meant by such a term. A total change in the forms of man's social organization is a distinct physical impossibility. It is as impossible as miracles are in the universe of Newton. Neither human nature nor the law of gravity can be repealed.

History is thus the ordered apprehension of the moral nature of things. It condemns in advance any over-optimistic attempts to achieve ideal or drastically rational political change. It tells us that what has never yet been witnessed in man's behaviour in the past can hardly be expected to appear in the present or future. J.-H. Meister in 1790 sums up the view very clearly and with a certain irony not uncommon at this time in the writings of those who felt the reassuring weight of the centuries behind them as they attacked the impertinent *a priorists*:

Il est possible qu'il se soit fait depuis quelque temps une grande révolution dans le monde moral, et que cette révolution merveilleuse en ait bouleversé tout à coup l'ordre et les principes. Mais avant cette époque mémorable, si l'on pouvait prendre un peu de confiance dans les résultats qu'offrent le plus évidemment l'histoire et l'expérience du cœur humain, n'aurait-on pas reconnu, sans peine, que ce qui agit le plus fortement sur la volonté de l'homme, c'est l'empire des choses et des circonstances; que ce pouvoir suprême n'est balancé que par celui des passions, et ne l'est encore qu'un certain temps; que les passions ont plus de force que les habitudes, les habitudes plus que les préjugés, les préjugés plus que les intérêts ordinaires de la vie, ces intérêts habituels plus que de simples idées de justice ou de convenance; qu'enfin de tous les ressorts qui déterminent nos actions et notre conduite, le plus faible, sans doute, est celui du raisonnement, quelque admirable qu'en soit la logique?

Si l'influence secrète d'une puissance surnaturelle n'avait pas changé tous les rapports, penserait-on de bonne foi qu'il ne faut point opposer d'autres barrières au mouvement inconstant des volontés et des passions humaines que les limites d'une idée métaphysique tracée plus ou moins heureusement? . . .

Serait-il encore permis de douter, si le seul gouvernement qui n'a jamais existé nulle part est infailliblement le plus parfait comme le plus admirable? . . .

J'ai le plus profond respect pour des révolutions de brochures et de philosophie, surtout lorsqu'elles sont appuyées par une coalition aussi terrible que celle de la populace et de l'armée; mais quelque décisifs qu'en soient les effets, je crains toujours un peu le retour de cet empire qu'il ne faut jamais oublier, celui des choses et des circonstances. . . .[1]

[1] J.-H. Meister, *Des premiers principes du système social appliqués à la Révolution présente*, Nice, 1790, pp. 120–7.

Meister, one of the more original thinkers in late eighteenth-century France, gives proof, not only in this work but in several others, of having been generally influenced by the whole Humian doctrine of human nature. See *De l'origine des*

The reformer of society must bear in mind not only man's unchanging passions in his lofty search for what is ideally right in government; he must pay attention also to more earthly matters, to what history, for example, has shown to be socially useful. Such is the opinion of the Abbé L.-S. Balestrier de Canilhac, who in 1790 devoted well over a hundred pages of the *Bibliothèque de l'homme public* to a critically-timed reprinting of Hume's political essays[1] and who provoked the resignation of his fellow editor Condorcet by defending the historical empiricism of Burke against the *a priorism* of Thomas Paine:

M. Paine raisonne dans son ouvrage, comme la plupart de nos législateurs modernes, en simple philosophe, constamment attaché aux principes du droit naturel et à leurs conséquences les plus rigoureuses. M. Burke raisonne, au contraire, en politique sage, qui a étudié les hommes et les effets des passions réunies dans les grandes sociétés. . . .

En politique il ne faut pas toujours considérer *le droit* mais *l'utile*. La seule raison nous apprend le droit naturel; mais il n'y a que l'expérience unie à l'observation qui puisse nous rendre certains de ce qui est vraiment utile. Qui doute que le peuple n'ait le droit, rigoureusement parlant, d'élire ses rois, et de les déposer même sans motif? Il ne faut pas être un grand philosophe pour prouver cette vérite; mais il faut être plus que philosophe pour décider la question sous le rapport de l'utilité, et c'est un grand principe de politique: *qu'il n'est pas toujours utile au peuple de faire tout ce qu'il a droit de faire.* Les vérités de droit sont immuables, celles d'utilité varient selon les circonstances, et le monde n'est jamais dans la même situation. Nous ne voulons pas dire pour cela que le gouvernement doit changer à tout moment de principes, mais il doit les modifier avec cette lenteur sage que la nature observe dans ses opérations.[2]

The eighteenth century had indeed witnessed the production of a good many rather long, geometrically assembled, highly indigestible *ex professo* treatises on natural law, most of which, when all was said and done, proved impeccably in many languages that man should be *just.* One sometimes has, on reading such productions, the classic impression of watching mountains give birth to

principes religieux, 1768, pp. 5–49; *Lettres sur l'imagination*, Londres, 1799, *passim; Mélanges de philosophie, de morale et de littérature*, Genève, 1822, pp. 212–15, 243–4.

[1] *Bibliothèque de l'homme public ou analyse raisonnée des principaux ouvrages français et étrangers* . . . par M. le Marquis de Condorcet . . ., M. de Peysonel . . ., M. Le Chapelier, et autres Gens de Lettres, Paris, 1790, I, tome 2.

[2] Ibid., 1791, IX. 247–8.

mice. The Age of Reason also spoke a good deal of natural rights but natural rights, too, the empirical politician might object, seldom appear to be more than tautological fictions: there are no natural rights as such, there are only the historical adjustments of different men's conflicting claims. The reformer of society should be guided, then, by positive law rather than by so-called natural law. He should consult Hume and Montesquieu, not the reason of the Age of Reason. Cerutti, a member of the *Assemblée législative* and one of the warmest eighteenth-century admirers of Hume's *History* ('l'histoire des passions anglaises, par la raison humaine') sums up the practical applications of this empirical view:

Un principe est . . . un résultat du calcul et de l'expérience. La politique n'est . . . pas un art de sentiment ni une science de système. Des idées neuves ne peuvent . . . prévaloir sur les idées antiques, par cette raison seule qu'elles ont le mérite de la nouveauté. On ne devient pas législateur en un moment. Ceux qui dédaignent de consulter les oracles de l'antiquité, ceux qui regardent en pitié, et le Sénat de Rome, et l'Aéropage d'Athènes, et le Parlement d'Angleterre, et les méditations de Montesquieu, et les observations de Blackstone, et les réflexions de Hume, de Robertson, de Ferguson, de Lolme, peuvent être des hommes de génie, mais leur génie est bien précoce, bien précipité, bien enfant, s'il faut le dire, pour quitter ainsi les vieillards de la sagesse.

Toutes les révolutions ont besoin du courage. Aussi rien ne les accélère comme la magnanimité des jeunes gens. Mais s'ils excellent à démolir le présent, ils n'excellent pas de même à fonder l'avenir. C'est l'oeuvre de l'âge mûr, des esprits mûrs, des idées mûres. Cette maturité, jetant de côté les passions toujours extrêmes et toujours imprévoyantes, s'occupe à poser des fondements solides et des bornes salutaires.[1]

The counter-revolutionist Count Ferrand, future minister of Louis XVIII and another admirer of Hume's *Stuarts*,[2] gives in 1793 yet another conservative's view of the rôle of history. History shows how human nature can be 'modified' but can never be 'changed'. Once he has a good understanding of the 'nature of things', the reformer will automatically avoid all abstractions and general principles which always appear simple since they ignore

[1] *Lettre de M. Cerutti adressée au café de Foix*, in *Œuvres diverses de M. Cerutti ou recueil de pièces composées avant et depuis la révolution*, Paris, 1792, II. 3–5; see also I. 4–7.

[2] See *L'Esprit de l'Histoire ou Lettres politiques et morales d'un père à son fils*, Paris, 1802, III. 400, 497–8.

difficulties but which are, in fact, invariably based on false hypotheses:

Il ne visera pas à une simplicité, à une unité de moyens, parce que la nature n'est pas plus simple dans l'homme moral que dans l'homme physique, parce que le but et les fins de la société sont si compliqués, qu'il est impossible de la faire agir avec des ressorts simples, qui seraient insuffisants, et par conséquent dangereux.

Bien convaincu de ces vérités générales, il examinera la situation particulière de l'Etat, mais sans prétendre à l'honneur de faire de grandes découvertes dans la moralité, dans les principes du gouvernement et dans les idées sur la liberté. Plus sa sagacité aura l'habitude d'observer, plus il croira que la science du gouvernement, si pratique, dirigée vers tant d'objets, exige plus d'expérience qu'aucun homme n'en peut acquérir pendant sa vie. Il appellera donc à son secours celle des siècles passés; il s'enrichira dans ce fonds commun, qui fournit, sans s'épuiser, aux besoins de tous les hommes; il ne regardera pas l'ancienneté d'une idée, d'une habitude, même d'un préjugé, comme un signe infaillible de réprobation; il croira qu'il est de bons préjugés, dont la conservation est utile, dont la destruction serait pernicieuse; que ces préjugés étant une première inspiration du sentiment qui conseille, ou qui adopte, avant que le jugement ait prononcé, doivent être un puissant agent sur la majorité du peuple, plus capable de sentir que de juger; et d'après cela, plus l'édifice qu'il doit réparer sera ancien, plus il s'en approchera avec une vénération religieuse, comme d'une enceinte sacrée où la majesté des siècles a déposé, sous la garde de l'expérience, la science pratique de la morale et de la justice; comme d'un établissement qui a vu passer les générations, et dont l'auguste et bienfaisante vieillesse avance dans l'éternité. Il sentira qu'un gouvernement qui a ces caractères, est un bien héréditaire, substitué par les aïeux à ceux qui doivent le transmettre à leur postérité qui le recevra, qui le possédera, qui le laissera comme les propriétés et la vie; que par là *le système politique se trouve dans un accord parfait avec l'ordre du monde;* que la marche de l'Etat imitant celle de la nature, il n'est *jamais totalement neuf dans ce qu'il acquiert, ni entièrement vieux dans ce qu'il conserve;* . . . .[1]

It is not difficult to see in the preceding passages echoes of Montesquieu, Hume and Burke. It would, moreover, be a comparatively simple matter to find scores of similar passages in the works of other conservatives of the period, all with essentially the same message: the facts of human nature, the lessons of history and experience, the moral nature of things, the science of man, in

[1] Antoine-François-Claude, Comte Ferrand, *Le rétablissement de la monarchie Françoise*, Liège, 1794, seconde édition, pp. 69–71.

short, cannot be ignored. Revolutionary innovators who disregard what the great historical empiricists have written, who make up new men and new constitutions with the scissors and paste of mere logic, are condemned in advance to failure: 'En considérant leurs symétries politiques et leurs applanissements', writes Mallet du Pan, also a counter-revolutionary admirer of Hume, 'on croit voir un ramas de fous travaillant à aligner les Alpes sur le module de la colonnade de S. Pierre.'[1]

Such being the case, what must one think of a 'revolution' in the affairs of men or of those who claim to be placing man in an entirely new world where all the old problems, the old injustices will be eliminated? For the conservative the answer is not difficult: one has very little to think or to do except to wait and, perhaps, if circumstances permit, to smile ironically at such naïvely enthusiastic but completely wasted efforts. A 'revolution' means exactly what it seems to mean etymologically: it is a wild and wasteful ride on a merry-go-round which, after going through the classical phases of saving everyone, ends up by, temporarily at least, enslaving everyone, and it ultimately leaves a nation in a social position much worse very often than the one it was in before the foolish political ride began. Revolutions go the full circle, they are 'horizontal', and we shall see that even in the Convention the hope of many of the more history-minded radical members was not that such a view was untrue but that somehow history could be deceived, that the merry-go-round could be stopped at a half-turn. 'Les révolutions', one of them tells us, 'ne marchent pas en ligne droite, mais parcourent un cercle. . . . Par conséquent chaque pas que l'on fait en avant ramène au despotisme, lorsqu'une fois on est parvenu au point qui lui était diamétralement opposé. . . .'[2]

All revolutions consequently resemble each other. If one has studied those of the past in a good historian one can predict with accuracy and profit the course of those of the present or future:

L'histoire romaine devient ainsi après deux mille ans, utile au génie politique qui décompose les événements, pour en fixer les causes, et qui

[1] *Correspondance politique pour servir à l'histoire du républicanisme français*, par M. Mallet du Pan, Hambourg, 1796, p. xiii.

[2] See *Opinion de L.-M. Revellière-Lépeaux*, député de Maine-et-Loire, 7 janvier 1793.

en connaît les éléments primitifs. Montesquieu, en adoptant cette méthode a plus donné à penser, dans un seul volume sur les Romains, que tous les historiens qui avaient, avant lui, rapporté jusqu'aux plus petits détails de l'histoire romaine. La plupart des historiens ressemblent à ces joueurs, qui notent et racontent le nombre des coups en gain ou en perte, tandis que le géomètre analyse le fond d'un jeu, fixe les chances et les désavantages, et n'a pas besoin de savoir des événements qu'il a en quelque sorte prévus.[1]

So great are the resemblances between revolutions that the observer may be tempted even to believe that revolutionary leaders consciously imitate the actions of their predecessors. We shall see that extreme royalists did in fact make the charge that the French revolutionists were imitating, point for point, procedures of the mid-seventeenth-century English revolution. Others seemed content with a less sinister account of similarities, explaining them as the unavoidable results of the 'nature of things':

. . . amour-propre, intérêt, esprit d'indépendance, terreur. Ils n'ont pas paru pour la première fois dans cette révolution; ils sont tous écrits dans l'histoire et seront toujours reproduits sous mille formes diverses par tous ceux qui entreprendront d'attaquer les gouvernements.

Il suffira pour s'en convaincre, de lire Tacite, Salluste, Tite-Live, de Thou, Vertot, Hume, Velly, et en général tous les écrivains qui nous ont transmis le souvenir des agitations qu'ont éprouvées les différents empires.

Ces similitudes ont été tellement frappantes que l'on a été assez généralement porté à penser que les chefs de la révolution avaient fait une étude particulière de toutes celles qui ont existé jusqu'à nos jours; qu'ils les avaient méditées longuement pour s'approprier tous les moyens par lesquels leurs précurseurs s'étaient assurés des succès dans cette carrière difficile . . .; mais il faudra convenir aussi qu'un grand nombre de ces ressemblances a été presque entièrement dû à la seule nature des choses qui . . . ne pouvait manquer . . . de présenter de fréquentes ressemblances.[2]

Although he was not above occasionally playing the very popular game of historical *rapprochements* himself, the celebrated lawyer, J.-M.-A. Servan, perhaps the eighteenth-century French

[1] G. Sénac de Meilhan, *Des principes et des causes de la révolution en France*, Londres, 1790, pp. v–vi.

[2] G.-M. Sallier-Chaumont de la Roche, *Essais pour servir d'introduction à l'histoire de la Révolution française*, Paris, 1802, p. 184.

political thinker who most admired Hume,[1] cautions that the sociology of revolutions is still in its infancy. It is undeniable, of course, that general laws governing human events exist: 'Sans doute,' Servan concedes, 'en se plaçant dans un certain point de vue élevé, il faut bien convenir que tous les événements du monde physique et moral tiennent à des causes générales. Mais de quoi sert cette vérité? Outre que ces causes sont très difficiles à découvrir, leur application aux cas particuliers est bien souvent impossible. . . .'[2] Montesquieu's historical determinism, in particular, sometimes goes too far in making a science out of politics. The solution, although the end result still leads to political conservatism, lies in a Humian scepticism:

J'ai trouvé dans les essais politiques de M. Hume, des réflexions qui, sous l'apparence du paradoxe, me semblent offrir une vérité piquante.

'Je crains, dit-il, que le monde n'ait pas encore assez vieilli, pour nous permettre d'établir beaucoup de propositions politiques qui soient généralement vraies, et dont la vérité puisse se soutenir dans les âges les plus reculés; notre expérience ne s'étend pas au-delà de trois mille ans; ainsi, non seulement la logique de cette science est défectueuse, mais nous n'avons pas même assez de ces matériaux dont nous devrions faire usage dans nos raisonnements. Nous ignorons jusqu'à quel degré précis la nature humaine peut raffiner sur les vertus et sur les vices.'[3]

What is the value of all the tantalizing analogies which can be seen when one compares the histories of mankind's various revolutions? Servan answers this question with another analogy:

L'homme qui joint à la plus grande sagacité naturelle le plus d'étude et d'expérience, ressemble dans ses conjectures sur l'avenir, au voyageur, ou au chauffeur, qui peut fort bien, à force d'exercice et d'habitude, juger avec assez de précision, de la vraie distance entre lui et les objets éloignés, tandis qu'un autre moins exercé, moins attentif, s'y trompe lourdement; mais ce même homme qui par l'observation des effets de l'ombre et de la lumière, par la comparaison des objets intermédiaires, détermine très exactement l'éloignement d'une montagne, d'une ville,

[1] See, for example, *Lettre à Monsieur Rabaut de Saint-Etienne sur l'humanité, par un aristocrate sans le savoir* (April 1790), in *Œuvres choisies de Servan, Avocat Général au Parlement de Grenoble*, Paris, 1825, III. 356–63 and, especially, *Correspondance entre quelques hommes honnêtes*, Lausanne, 1795, III. 136–78.

[2] *Des révolutions dans les grandes sociétés civiles considérées dans leurs rapports avec l'ordre général*, in *Œuvres choisies de Servan*, V. 70.

[3] Ibid., pp. 76–77.

ou de tel autre objet éminent, ne pourra jamais deviner, si en allant à cette montagne, à cette ville, quelque précipice qui l'arrêtera, et où peut-être il se perdra en essayant de les franchir.

Etudions tant que nous voudrons et tant que nous pourrons, nous ne saurons jamais qu'un peu du présent, beaucoup moins du passé, et presque rien, si ce n'est même rien du tout, de l'avenir.

C'est une magnifique expression que celle du *flambeau de l'histoire*; cela figure très bien dans un vers, ou dans une phrase harmonieuse, mais quand on veut la réduire à l'exacte vérité, il se trouve que ce *flambeau* n'est qu'une torche. . . . En un mot l'histoire avertit bien plus qu'elle ne guide; c'est un fanal sur un écueil, mais ce n'est pas une boussole et une carte.[1]

Servan's rather balanced if sceptical attitude is fairly rare among French thinkers of the Right at this time. We shall have occasion to cite various counter-revolutionary texts which betray a great deal more confidence in the prophetic value of history and which draw, in minute detail, historical analogies intended to condemn the simple optimism and criminal tampering of the revolutionary leaders. This almost literal belief in historical parallels extended, moreover, well into the early nineteenth century and is effectively illustrated by the following anonymous and rather curious document purporting to be a history of the session of 1828, written in advance by the great Scottish prophet of prophets, David Hume.

The 'editor' of the *ultra* work in question begins by telling his readers that he, at first, had intended to write his own history of the session, 'lorsque je m'aperçus', he goes on to say, 'qu'elle avait été écrite longtemps d'avance, et avec la plus minutieuse exactitude, par David Hume, dans son histoire des Stuarts.'[2] Happy at finding his work already done, the writer abandons his original project and begins to copy:

. . . je présente à mes lecteurs le tableau, tracé par une main nécessairement impartiale, de ce qui vient de se passer sous nos yeux. Heureux si par un rapprochement aussi frappant, je pouvais ouvrir les yeux de tant d'hommes honnêtes qu'on trompe avec de belles phrases. . . .

Ils verront que, dans tous les temps et dans tous les pays, la marche des révolutions est uniforme; que dans ce siècle de perfectibilité nous

[1] *Correspondance entre quelques hommes honnêtes*, III. 72–78.

[2] *Histoire abrégée de la session de 1828, écrite à l'avance par David Hume*, Paris, 1829, *Avis de l'éditeur*, p. 3.

n'avons pris la peine de rien inventer, et que nous ne sommes que les copistes serviles des Anglais du dix-septième siècle. . . .

Aujourd'hui ne pourrions-nous dire comme les royalistes anglais en 1641; 'Jamais souverain eut-il plus de modération en partage avec plus de justice, d'honneur et de grandeur d'âme? Quelle pitié qu'un tel prince soit sans cesse harcelé par des soupçons, des calomnies et des plaintes! Supposé qu'il y ait des abus, n'y a-t-il d'autres moyens d'en prévenir le retour que l'entière abolition de l'autorité royale? . . . L'autorité n'est pas moins nécessaire au gouvernement que la liberté; elle est nécessaire pour le soutien de la liberté même. Quelle folie lorsque tout est heureusement réglé par d'anciennes institutions, de faire le dangereux essai d'une constitution nouvelle, de préférer à la sagesse éprouvée de nos ancêtres, les fantaisies mal digérées de quelques turbulents innovateurs!' (Hume, tome XIV). . . . L'historien anglais donne l'explication de beaucoup de beaux discours, la mesure de beaucoup de grands hommes, et la clef de beaucoup de grands mystères.

Les hommes en effet sont les mêmes dans tous les siècles et dans tous les lieux; l'adresse des uns exploite les passions ou la crédulité des autres; et l'ignoble devise de la révolution de 1789: ôte-toi de là que je m'y mette, fut et sera toujours celle de toutes les révolutions.[1]

The prime examples cited in the preceding note suggest the extent to which the idea that the French revolution paralleled the English revolution and paralleled it not only closely but, for

[1] Ibid., pp. 3–15.

In his *Analogies de l'histoire de France et d'Angleterre ou 1828 et 1640*, Louis de Bonald also invites the French to study Hume at this time: 'C'est dans l'histoire des derniers Stuarts et particulièrement dans celle du plus malheureux de tous qu'il faut étudier notre propre histoire, celle de ces temps-ci.' Those who felt in 1828 that there was no danger of revolution were especially urged to re-read the events of Charles I's reign: 'Ils reconnaîtront, chez les deux peuples, et en 1828 comme en 1640, les mêmes causes de révolution, les mêmes moyens, les mêmes effets. . . .' (See *Œuvres complètes de M. de Bonald*, publiées par M. l'Abbé Migne, Paris, 1859, III. 913.) Joseph de Maistre, much earlier, had already included as the final chapter of his famous *Considérations sur la France* (1796) a similar 'posthumous' work entitled 'Fragment d'une histoire de la révolution française par David Hume'. That de Maistre considered it an important and integral part of his text is made clear in the following letter to de Bonald from Turin, 15 November 1819: 'Tout ce que vous me dites dans votre dernière lettre sur la Révolution d'Angleterre comparée à la vôtre est parfait. J'avais donc bien raison d'en faire le dernier chapitre de mes *Considérations* et bien raison encore de me courroucer contre le sauvage éditeur qui s'est avisé de le retrancher de son autorité dans la dernière édition.' (*Œuvres complètes*, XIII. 192.) See also de Bonald's letter to de Maistre in 1819: 'Cette déplorable histoire est la nôtre de point en point, et jusque-là les deux révolutions ont eté calquées l'une sur l'autre.' (Ibid., XIV. 348.)

many, identically, caught hold of the conservative imagination in revolutionary France. It is, in fact, through the counter-revolutionists' all but total acceptance of this idea that the influence of Hume's history had its effect from 1789 to 1800. For most Frenchmen of the time, no other history of the Stuart period existed; and Hume's manner of relating the events of the English revolution, his frequent reflections on those events, the guaranty provided by his long-standing reputation for nearly superhuman impartiality were all factors which served to increase the authority of his account in support of the doctrines of the Right.

A careful examination of all types of rightist literature of this early counter-revolutionary period would show, I think, that Hume's influence, though in some ways more subtle and diffused, is greater before the turn of the century than even the sensational but somewhat speculative impact of Burke. Burke's shouting, cranky pamphlet on the Revolution caused more amusement than concern among those it was meant to annihilate. Jokes were made about the probable insanity or at least senility of this raving Englishman who had been considered a frank liberal in France until the appearance of his *Reflections*. Burke's new tone could convince only those who wanted to be convinced. On the other hand, Hume's *Stuarts*, widely read during the thirty years preceding the Revolution had had what we might call a subliminal influence even on the hostile, on those who did not want to be convinced and who were forced by the resulting intellectual tension to rewrite history in a more suitable form or to reject its authority altogether.

Through his popular description and analysis of the English revolution, Hume had helped to condition the minds and to form the prejudices, both negative and positive, of the generation which was to be so vitally concerned with similar events. He had provided in advance an almost irresistible set of categories to impose on France's own revolutionary events—a formula of response most suited to conservatives, it is true, but which, even as late as the period in which Louis XVI was tried, a fair number of *conventionnels*, I will not say accepted, but at least felt obligated to consider. Mailhe's report is only the most outstanding example of the need that was felt by many to formulate revolutionary activity in terms of the parallel activity which seventeenth-century England had witnessed.

The many conservative parallels, and there are almost none which do not make specific use of Hume, were not thus just the fashionable and flimsy games of idle pundits. In most cases, historical analogies were pointed out with deadly seriousness and were consciously intended to provoke or encourage a vigorous counter-revolutionary response. I will cite here one of the earliest of these *rapprochements* which, brief as it is, serves as a good example. It is revealed in an anecdote which we find in Soulavie's *Mémoires* and is not a published document, but many documents published subsequently make a similar point:

Le comte d'Artois, le jour que M. Necker avait réussi à doubler le tiers, au mois de décembre 1788, au mépris de l'avis des princes et des notables, avait substitué dans le cabinet du roi le portrait de Charles Ier à celui de Louis XV. Le jour où Louis XVI demanda à M. Necker de rester au ministère, ce jour où le peuple de Versailles témoigna, par ses attroupements, l'intérêt qu'il prenait en M. Necker, M. d'Artois enleva cette image trop silencieuse et substitua une gravure récemment publiée, où le roi Charles étendu sur le carreau reçoit du bourreau le coup de hache. La leçon ne fit pas sur le roi une impression différente.[1]

As Soulavie suggests, there is perhaps good evidence to show that such *rapprochements* may have had, at least on Louis XVI, an effect opposite to that intended. But not all the parallels were conceived so brutally. Some were published to lend hope to the royalists in their darkest hour, to console them by showing that history was on their side, that all would come out right in the end and that they should therefore continue their faithful support of the counter-revolution. Others were quite obviously published to shame the revolutionaries, to humiliate the pride of those who ignorantly proclaimed that the bonds of history had been broken, that their revolution was new and without precedent. Pointing to the Stuart parallels, the royalist felt he could prove conclusively that the revolutionaries were, to the contrary, not at all original; they were not even original in their crimes and their wasted and bloody efforts were condemned to futility once the whole sorry mess had gone the full circle. Some parallel makers, with their studied analogies, seem even to have cherished the rather sanguine hope of converting the radical enthusiasts to conservatism. Chateaubriand tells us, for example, that it is important to show

[1] J.-L. Soulavie, *Mémoires historiques et politiques*, VI. 312–13.

there is nothing new under the sun since a man 'bien persuadé qu'il n'y a rien de nouveau, perd le goût des innovations'.[1]

One last more general reason for the proliferation of parallels during this period should not be neglected. They obviously provided a certain intellectual and aesthetic satisfaction to the hundreds of amateur pamphlet-historians who sprang up everywhere and who found it understandably difficult to give immediate meaning to the confusion and chaos of contemporary events. For these, the obvious parallel with Stuart history furnished a readily available short-cut to the time perspective and allowed the chronicler of current happenings to speak with the borrowed authority of the ages. Here for the asking was a pre-fabricated dramatic structure ready to be imposed on events only an hour old. Here, Hume seemed to say, was the beginning, there was the middle, and finally, there would be the happy conclusion. Some parallels end, in fact, with wistful invocations to General Monk! The making of historical parallels was not new at this time nor has it entirely disappeared from serious modern historical literature. One would probably have difficulty finding, however, a period in history in which such analogies were more widely used and in which they had more real influence.

2. *History as the superstition of slaves*

If we turn now to the opinions of the Left on this matter we will see that the revolutionary ideologists disagreed violently with the basic assumption on which such historical conservatism rested: namely, the idea of a stable human nature, of an inflexible moral 'nature of things'.

True enough, if man at birth is shown to be a creature of innate principles, of unchanging passions, of totally predictable motivation, why then his range of potential behaviour would be strictly limited; nothing really new could ever be expected of him; his 'original sin' would be the despair of all social reformers and all efforts to change and improve his form of social organization would be predestined to failure. But original sin, even in its naturalistic interpretations, had been driven out with the advent of Lockian epistemology. Man is not, Locke tells us, born with *a*

[1] F.-R. de Chateaubriand, *Essai sur les Révolutions* in *Œuvres complètes de M. le vicomte de Chateaubriand*, Paris, 1834, I. 202.

human nature, his mind is a *tabula rasa*; his heart, too, others said, is a blank sheet. Man is merely what, not nature, but nurture makes him. Good education for the individual and for the society, good legislation, can change man, not overnight, of course, but at least in a generation. Thus the so-called nature of things is no longer a great stumbling block; history becomes bunk, and progress, even indefinite progress, becomes a real possibility.

No one, perhaps, argues the case for a rejection of history more cogently than the Abbé Sieyès:

> Assez d'autres croiront devoir demander aux siècles barbares, des lois pour les nations civilisées. Nous ne nous égarerons pas dans la recherche incertaine des institutions et des erreurs antiques. La raison est de tous les temps; elle est faite pour l'homme; et c'est surtout quand elle lui parle de ses intérêts les plus chers, qu'il doit l'écouter avec respect et confiance. . . .
>
> Commandez une pendule à un horloger, et voyez s'il s'amusera à extraire de l'histoire, vraie ou fausse, de l'horlogerie, les différents moyens dont l'industrie naissante a pu s'aviser pour mesurer le temps. . . .
>
> Toujours ardents à profiter, pour la jouissance, des moindres progrès que nous voyons faire aux arts de commerce et de luxe, rentrerons-nous toujours dans une indifférence honteuse, dès qu'il s'agit des progrès de *l'art social*, de ce premier des arts dont les combinaisons savantes recèlent le bonheur du genre humain?[1]

We should note that, with the eighteenth century's empirical connotation for the word *science*, Sieyès prefers to speak of an *art social* and not a *science sociale*. The choice of words is not insignificant for it is the conservative's privilege to speak at this time of history as a sacred repository of all the empirical data from which could be derived a science of human nature. It is the conservative who speaks also of general psycho-physical laws as governing with Newtonian regularity the processes of moral phenomena. Those who reject history are forced, on the other hand, and not without considerable embarrassment, to resort to an almost pre-scientific moral indeterminism and to claim, paradoxically for this monistic age, an almost spiritually independent status for man's moral and political being:

[1] E.-J. Sieyès, 'Vues sur les moyens d'exécution dont les Représentans de la France pourront disposer en 1789', in *Collection des écrits d'Emmanuel Sieyès*, édition à l'usage de l'Allemagne, Paris, pp. 8–10.

Nous voyons tous les jours un pédantisme niais s'essayer avec confiance à décrier le philosophe qui remonte aux principes de l'art social. L'utile, la féconde méditation, ne paraît au lourd érudit que l'ouvrage de la paresse; et lorsque l'homme supérieur a laissé par dégoût autant que par sagesse, le triste tableau des erreurs de nos pères, la médiocrité s'empare de la matérielle occupation de noter assidûment toutes les pages de l'histoire; elle voit dans le seul talent de lire et de transcrire le mérite par excellence, et la réponse à toutes les questions.

Malheureusement les philosophes eux-mêmes qui, dans le cours de ce siècle, ont rendu de si grands services aux sciences physiques, paraissent autoriser cette ridicule confiance, et prêter la force de leur génie à des déclarations aveugles. Dégoûtés avec raison de la manie systématique de leurs prédécesseurs, ils se sont attachés à l'étude des faits, et ils ont proscrit toute autre méthode; jusque-là ils ne méritent que des éloges; mais lorsque, sortant de l'ordre physique, ils ont voulu employer et recommander cette méthode jusque dans l'ordre moral, ils se sont trompés. Avant de prescrire une même marche à toutes les sciences, il aurait fallu consulter la différence de leur objet et de leur génie.

Que le physicien se contente d'observer les faits, de les recueillir, d'en saisir les rapports; rien de plus sensé. Il a pour objet de connaître la nature; et puisqu'il n'a pas été appelé à aider de son conseil ou de sa main, le plan du système du monde, puisque l'univers physique existe et se maintient indépendant de ses méditations correctrices, il faut bien qu'il se borne à l'expérience des faits. Le physique ne peut être que la connaissance de *ce qui est.*

Mais les bornes de la science ne sont pas celle de l'art. L'art plus hardi dans son vol, se propose de plier et d'accommoder les faits à nos besoins et à nos jouissances; il demande ce qui *doit être* pour l'utilité des hommes. . . .[1]

The historico-scientific method in politics, Sieyès affirms, leads not to science but to superstition. It is true that history can provide some useful information to the legislator who has a meditative turn of mind, but he must also look beyond mere facts. Most historical facts are, moreover, entirely unedifying:

Ah! si le chemin de l'expérience est long pour le physicien, au moins est-il utile; et il est sûr, en avançant sans cesse, d'aggrandir toujours la sphère de ses connaissances. Quelle différence pour le législateur! que les événements doivent peser sur son cœur! et qu'il doit se sentir pressé de sortir enfin de l'effroyable expérience des siècles. . . .

Défiez-vous de l'influence que peut avoir sur l'esprit de vos Repré-

[1] Ibid., pp. 40–41.

sentants, l'idée déjà trop propagée par vos savants, de fonder la morale, comme la physique, sur la base de l'expérience. . . .

Jamais il n'a été plus pressant de rendre à la raison toute sa force, et d'ôter aux faits celle qu'ils ont usurpée pour le malheur de l'espèce humaine. Cette considération me commande; oui je donnerai libre cours à mes plaintes et à mon indignation contre cette foule d'écrivains, qui se consument à demander au passé, ce que nous devons être dans l'avenir; à chercher dans de misérables traditions, tissues de déraison et de mensonges, les lois restauratrices de l'ordre public; qui s'opiniâtrent à fouiller dans toutes les archives, à compulser, à compiler d'innombrables mémoires, à rechercher, à révérer jusqu'aux moindres fragments quelque apocryphes, obscurs ou inintelligibles qu'ils soient, dans l'espérance de découvrir, quoi? de vieux titres, comme si, dans leur extase gothique, ils aspiraient à mettre la nation en état de faire ce qu'on nomme *des preuves*.[1]

Legislators will find nothing useful searching in historical archives; the true archives of man lie in his heart:

. . . la lumière de la raison doit enfin s'allier avec le sentiment de la liberté. Nous saurons nous placer de nous-mêmes, dans le chemin qui conduit à l'ordre social; et là, puisqu'il faut se proposer d'aller en avant, nous n'aurons pas la ridicule faiblesse de prendre pour guides, des gens qui ne savent que regarder en arrière. . . .

. . . hâtons-nous d'abjurer une superstition d'esclaves; cessons de nous défendre contre les lumières qui nous pressent de toutes parts, et dans le grand jour qui se prépare pour nous, montrons-nous instruits de nos droits; ne souffrons pas que nos Représentants chargés de fixer les destinées de vingt-six millions d'hommes, s'abaissent à de vaines querelles, offrant à l'univers attentif, le tableau ridicule et honteux d'une tourbe théologique, qui se dispute des textes, qui déchire à l'envi la raison, et finit tout ce bruit par la plus profonde nullité.[2]

There are thus no lessons from the past worth worrying about. History is largely irrelevant. It is not, for example, a valid argument to point out that certain political institutions deserve respect because they are old and therefore good. All human institutions are old, and despotism is perhaps the oldest of all. The French would be wrong to follow the examples of past generations or of other nations. They must have the ambition and courage to strike out on their own, to elaborate independently the ideal forms of political government and to serve themselves as a model for other nations and for future generations.

[1] Ibid., pp. 42–45. [2] Ibid., pp. 50–53.

Thomas Paine in 1791 stresses the same necessity of emancipation from the tyranny of the old historical adjustments: 'Every age and generation', he writes, 'must be as free to act for itself *in all cases* as the ages and generations which preceded it. The vanity and presumption of governing beyond the grave is the most ridiculous and insolent of all tyrannies. . . . Every generation is, and must be, competent to all the purposes which its occasions require. It is the living and not the dead, that are to be accommodated.'[1] Paine's own description of how he set about writing his highly influential pamphlet *Common Sense* is typical of this radical rejection of history: 'I saw', Paine wrote in 1792, 'an opportunity in which I thought I could do some good, and I followed exactly what my heart dictated. I neither read books, nor studied other people's opinions. I thought for myself.'[2]

The inventory of Robespierre's Paris library seems to indicate that he too was not an avid reader of history.[3] Moreover, the Incorruptible's famous diatribe on the *philosophes* might possibly be interpreted as betraying an anti-history attitude. It was quite obviously directed as much against their learning, which Robespierre seems to equate with sophistry, as against their religious disbelief. He praises Rousseau, on the other hand, for the *pureté de sa doctrine* 'puisée dans la nature et dans la haine du vice'.[4] The virtue of unlettered patriots, he affirms, is to be contrasted with the craven neutrality of the once-celebrated intellectuals:

Les hommes de lettres, en général, se sont déshonorés dans cette Révolution, et, à la honte éternelle de l'esprit, la raison du peuple en a fait seule tous les frais.

Hommes petits et vains, rougissez, s'il est possible![5] Les prodiges qui ont immortalisé cette époque de l'histoire humaine ont été opérés sans vous et malgré vous; le bon sens sans intrigue et le génie sans instruction ont porté la France à ce degré d'élévation qui épouvante votre bassesse et qui écrase votre nullité. Tel artisan s'est montré habile dans

[1] *The Rights of Man*, Part I, Everyman's Library, p. 12.

[2] Ibid., Part II, p. 223, note 1.

[3] See G. Bapst, 'Inventaire des bibliothèques de quatre condamnés', *La Révolution Française*, July–December 1891, XXI. 534.

[4] 'Sur les rapports des idées religieuses et morales avec les principes républicains et sur les fêtes nationales', séance du 7 mai, 1794, in *Œuvres de Robespierre*, ed. A. Vermorel, Paris, 1867, p. 324.

[5] At the risk of sounding facetious in defence of outworn perspectives, one might observe that it was no longer possible, thanks to the tidy efforts of this gentleman from Arras, for a good number of them to blush at this time.

la connaissance des droits de l'homme, quand tel faiseur de livres, presque républicain en 1788, défendait stupidement la cause des rois en 1793; tel laboureur répandait la lumière de la philosophie dans les campagnes, quand l'académicien Condorcet, jadis grand géomètre, dit-on, au jugement des littérateurs, et grand littérateur au dire des géomètres, depuis conspirateur timide, méprisé de tous les partis, travaillait sans cesse à l'obscurcir par le perfide fatras de ses rapsodies mercenaires.[1]

Ironically, Condorcet himself not long before, although he did not attack history *per se*, had assailed the old historians on much the same grounds:

L'histoire moderne a jusqu'ici été corrompue, tantôt par la nécessité de ménager les tyrannies établies, tantôt par l'esprit de parti. . . .

. . . Voltaire même, le premier des historiens modernes, si grand dans la partie morale de l'histoire, n'a pu dans la partie politique s'abandonner à son génie. Forcé de ménager un des ennemis de l'espèce humaine pour avoir le droit d'attaquer l'autre avec impunité, il écrasa la superstition, mais il n'opposa au despotisme que le cri de l'humanité et les règles de la justice personnelle; il lui reproche ses crimes, mais il laisse en paix reposer entre ses mains royales le pouvoir de les commettre.

Il nous faut donc une histoire toute nouvelle, qui soit surtout celle des droits des hommes, des vicissitudes auxquelles ont été partout assujetties et la connaissance et la jouissance de ces droits. . . .[2]

Other republicans had even more severe recommendations. The reading of history, some suggested, should be sternly limited; that of the ancients and that of one's own country sufficed.[3] That of one's own country, agreed Mercier, provided it was first properly purged: 'L'histoire de France est à brûler et à recommencer; elle doit aller rejoindre les gros livres de *jurisprudence* et la philosophie scolastique. . . .'[4] In 1798, the *idéologues* in *La Décade* go even farther: 'Tous les livres d'Histoire sont à refaire; tous les livres de Législation politique, civile et criminelle, sont à refaire; tous les livres de Morale, mêlés jusqu'ici de mysticité sont à refaire.'[5]

[1] Ibid., p. 325.

[2] *Sur l'instruction publique*, '5ème mémoire', in *Bibliothèque de l'homme public*, XI, tome 9, pp. 57–59.

[3] See J.-J.-G. Levesque, *Essai sur la manière d'écrire et d'étudier l'histoire*, Paris, An III, pp. 79–80.

[4] *De J.-J. Rousseau considéré comme l'un des premiers auteurs de la Révolution*, Paris, 1791, II. 194.

[5] See *La Décade philosophique, littéraire et politique*, XVII. 493.

Once history was burned it could of course be rewritten along republican lines for those who still felt some need of it. We shall see that such revolutionary figures as Mirabeau, Brissot, Condorcet, Mme Roland, and others did indeed actively publicize Catherine Macaulay's history of the English revolution as most suitable to replace the hated royalist account by Hume. For others, however, the history of former revolutions was totally irrelevant. Carra, speaking during the Convention debates on Louis XVI's trial, exemplifies the new attitude:

Ce sont des résultats du gros bon sens, des rapprochements calculés de sang-froid, des idées simples, des raisonnements pris dans la conscience du cœur humain et dans la moralité de l'esprit, que j'essaie de présenter à votre sagesse, à vos lumières. Je ne citerai point l'histoire, parce que l'histoire n'a rien qui puisse se comparer à notre révolution . . . ; parce que l'histoire, ainsi que je l'ai observé depuis la révolution n'a fait qu'égarer les rois et leurs ministres dans l'application qu'ils en ont faite pour les événements futurs; parce que notre révolution étant le produit des progrès bien décidés de la raison et de la politique universelles, elle ne peut avoir en rien le caractère des révolutions précédentes, ni souffrir des applications rétrogrades, ou des données positives prises dans l'histoire. Tout est neuf dans notre révolution. . . .[1]

Everything was new in Carra's revolution—a radical sentiment which was very neatly answered by Bancal who summed up in his reply the traditionalist defence of history: '. . . oui, tout est neuf, excepté les hommes, qui sont les éléments des révolutions, et qui sont sujets à des passions dans tous les pays et dans tous les siècles.'[2]

Saint-Just even implies that holding to the old cyclical view of revolutions was part of the Girondist conspiracy. In his report of 1793 to the Comité de salut public concerning the Girondins arrested after 31 May and 1 June, he made the following accusation: 'Les détenus . . . n'ont point fait un pas qui ne conduisît à la monarchie. . . . Les hommes habiles, et pervers en même temps, ont fini par sentir qu'il fallait suivre le peuple, persuadés que la ligne que parcourent les révolutions est horizontale, et que par les

[1] *Discours contre la Défense de Louis Capet, Dernier Roi des Français,* par le Citoyen Carra, député de Saône-et-Loire, prononcé à la séance du 3 janvier 1793.

[2] *Discours et projet de décret de Henri Bancal,* député du Puy-de-Dôme, p. 4.

excès, les malheurs et les imprudences qu'elle entraîne, on retourne au point d'où l'on était parti. . . .'[1]

Quite to the contrary, revolutions progress vertically not horizontally; they are the instruments of man's moral ascent. To say that similar attempts had been made before and had necessarily failed, to identify the French revolution and the English revolution —these were counter-revolutionary ideas and a subtle form of treason: rather like pointing out that the total number of victims of the Bastille in all the centuries of its existence probably never equalled the number of prisoners confined in the Châtelet and the Abbaye during the first two or three glorious years of the *règne de la liberté*.

[1] 'Rapport sur les trente-deux membres de la Convention détenus en vertu du décret du 2 juin', in *Œuvres complètes de Saint-Just*, ed. Charles Vellay, Paris, 1908, II. 10.

III

FROM 1789 TO THE TRIAL OF LOUIS XVI

1. Prophetic parallels and the counter-revolutionary lessons of Hume

ABBÉ MAURY figures most appropriately at the beginning of this chapter dealing in part with examples of Hume's influence on some of the early counter-revolutionary leaders. Maury, generally recognized as the leading orator of the Right in the Assemblée constituante, had been since 1785 a member of the French Academy and was eventually to be named a cardinal of the Church. He seems to have been a witty, rather forceful person and an extemporary speaker of some brilliance. It is not too inappropriate to contrast him, as contemporaries often did, with Mirabeau, his opposite number on the Left.

Like his personal friends Gerdil and Bergier, Maury was fond of quoting Bossuet in defence of the *ancien régime* but, like them too, he occasionally found it useful to invoke also the authority of that new Bossuet, the historian David Hume. Long before the Revolution he had commended Hume as a loyal and impartial historian worth using to attack the 'English bias' of the *philosophe* Voltaire. In 1777, for example, he quite happily pointed out that the Scottish historian disagreed with the great Voltaire on the quality of English eloquence.[1] Voltaire had devoted one of his famous philosophical letters to praising Bacon, and Maury points out at this time—as Joseph de Maistre was to later—that Hume had attacked the inflated reputation of this culture hero of the *encyclopédistes* and had rightly put him well below Galileo in importance. On at least one occasion we even find the Abbé adducing proofs from Hume in his sermons, as in his panegyric of Saint Louis delivered to the assembled members of the French Academy in the chapel of the Louvre on 25 August 1772.[2]

[1] *Discours choisis sur divers sujets de religion et de littérature*, par M. l'Abbé Maury, Paris, 1777, p. 132. See also *Œuvres choisies du cardinal J.-Sifrein Maury*, Paris, 1827. II. 142–51.

[2] Ibid., III. 361–2. Maury quotes Hume's portrait of the French king.

Hume is not infrequently mentioned in Abbé Maury's speeches delivered during the early revolutionary debates. Defending the rights of the throne in 1790, he accused the National Assembly of an illegitimate attempt to deprive the Crown of its traditional prerogative to declare war and make treaties. The rôle of the Assembly, as Maury saw it, was not to establish a new constitution but to correct with the help of the king any current abuses in government and to revive, to that end, the ancient constitution of France. History, he asserted, provides a warning to those who dare to attempt more radical reforms and who, wishing to extend illegitimately the powers of popular representatives, reduce the monarch's importance to that of being merely a 'republican' figurehead:

On sait que le cardinal Mazarin fit les plus grands efforts, après la mort tragique de Charles Ier, pour engager les Anglais à introduire dans leur île un gouvernement purement républicain. Mazarin . . . avait compris combien cette forme de gouvernement . . . affaiblirait par ses lenteurs et par ses divisions intestines, la puissance politique de cette nation; mais les Anglais après avoir essayé . . . de *se passer d'un roi* selon l'expression de M. Hume, sentirent que leur parlement avait besoin du contre-poids de l'autorité royale; ils relevèrent le trône de leurs mains patriotiques et depuis un siècle ils n'ont plus tenté d'ébranler ce fondement sacré de leur constitution. Serait-il possible, messieurs, d'oublier dans cette assemblée cette grande leçon que l'Angleterre a donnée à l'Europe?[1]

A reader of the *Political Discourses* as well, Maury cited Hume in July 1790 against the fiscal policies of Necker:

C'est lui seul, il faut l'avouer, qui en donnant à nos finances une prospérité apparente, en assurant contre toute vérité qu'il soutenait une guerre sans augmenter les impôts, a opéré la ruine du royaume, par des emprunts exorbitants. L'appât qu'il présentait aux prêteurs, a singulièrement renforcé son crédit personnel, qui nous est devenu si funeste. *Il faut*, dit M. Hume, *qu'une nation anéantisse le crédit public, ou que le crédit public anéantisse la nation. . . .*[2]

Abbé Maury had already quoted Hume's testimony in his maiden speech of September 1789 on the question of the royal veto, again to the effect that the king's authority must not be

[1] *Opinion sur le droit de faire la guerre et de conclure les traités de paix, d'alliance et de commerce;* prononcée dans l'assemblée nationale le 18 mai 1790, ibid., IV. 99–100.

[2] *Opinion sur les finances et sur la dette publique*, July 1790, ibid., IV. 172.

weakened, that revolutions are futile, that Charles II, for example, had found the source of his restored power in the effects of his unfortunate father's execution.[1] Maury's greatest Hume-inspired parliamentary triumph was to come, however, in 1790 during a verbal exchange with his noted enemy Mirabeau concerning the sovereignty of the people.[2]

Maury began his attack on the concept of the people's sovereignty with an appeal to the traditional arguments of Fénelon and Bossuet on the subject. The theory of contract is a fiction. Society took its origins in man's natural, that is, God-given, sociability. Authority and subordination are thus also divine in origin. Express or tacit consent of a primitively 'free' people may *seem* at times to have been the source of government, but this is a fallacious appearance. Free consent is sometimes the *channel* of authority, it is not the *source*. 'Il résulte de cette théorie', Maury continues, 'que la religion nous donne une idée aussi juste que lumineuse de l'autorité qui régit les peuples, quand elle la fait émaner primitivement de la

[1] *Discours sur la sanction royale*, ibid., V. iv.

[2] A note of caution is necessary here. That Maury was the only rightist orator at this time who could match the vigour of Mirabeau seems little in doubt. That such was the opinion of contemporaries is evidenced in the following not entirely biased 'Anagramme-Epigramme sur deux chefs de parti très connus' which we find in the *Actes des Apôtres*, 1789, I, No. 28, p. 16:

Deux insignes chefs de parti
D'intrigue ici tiennent bureau,
Chacun à l'autre est assorti,
Même audace & voix de taureau;
L'on pourrait faire le pari
Qu'ils sont nés dans la même peau;
Car retournez *abé Mauri*,
Vous trouverez *Mirabeau*.

There are many anecdotes attesting to Abbé Maury's quick wit. The following example of it is related by Montlosier who describes how one day the future Cardinal was walking near the market place: 'Des femmes de la Halle l'ayant aperçu vont à lui: —"Bonjour mon vigoureux!" —"Bonjour, mesdames." —"Tu as bien de l'esprit, mais tu as beau te débattre, tu n'en seras pas moins f. . . .". —"Oh! mesdames, vous savez bien qu'on n'en meurt pas". Les voilà qui rient et qui lui sautent au cou pour l'embrasser.' (*Mémoires de M. le Comte de Montlosier sur la Révolution française*, Paris, 1830, II. 314.) There is evidence to show, nevertheless, that Maury's powerful lungs and sharp wit were not always sufficient for the task of overcoming the increasingly impatient heckling of the opposition benches (see, for example, the *Journal des débats*, Nos. 153 and 382). Although he remained at his post until 1791, he more than ever took to publishing dictated versions of his speeches. It is thus very likely, as Aulard points out, that 'les passages les plus célèbres de l'abbé Maury . . . n'ont jamais été *dits* par lui.' (F.-A. Aulard, *Les orateurs de l'assemblée constituante*, Paris, 1882, p. 234.)

Divinité. En nous présentant l'Etre suprême comme l'auteur immédiat de la souveraineté, le protecteur et le vengeur des lois, elle nous montre, sous ce point de vue, toute société humaine comme une véritable théocratie. . . .'[1]

Preparing to go on with the practical applications of this pious theory, Maury, as he tells the story, was interrupted by that foolish fellow Mirabeau who shouted:

—'C'est se jouer de l'Assemblée que de venir lui faire des leçons de théologie. Il n'y a jamais eu que des fanatiques et d'ignorants théologiens, qui aient professé une pareille doctrine sur l'origine prétendue de la souveraineté. Je vous défie de citer un seul homme de bon sens qui ait soutenu cette ineptie!'

Quite unruffled and wisely prepared in advance to answer such an impertinence, Abbé Maury took up the challenge:

—'J'accepte un si généreux défi, M. de Mirabeau, en vous faisant observer, d'abord, qu'il n'est pas surprenant que l'esprit humain soit obligé de recourir à Dieu, pour assigner un inébranlable appui à la souveraineté, puisqu'on ne peut sans son intervention, donner aucun fondement solide à la morale même. Je vais donc vous citer, parmi les défenseurs de ma doctrine, non pas un théologien, mais l'un des plus célèbres écrivains de notre siècle, sur les matières politiques, un philosophe anglais que personne encore n'a soupçonné de superstition. Voici ce que je lis dans le vingt-cinquième essai moral et politique de David Hume: . . .'

If we are to believe Maury's account, he then recited to the assembled representatives of the French nation the 'theocratic' passage already used for a similar purpose in 1769 by his friend, Cardinal Gerdil,[2] omitting, however, and hardly because of its length, the last half. His conclusion is triumphant:

—'En avez-vous assez, M. de Mirabeau? Je vous fais grâce de dix citations pareilles. Vous voyez que les autorités les plus imposantes viennent déjà se réunir, en faveur de mon opinion, aux raisonnements les plus péremptoires, tandis qu'il ne vous reste que des assertions que je démens et des défis dont je profite.

'Je dis donc avec M. Hume à tous les philosophes à vue courte, que ce n'est pas du peuple, mais de Dieu seul qu'émane le pouvoir

[1] *Opinion sur la souveraineté du peuple,* prononcée dans l'Assemblée Nationale en 1790 par M. l'Abbé Maury et publiée sur les manuscrits autographes de l'auteur par Louis-Sifrein Maury, son neveu, Avignon, 1852, pp. 95–96.

[2] See *supra,* pp. 37–38.

souverain. Dieu, dont la féconde et magnifique nature crée tout l'ensemble de ses décrets dans l'immensité de sa pensée, a créé aussi cette autorité tutélaire, en appelant le genre humain à l'état social. . . .'[1]

Abbé Maury leaves it to be understood that, after such a complete answer, his opponent Mirabeau was, momentarily at least, struck dumb with defeat. Of course, at least in this last example, Maury is merely continuing the practice of *rétorsion* in the tradition of Gerdil, Bergier, Nonnotte, and others, and it would be a mistake to imagine on his part anything more than a polemical attachment to Hume's statement. His perhaps more sincere opinion of Hume he confided privately years later to another counter-revolutionary ideologist, Count Joseph de Maistre, when they met in Venice during the winter of 1799. There they had an extensive conversation on various literary subjects and one of these was the question of Hume's merit as an historian. De Maistre notes without comment that Maury judged Hume to be 'un historien médiocre qui s'est fait une réputation d'impartialité par la manière dont il a parlé des Stuarts'. The English were really superior only in their novels, of which *Clarissa Harlowe* and *Tom Jones* seem to have been the good Cardinal's favourites.[2]

It is not difficult to find other counter-revolutionary figures who make at this time less spectacular but undeniably influential use of Hume's writings. In this regard, his statements on the empirical nature of the British constitution, denying that before the seventeenth century it formed a 'regular plan of liberty', were found of special interest.

Traditionalists were disturbed from the very beginning of the revolutionary debates by the radical claim that France had no constitution. It was of no use to speak, as Fénelon, for example, had spoken years before, of an ancient 'unwritten' constitution. A constitution, as Thomas Paine wrote in 1791, 'is not a thing in name only, but in fact. It has not an ideal, but a real existence; and wherever it cannot be produced in a visible form, there is none.'[3]

[1] Ibid., pp. 96–98.

[2] See *Œuvres complètes de J. de Maistre*, VII. 503. Worth mentioning here also is the use made at about this same time of Hume's position on divorce by another representative of the clergy in the National Assembly, the Abbé Armand de Chapt de Rastignac, in his work *Accord de la Révélation et de la Raison contre le divorce*, Paris, 1790, pp. 332–3, 339, 347–8.

[3] *The Rights of Man*, Part I, p. 48.

A constitution, in short, had to be something that one could roll up and put in one's pocket. The English had no constitution until Magna Carta; France in 1789 was in rather the same position as England before the granting of the Great Charter.

Along with others on the Right, the extreme royalist de Montjoie took exception to this view. The revolutionists, he accused, talked endlessly about constitutions without having the most elementary understanding of what that word meant. Constitutions are not theoretical *a priori* constructions, they are as natural as gravity itself. It is impossible for a nation not to be constituted and France was no exception:

> Nos parlements, nos assemblées du clergé, nos provinces à états et sous-états, n'étaient point une constitution; mais l'existence de ces institutions, la manière dont elles étaient organisées et se liaient à l'ensemble du gouvernement, formaient la constitution française.
>
> Je désire bien ardemment que de l'anarchie actuelle, il sorte une constitution raisonnable, mais ce n'est pas moi qui ai creusé cet abîme d'anarchie, ce sont ceux qui, en 1789, ont fait croire ou laissé croire aux Français, qu'ils n'avaient point de constitution. . . .
>
> Un peuple policé ne saurait être sans constitution, car un peuple policé ne saurait être sans une forme de gouvernement.[1]

What de Montjoie and others who took this position are really doing, of course, is rejecting the contract theory of the origin of government in one of its various manifestations. Hume's political empiricism helped to support this anti-*a priori* line of argument. His *History*, de Montjoie pointed out, underlines the fact that constitutions are nothing more than the products of time and of circumstance. One cannot say that the British nation had a fixed constitution in all the years of its political existence since Magna Carta. The British constitution had been a fluctuating and ill-defined thing throughout the ages. Hume had in fact viewed the 'usurpations' of the Stuart kings with more leniency than most historians precisely because of his belief in the extenuating circumstances provided by such constitutional variation. Speaking, for example, of the constitution under James I, de Montjoie asserts:

> . . . elle a été engendrée par de violentes innovations. Elle ressemble si

[1] F.-L.-C. de Montjoie, *Histoire de la Révolution de France et de l'Assemblée Nationale*, Paris, 1792, cinquième partie, pp. 127–8.

peu à celle qu'avaient les Anglais sous Jacques II, que M. Hume fait de l'une et de l'autre, deux constitutions absolument différentes. Voici ses paroles qui sont remarquables:

'Ceux à qui la nation anglaise est redevable de ses privilèges, doivent être loués avec réserve, et sans la plus légère rancune contre les partisans de l'ancienne constitution.'

Ce n'est donc pas parce que les Anglais ont eu dans le treizième siècle une grande charte, que l'Angleterre se trouve constituée comme elle l'est aujourd'hui.[1]

From the *tabula rasa* political view of France without a constitution naturally followed for many revolutionary theoreticians the conclusion that the National Assembly was invested with the primary status of a *convention nationale* representing all the authority of the nation in its pre-constituted state. Radical attempts to grace the National Assembly with this title were of course vigorously opposed by members of the Right. Both citing Hume on the question, Calonne and Lally-Tollendal[2] insisted that to call the National Assembly a *Convention* would be to imply with impudence and quite erroneously that all preceding government had been entirely dissolved, whereas France's national parliament had in fact been convoked by the king in conformity with the 'constitution' and with all the ordinary formalities 'ainsi que l'ont été toutes les Assemblées Nationales depuis Charlemagne. Donc nous n'étions point *Convention Nationale*.'[3]

The details of the semantic controversy just noted may seem trivial in retrospect. What was certainly not trivial, however, was the amount of political power being hotly disputed, and it is significant, I think, that Hume's authority was brought into the question by two such important members of the Right. Also wishing to show that France before the Revolution was not entirely without legal foundation, another noted traditionalist, Jean-Joseph Mounier, quoted Hume's opinion that the privileges of English peers and the liberty of the English Commons had in fact originated in France. Consequently, Mounier asserted in 1792, if the French had adopted the British constitution they

[1] Ibid., p. 127.

[2] *De l'Etat de la France, présent et à venir*, par M. de Calonne, ministre d'Etat, Londres, 1791, pp. 360–1; *Mémoire de M. le Comte de Lally-Tollendal, ou Seconde Lettre à ses Commettans*, Paris, 1790, pp. 107–8.

[3] Lally-Tollendal, op. cit., p. 109.

would only have repatriated what was to begin with their own.[1]

It can be easily seen that, with the parties of the Right, Hume's reputation and authority as an historian are in this period as great or even greater than they were during the thirty years preceding the Revolution when he was read under circumstances so different. Barnave in 1792, for example, called Hume 'le meilleur des historiens modernes'[2] and Lally-Tollendal in the same year cited Hume-inspired political lessons to Burke.[3]

Hume's interpretation of the Long Parliament's activities as a series of cunning usurpations seems to have been particularly useful to those rightists who at this time wished to attack the National Assembly's claim that it fully represented the true wishes of the nation. What was this *nation*, royalists liked to ask, this fantastic creature whose mandate was always being invoked, which was presumably all of France but which apparently made its wishes known only to a few and at the bidding of a few? Attacking a current practice of some parties in the National Assembly, the Comte d'Antraigues, who was later to play an active cloak-and-dagger rôle in the counter-revolution, quoted Hume against the demagogic use of *adresses* or petitions:

Nous savons trop par quels petits moyens on se procure des faisceaux d'adresses.

Mais je dis que des adresses sont des éloges pour l'assemblée à qui elles sont présentées, mais que jamais elles ne peuvent suppléer à des formes essentielles qui sont de rigueur. Les adresses de mille municipalités ne peuvent représenter le décret d'un baillage; c'est comme si le consentement partiel et isolé des individus qui composent l'assemblée nationale, pouvait former un décret.[4]

In a three-page note attached to this passage, d'Antraigues reproduces Hume's description of the similar abuse of petitions by

[1] *Recherches sur les causes qui ont empêché les Français de devenir libres et sur les moyens qui leur restent pour acquérir la liberté*. Genève, 1792, I. 210. In this same work Mounier, quoting Hume's sentiment that despotism is preferable to popular anarchy, urges the French to rally round Louis XVI and place absolute power in his hands for the period of one year. (Ibid., II. 213–15.)

[2] *Introduction à la Révolution Française* (1792) in *Œuvres de Barnave*, Paris, 1843, I. 72.

[3] *Seconde Lettre de M. de Lally-Tollendal à M. Burke*, Londres, 1792, p. 35. The French jurist J.-V. Delacroix also calls Hume 'le plus impartial des historiens' in his *Constitutions des principaux états de l'Europe et des Etats-Unis de l'Amérique*, Paris, 1791, II. 206.

[4] *Quelle est la situation de l'Assemblée Nationale?* (1790), pp. 41–44.

the Long Parliament. The petitions were, Hume tells us, a fraudulent device of popularity, accepted only from groups favourable to the Puritan faction and used to incite the people to civil discord. All petitions which favoured the monarchy or the Church were, on the other hand, immediately rejected. D'Antraigues concludes with the darkly prophetic comment: 'Je n'ajoute aucune réflexion à ce passage, la prudence seule me prescrit de prouver que je ne l'ai pas inventé, qu'il existe, et si c'est un crime de présenter de pareils tableaux, il faut l'imputer à M. Hume, *Histoire de la Maison de Stuart*, année 1642 . . . 7 ans avant l'assassinat de Charles Ier, 11 ans avant que Cromwel fût déclaré protecteur.'[1]

Comparisons such as that by d'Antraigues, viewing at the same time the activities of the Long Parliament and those of the revolutionary assembly, form the basis of most parallels drawn between the English and French revolutions published by conservatives at this time.

Fairly typical of these are the *tableaux* which appeared in the ultra royalist journal *Les Actes des Apôtres* in 1790. Beginning in January of that year and with a peculiar light-heartedness (since at first the *apôtres* seemed to believe that it would take to push back the Revolution no more than a timely dose of *Hudibras*),[2] the editors presented their readers with the 'Tableau parlant, Fragment de l'histoire d'Angleterre'.[3] Although it is an account largely from Hume of the seventeenth-century revolution in England, the *tableau* is presented as depicting exactly events taking place in revolutionary France: '. . . le dessein était formé d'anéantir à la fois l'église et la monarchie. Le conseil du monarque avait été de mauvaise foi; la nation était irritée, ses représentants ambitieux et

[1] Ibid., pp. 43–44. The same passage from 'le sage Hume' is quoted against the Convention in December 1792 by Dugour: *Mémoire justificatif pour Louis XVI*, Paris, 1793, pp. 119–21.

[2] 'Enfin de la folie
Le peuple guérira,
Et de sa maladie
Les auteurs punira.
Je crois qu'après cela
Tout se rétablira;
Je crois qu'après cela,
Ça ira, ça ira.'
(*Les Actes des Apôtres*, No. 173, p. 16.)

Hume's name, along with those of other conservative heroes, figures in some of their light verse against Robespierre. See, for example, ibid., No. 15, pp. 5–6.

[3] Ibid., II. 5–25.

pervers. Le ministre parlementait, le gouffre se creusait et déjà l'horizon se chargeait de sang.'[1]

At the end of this historical sketch the editors state its purpose and promise more of the same:

Nous terminerons à cette époque, la première partie de notre introduction, qui forme un vrai *tableau parlant*: des événements semblables ont depuis développé ailleurs les mêmes passions. Nous laissons au lecteur à en faire lui-même l'application, et en présentant aux sujets fidèles, aux citoyens éclairés, le tableau des troubles d'une grande nation, puissions-nous épargner à celles qui veulent se régénérer, les erreurs et les horreurs dont la fière Albion aura toujours à rougir aux yeux de la postérité.[2]

Volume III followed with the 'Tableau de comparaison' continuing the account of Stuart history from 1641. Written in April 1790, and still inspired by the wise prophet David Hume, the new sketch pictures the unfortunate king 'luttant, pour sa prérogative royale, contre un parlement composé de factieux qui avaient résolu de fonder la république sur les débris de la monarchie et de l'église'.[3] In Volume IV we are presented with the 'Tableau royal' which quotes in full Hume's portrait of Hampden as describing perfectly the typical French revolutionist: 'On doit prendre garde seulement, malgré son généreux zèle pour la liberté, à quel titre il mérite la qualité de bon citoyen. Au travers de toutes les horreurs de la guerre civile il chercha l'abolition de la monarchie, et la ruine de la constitution, but que tout ami sincère de la patrie devait éviter, quand il y aurait pu parvenir par des voies paisibles.'[4] Hampden's portrait is then contrasted with that of the virtuous Falkland whom another Hume disciple, Lally-Tollendal, had already seen himself as imitating when he resigned from the Assembly in 1789. In addition, the *apôtres* note the existence in both countries of a 'simulacre d'assemblée nationale' which 'au mépris de la constitution déjà existante, ne manqua pas pour affermir son autorité, de décréter le principe, que tout pouvoir émane du peuple.'[5] Finally less concerned with pointing out parallels, the editors optimistically attempt a number of predictions. They meditate without sorrow on the fate of Charles I's judges: 'ce n'est pas, sans un secret plaisir que nous anticipons sur les événements, en annonçant qu'il y en eut 27 de

[1] Ibid., II. 21. [2] Ibid., II. 22. [3] Ibid., III. 5.
[4] Ibid., IV. 15–16. [5] Ibid., IV. 28.

pendus dix ans après, lors du rétablissement de Charles II sur le trône de ses pères.'[1] Of course, bringing attention to this last fact was somewhat gratuitous. If the inexorable parallel between the two revolutions seemed to waver in one respect it was that the French in 1790 were too wise to rush headlong into the crimes of seventeenth-century England: 'Louis XVI a déjà triomphé des méchants; espérons que la monarchie triomphera de même de la république, et qu'un jour enfin nous aurons la traduction en français des hiéroglyphes constitutionnels que l'on grave à bâtons rompus sur l'obélisque national.'[2]

To celebrate this anticipated happy change in the course of the French revolution, a fourth and final tableau was prepared, the 'Tableau de la résurrection', depicting, of course, the restoration of the monarchy in England. Events in France at the end of 1790 stubbornly refused, however, to follow true to form. Ruefully the *apôtres* conceded in Volume V that the promised last instalment would have to be postponed for a time; the task, it seems, was even beyond the strength of *Hudibras* and renewed meditation on the darker parallels was necessary:

Peuple malheureux . . . on cherche à caresser tes passions par le mot de *république*; on travaille à t'en inspirer le désir; on veut qu'il t'exalte, qu'il t'égare comme celui de la liberté t'a déjà égaré. . . . Ecoute un moment, apprends ce qui se passait il y a cent cinquante ans chez tes voisins, compare les événements, les moyens, les effets; compare et juge, afin que, s'il se peut, les malheurs des peuples ne soient pas perdus pour toi.

Cromwel et son parlement passent à travers les siècles en horreur à tous les hommes, et voués à l'exécration de nos derniers neveux; cependant ils eurent les noms de *patriotes*, de *défenseurs des lois*, de *protecteurs du peuple*; tout ce qu'ils firent, ils le firent, dirent-ils, pour le bien de ce peuple, pour la conservation des droits de la nation, et au nom de la liberté. Animés par de si nobles motifs, ils désolèrent leur patrie, dressèrent des échafauds et firent tomber la tête de tous ceux dont la vertu leur faisait ombrage: ils attaquèrent le trône, poursuivirent leur roi, l'emprisonnèrent, en protestant de leur respect et de leur amour pour sa personne, et enfin . . . eh bien! tant de forfaits aboutirent à mettre la souveraineté entre les mains de quarante petits tyrans, et à faire déclarer l'odieux Cromwel, *protecteur du bon peuple de la république*.

Ecoute encore: à peine le monstre fut-il expiré, que le charme se

[1] Ibid., IV. 29. [2] Ibid., IV. 31.

rompit, et que les yeux des Anglais se dessillèrent. Ils poursuivirent ses complices, et assouvirent leur vengeance sur sa mémoire; ils pendirent et brûlèrent dans toutes leurs villes les effigies de l'usurpateur; et ayant déterré son corps, ils le traînèrent dans la fange, et l'attachèrent aux fourches patibulaires, digne salaire de sa scélératesse et de sa tyrannie. . . . Peuple français, épargne-toi les crimes; ils mènent à leur suite la misère et la honte, les remords et l'esclavage.[1]

We have in the last quotation a good average view of Stuart history as interpreted by the French of the Right. Important to note also, it is seen as David Hume's view. Even when the parallels do not quote him explicitly—and this is exceptional—his tremendous hold over French conservative opinion is still felt and his explanation of the events of the past century and a half becomes the explanation of what is seen as only the eighteenth-century French version of a similar evil cycle in the course of human history. The *apôtres* have been only temporarily delayed in their presentation of the already prepared 'Tableau de la résurrection'. Ultimately it must come to that for, as they themselves express it, 'l'histoire a déjà présenté les mêmes causes, les mêmes effets'.[2]

Very similar to the *tableaux* of the *Actes des Apôtres* are the parallels drawn also in 1790 by Angélique-Marie Darlus du Taillis, Comtesse de Montrond, in her work *Le Long Parlement et ses crimes, rapprochemens faciles à faire*. The book is a 143-page history of the Long Parliament again summarized from Hume and illustrating the harmony of his account with a royalist interpretation of 'equivalent' events in France. With regard to the causes of the two revolutions, in both cases the antecedent actions of the reigning monarch are exonerated. The Countess underlines, for example, Hume's statement that the allegedly unconstitutional levy of ship-money by Charles I proved subsequently to be very useful to the British navy in its encounters with the Dutch. As for the individual members of the Puritan parliament, Countess Montrond affirms that 'le grand nombre étaient des ambitieux et des hypocrites: le cri universel était moins la restauration de l'Etat, que l'humiliation du Roi et l'abaissement de la Couronne.'[3] Later her work draws a further parallel between the English patriots and the French revolutionary leaders: 'Ces impies imposteurs prétendaient à la Sainteté, comme nos Démagogues à l'Humanité.'[4]

[1] Ibid., V. 43–44. [2] Ibid., V. 63.
[3] *Le Long Parlement et ses crimes*, Paris, 1790, p. 9. [4] Ibid., p. 108.

The suffering multitude is deceived by such unintelligible slogans: '*Heureux les Anglais*, dit M. Hume, *si cette Chambre s'était conduite avec modération*, et si dans la plénitude d'un pouvoir usurpé, elle en avait fait bénir l'usage. Heureux les Français, dira un jour le *Tacite* de nos infortunes; mais qui peut les juger aujourd'hui ces infortunes versées à grands flots sur un Peuple abusé!'[1]

Holding to a cyclical view of history, the Countess invites her French readers to compare events in both revolutions and to reflect seriously on them. The results of France's upheaval must inevitably be the same: 'Les Français égarés éprouveront des remords, qui bientôt seront suivis du retour de leur amour pour le meilleur des Rois, le plus courageux des Rois; les sentiments confondus de repentir et d'amour, les précipiteront aux pieds de ce Monarque si sensible, si *self-denying*, et leur erreur même deviendra un lien plus fort qui les tiendra dévoués à jamais à leur généreux Souverain.'[2]

Rarely, if ever, do the people profit from revolution; the new government is likely to be worse than the old one: 'Et jamais la vérité de cette maxime, dit M. Hume, ne fut plus profondément sentie que dans la présente situation de l'Angleterre.'[3] The English had managed to pull down the throne but, far from finding themselves happy, they were soon crushed with an unprecedented burden of taxes and subjected to a tyrannical administration in which there was not even the shadow of justice and liberty.

History cannot be deceived. Inevitably the French revolution too would go the full circle and a Cromwell would appear on the scene: 'Une funeste expérience prouva aux Anglais, comme les exemples anciens l'avaient appris, qu'une violence contraire aux lois, de quelque prétexte qu'elle puisse se couvrir, et quelque but qu'elle se propose, doit infailliblement aboutir au gouvernement arbitraire et despotique d'un seul.'[4]

Comtesse de Montrond's *rapprochements* clearly illustrate how the parallels were not just idle works of analysis and prediction. Hers is a work heavily charged with emotion:

L'esprit dans lequel j'écris cette Histoire, me faisant voir sans cesse Louis XVI à côté de Charles Ier, dans les oppositions comme dans les similitudes, il en résulte un tel accroissement de sensibilité pour les

[1] Ibid., p. 16. [2] Ibid., pp. 84–85.
[3] Ibid., pp. 100–1. [4] Ibid., p. 143.

malheurs de Charles Ier, et de reconnaissance pour le courage de Louis XVI, que souvent, je suis forcée d'interrompre mon pénible travail, et je ne sais pas s'il me serait possible d'amener le Roi d'Angleterre jusqu'au terme de sa vie; si mes larmes sont cruelles, si elles coulent à torrents, elles élèvent du moins une consolation dans mon cœur! Je ne suis pas seule, Française, je ne suis pas seule embrasée de cet amour pour mon Roi. . . .[1]

There is even some hint in her book that if Louis were to choose, as Charles had chosen earlier, to raise the Royal Standard against these vile usurpers, he would not be lacking in support: 'Songez, ah! songez souvent, que des milliers de Français vous adorent, qu'ils se taisent pour s'unir à votre résignation, et à celle de votre compagne, qu'ils honorent et chérissent; que si votre intérêt le demandait, ou seulement le permettait, des légions sans nombre voleraient à votre secours. . . .'[2]

Another of the 'écrivains noirs', François Suleau, published more *rapprochements* in 1791 and 1792, again with the intention of rousing the French and especially Louis XVI to more vigorous counter-revolutionary action.

Side by side, in two columns of his journal, he compared what he called the 'Drame Anglais' and the French 'Imitation qui passe les bornes de la parodie'. Throughout the account of the *Imitation* column we find comments such as the following: 'Ces rapprochements sont frappants', 'Tout comme chez nous', 'Rien ne cloche dans le parallèle des circonstances', 'Même verbiage', &c. Suleau gives proof, in fact, that he must have believed in an almost complete identification of the two revolutions: 'Nos tribuns', he wrote, 'ont copié servilement tous ces diaboliques stratagèmes et je n'ai pas besoin de dire qu'ils ont obtenu les mêmes résultats. *Nil sub sole novum.*'[3] We are not surprised to learn, even, that the Puritans had their own Faubourg St. Antoine: 'La comparaison se soutient avec une justesse admirable jusque dans les accessoires les plus malheureux. . . .'[4]

Suleau, as he draws his parallel, is no less explicit and no more innocent of purpose than the Comte d'Artois had been in performing those portrait antics to which we have already referred. His is a warning to princes 'qui s'abandonnent aux vertiges, toujours funestes, de la pusillanimité, quand ils croient ne suivre que les

[1] Ibid., p. 103. [2] Ibid., p. 45.
[3] *Journal de M. Suleau*, Paris, 1792, No. XII, p. 78. [4] Ibid., p. 85.

conseils de la prudence'.[1] Pointing to Charles I's initial 'co-operation' with the Puritans, Suleau warns:

Guidé par la terreur, il résolut de les apaiser par toutes sortes de condescendances. Il jugea que le torrent était trop fort pour s'y opposer, acquiesça sans hésiter à toutes leurs mesures, et il paraît même qu'il était sincèrement disposé à se réconcilier avec les factieux.

On sait comme ce système a réussi à Charles Ier! Louis XVI serait bien mal conseillé, s'il adoptait cette honteuse politique. Sans doute il est des circonstances tellement critiques, que la vigueur y serait inévitablement funeste; Louis XVI en est là; mais alors il faut du moins sauver son honneur, et s'abandonner avec dignité aux événements.

Tout cela est d'une similitude effrayante.[2]

Citing Bossuet rather than Hume but delivering essentially the same message, the Abbé Marie-Nicolas-Silvestre Guillon published in 1792 his *Parallèle des Révolutions*—a work which went through at least four editions during that year.

Guillon praises Charles I as a just, moderate and magnanimous prince, perhaps the most honest man of his century and one whose only fault was an excess of clemency. He minutely notes parallels between the French and English revolutions, using a highly emotional *style haché* quite reminiscent, not of Bossuet, but of a bad eighteenth-century *drame*:

O courage de la fuite! ô mon roi! que vous avez de vertus, puisque vous êtes malheureux! Mais . . . pressentiments terribles: il partit aussi cet infortuné Charles premier . . . et Strafford et Montrose!. . . . Palais de Whitehall! théâtre lugubre où fume encore le sang d'un roi immolé par son peuple, serait-il parmi nous des Cromwel? Non, non, subalternes ligueurs, ils ne se sont montrés capables ni de ces savantes hypocrisies, ni de ces forfaits vigoureux qui bravent la lumière, et veulent le génie pour les enfanter, l'héroïsme pour les exécuter; mais des Bradshaw ou des Chabroud, des Ireton ou des Grégoire, des Fairfax, ou des Lafayette, . . . affreux souvenirs! parallèle jusqu'ici trop ressemblant! . . .[3]

[1] Ibid., p. 77. [2] Ibid., pp. 82–83.

[3] *Parallèle des Révolutions*, Seconde édition, Paris, 1792, p. 297. As a matter of fact, the title *Cromwel* had been used rather generously and indiscriminately from the very beginning of the Revolution by both the Right and the Left as the supreme political insult. Within the space of only a few years it was applied variously to, among others, Necker, Mirabeau, Lafayette, Dumouriez, Danton, Robespierre, the entire Directoire, and, of course, Bonaparte. Curiously enough, too, it is the royalists who most often saw Cromwell as a great genius, albeit evil, and far superior to the revolutionary leaders, the 'hommes de boue', of the

Abbé Guillon makes parallels with other revolutions as well as with that of the Puritans, but all his evidence is chosen to prove the cyclical nature of such violent occurrences. Like the Comtesse de Montrond, he predicts the eventual replacement of popular anarchy by a dictatorship. History shows no exceptions to the rule that the usurpations of the multitude are followed by the tyranny of one man.[1] There is nothing new in the French revolution. It is a base imitation from start to finish:

Que l'on parcoure la suite de ces hérésies qui ont menacé la tranquillité des empires en ébranlant les colonnes de l'église et de la vérité; toutes vous offriront, jusque dans les moindres détails, l'image de ces événements dont nous sommes les témoins. Changez les noms, changez le lieu de la scène; que reste-t-il à notre révolution? rien que ses lâchetés et ses forfaits. Que dis-je? Plagiaires dans leurs systèmes persécuteurs comme dans leurs plans politiques, ils n'ont pas même su inventer des crimes![2]

One critical detail of the French parallel with the English revolution was still seen as different in 1792, but Guillon, with a certain grisly tenacity (for most of the 'Stuart prophets' avoided before January 1793 going this far), does not fail to note it: 'Les registres de Whitehall', he writes, 'vous diront que, pour compléter la ressemblance, il faut à la révolution un crime de plus, et que ce crime n'est pas loin peut-être.'[3]

We shall deal later with other specific *rapprochements* made for various purposes by counter-revolutionary writers during the trial of Louis XVI and after the Reign of Terror. Those that we have noted for the period from 1789 to 1792 by no means exhaust the bibliography on the subject but they are fairly indicative of the sort of thing commonly done at this time.[4]

Convention. (See, for example, the Comte d'Antraigues' *Adresse à l'ordre de la noblesse de France*, Paris, 1792, p. 99; also the opinion of La Harpe expressed in December 1794: '. . . un Robespierre et ses complices! C'est à côté d'eux que l'on nomme Cromwel! Il n'en est pas un (et l'histoire le prouvera) que Cromwel eût voulu pour sergent dans son armée. . . .' —*Lycée ou cours de littérature ancienne et moderne*, VIII. 17.)

[1] Ibid., p. 292. [2] Ibid., p. 414. [3] Ibid., p. 417.

[4] Mention should perhaps be made here of what seems to have been a veritable Strafford cult at this time among various French conservatives inspired, I think, by Hume's quite favourable account of Charles I's minister. Already in 1788, Linguet, drawing the parallel between a French trial of that year and that of Strafford, had exclaimed prophetically: 'Dieu veuille que les faits subséquents ne

Perhaps the entire spirit of the parallels can be best summed up iconographically. The frontispiece of an anonymous work entitled *L'Angleterre instruisant la France ou Tableau historique et politique du règne de Charles Ier et de Charles II*, published in Paris early in 1793, provides a good contemporary example. The legend of the engraving reads: 'L'Angleterre instruisant la France; le huit février, 1649' followed by:

> Je commis un grand crime.
> Prenez bien garde de suivre mon exemple.
> Si du Dieu de bonté vous voulez implorer la clémence,
> Ouvrez les cachots, et brisez les fers de l'innocence.

Pictured are two women standing; one is showing the other a book on which can be read the words 'Lisez et tremblez'.

It is an irony of history that this same idea of England teaching France could have changed so much in meaning in the sixty years since Voltaire's *Lettres philosophiques*. At that time, England's

se ressemblent pas! . . .' (*Annales politiques, civiles et littéraires du dix-huitième siècle*, 1788, XV. 339; see also his *La France plus qu'Angloise*, Bruxelles, 1788). At about this same time, Lally-Tollendal with the parallel of his father in mind gave private readings of his tragedy *Le Comte de Strafford* at Versailles: 'Ma tragédie devint une prophétie littérale, on me pressa de la faire représenter. . . .' But his *Strafford* was not made, he tells us, to compete with such *école des Rois* tragedies as *Brutus, César, Guillaume Tell*, or *Charles IX*; (see his dedicatory remarks in *Le Comte de Strafford: tragédie en cinq actes et en vers*, Londres, 1795, in which Hume is praised as 'attaché particulièrement au caractère d'impartialité' and is contrasted with Rapin-Thoyras 'qui ne connaissait guère d'autre vertu que celle d'être presbytérien et d'être révolté'—pp. 327–8).

It is possible that Strafford's execution was tacitly used as a conveniently euphemistic symbol of the frightening consequences of revolution by those royalists who, before Louis XVI's close arrest, wished to avoid indelicate references to regicide. Cazalès, another faithful Hume reader, refers in 1790 to Strafford as 'ce ministre qui joignait tant de talents à tant de vertus [et qui] fut traîné sur un échafaud; mais l'Angleterre le pleura, mais l'Europe entière honora sa mémoire, et son nom est un objet de culte pour tous les sujets de l'empire calmé. Tel est l'exemple que doivent suivre, tel est le modèle que doivent se proposer tous ceux qui sont appelés par la confiance de leur roi, dans ces temps difficiles, au maniement des affaires publiques.' (*Discours et opinions de Cazalès*, Paris, 1821, pp. 114–15.) In 1792 Barnave in yet another parallel of the English and French revolutions wrote: 'Il y a eu de part et d'autre trois couches de patriotes. D'un côté, Strafford, les presbytériens et les indépendants: de l'autre, Mounier, les constitutionnels et les républicains. M. de Lally ayant fait sa tragédie de *Strafford*, semblait avoir pressenti cette analogie par l'intérêt qu'il donnait à un homme qui avait occupé la place correspondante à la sienne.' (*Réflexions politiques sur la Révolution* in *Œuvres de Barnave*, Paris, 1843, II. 69–70.) Lally-Tollendal tells us, however, that he saw himself as a Falkland. (See *Seconde Lettre à ses Commettans*, January 1790, p. 169.)

'lessons' were feared by traditionalists in France. These were the lessons of Voltaire. Now traditionalists almost religiously sought other examples from England. These were the lessons of David Hume.

2. The Long Parliament: Brissot versus Clermont-Tonnerre

To illustrate the intensity of the revolutionary debates provoked by differing views of Stuart history and, what is more important, to show how Stuart history influenced in an immediate sense the formulation by both sides of many political problems of the day, let us examine at some length a controversy on the subject which raged during the summer of 1790 between the two important figures, Clermont-Tonnerre and Brissot.

Brissot is a particularly good example to choose here as representing the Left since he was probably influenced more than any other French revolutionary strategist by the examples of English civil-war history. We have already noted in our chapter on Hume's pre-revolutionary fortunes that the Girondin leader was one of the first in France to reject Hume's royalist interpretation of that period. His own admiration for English parliamentary heroes knew no bounds. His very name, Brissot de Warville—anglicized from the French place name Ouarville where his family held property—is a youthful tribute to his long-standing political anglomania. In its essentials, this anglomania remained as one of his most notable characteristics until his death by decapitation in Paris in 1793.

Also destined to be a victim of the Revolution, Stanislas Clermont-Tonnerre represents equally well, as a constitutional monarchist, that section of the rightist opposition most strongly influenced by the familiar Hume version of Stuart history.

A dispute over the famous *Comités de recherches* was the original issue which sparked their important debate, especially valuable to us as illustrating how the lines of battle on the current significance of the English revolution were drawn up. This controversy is also an illustration of the extent to which Hume's account for many traditionalists had come to be more than merely one man's history of that revolution but rather a body of essential, undeniable political facts, the profound appreciation of which was absolutely necessary for a correct understanding of the revolution in France.

The *Comité de recherches* of which Brissot was a member had been established by the Assembly in October 1789 and authorized to receive denunciations and evidence of conspiracies as well as to arrest, to question, and to hold suspects. Brissot had already defended his committee on several occasions against the accusations of various critics.[1] In August 1790 he found it necessary to return once more to this defence against charges made by Clermont-Tonnerre that such committees represented an inquisitorial device of despotism and had a public effect rather similar to what might be expected from a re-establishment of the Bastille.

Quite to the contrary, Brissot maintained, the powers of the committee were legal and constitutional, the popular party approved of them, they did not in any way resemble those of the Inquisition or the horrors of the Bastille and, finally, such extraordinary measures of security were necessary in a time of crisis when the Revolution had so many enemies. 'Comment pouviez-vous croire', he asks Clermont-Tonnerre, 'que des hommes qu'on dépouillait de privilèges usurpés, dont ils jouissaient depuis une longue suite de siècles, se soumettraient, avec une patience héroïque, à la volonté de ceux qu'ils opprimaient? Comment n'avez-vous pas vu qu'ils se révolteraient contre cette égalité de droits qui les faisait descendre au niveau des autres hommes? . . .'[2]

Brissot continued his self-apology by giving Clermont-Tonnerre one of those classically familiar revolutionary lessons on how people sometimes have to be forced to be free and even killed to be made equal: 'Rappelez-vous l'axiome si trivial et si vrai: *qui veut la fin, veut les moyens*.'[3] Then, having on other occasions already told his readers that there was great merit in the English idea of defining the crime of *lèse-nation*, that the Long Parliament had *many* salutary lessons to teach the National Assembly on how to choose its ambassadors, deal with king's ministers, &c.,[4] he proceeded to justify the *Comités de recherches* on the same authority: 'Et le long parlement d'Angleterre, dans le temps où le

[1] See, for example, *Le Patriote Français*, 25 November 1789, 30 January and 25 February 1790.

[2] *J.-P. Brissot, membre du Comité de Recherches de la municipalité à Stanislas Clermont* (*ci-devant Clermont-Tonnerre*) *membre de l'Assemblée Nationale* . . ., Paris, 28 août 1790, p. 8.

[3] Ibid., p. 11.

[4] *Le Patriote Français*, 10 August 1789, 8 and 22 January 1790.

patriotisme le plus pur l'animait, n'avait-il pas aussi son comité de sûreté ou de recherches? La République lui dut plus d'une fois son salut. Je vous le demande,' Brissot again asked, 'la France n'était-elle pas, en 1789, et n'est-elle pas encore aujourd'hui dans une crise assez violente, pour nécessiter l'institution de ces comités de sûreté?'[1]

Clermont-Tonnerre's answer, the *Nouvelles Observations sur les comités des recherches*,[2] was not long in making itself heard:

Je vais surmonter l'horreur que m'inspire le *long parlement* anglais, m'occuper un instant de ce monstre de politique et d'immoralité, et chercher avec J.-P. Brissot à découvrir quel est l'instant *où il lui a vu les principes du plus pur patriotisme.*

L'histoire exécrable du long parlement nous présente deux périodes: —on le voit d'abord entêté des rêveries presbytériennes, en faire le véhicule de l'ambition de quelques membres; on voit ceux-ci habiles à saisir, à diriger dans le sens de leurs vues la tendance que tout corps politique a par sa nature vers le pouvoir et l'action; on voit ce corps insensé usurper successivement toute la prérogative royale, former et signer une ligue, nommer aux emplois, lever une armée, faire la guerre au roi, l'acheter des Ecossais auxquels il s'était abandonné,commencer une procédure contre ce malheureux prince, détruire la chambre haute qui refusait de participer à ce forfait, et le consommer seul: voilà le *crime* du long parlement. Voici maintenant son *opprobre*: après l'assassinat du roi, accablé de son forfait, il tombe dans le mépris et l'avilissement; l'armée l'insulte, le peuple le brave; Cromwel s'en lasse; il dit un mot, et le long parlement disparaît. —Je le demande à J.-P. Brissot, à quelle époque attache-t-il l'idée du patriotisme le plus pur? Quand le parlement fut-il patriote? est-ce lorsqu'il foula sous ses pieds la tête sanglante de son roi? est-ce lorsqu'il rampa lui-même aux pieds d'un usurpateur? Aperçoit-il de loin ce Cromwel dont la coupable grandeur fut l'effet inévitable des crimes du long parlement? S'il le voit, qu'il le dénonce, afin que nous l'étouffions dans son berceau.

Dans quel temps vivons-nous donc? quelle idée avons-nous de la liberté et du patriotisme, s'il existe un homme qui ose nous proposer comme un modèle le long parlement d'Angleterre, cette assemblée régicide et lâche qui fit acheter le despotisme aux Anglais par sept années de trouble et d'anarchie?[3]

[1] *Brissot à Stanislas Clermont*, p. 7.

[2] See in *Œuvres complètes de Stanislas de Clermont-Tonnerre*, Paris, an III, volume III.

[3] Ibid., III. 341–2.

Brissot in a prompt reply showed that he had long since been emancipated from such a view of the English revolution, that he had read historians other than Hume:

Mon idolâtrie pour la liberté, ma profession de foi, datent d'un temps où Stanislas Clermont rampait dans l'œil de bœuf au milieu du troupeau servile des courtisans, qui ridiculisaient alors ces idées philosophiques et politiques, dont ils font bravement parade, aujourd'hui qu'elles triomphent.

Au moment où j'ai désespéré de la destruction du despotisme, trop fier pour me courber sous son joug insolent, trop ennemi de l'inégalité, pour en laisser l'odieux spectacle à mes enfants, j'étais passé en Amérique, pour m'y fixer au sein d'une république.[1]

We remember that Brissot in 1784 had expressed the wish that the history of this new republic in America would be written by that most patriotic of English historians, Catherine Macaulay. It is with her account of the English revolution that he now answers Clermont-Tonnerre:

Le long parlement anglais vous inspire de l'horreur. Je le crois: l'histoire d'une république doit crisper aisément les nerfs d'un courtisan.

Vous l'appelez un *monstre de politique et d'immoralité*. —Vous êtes surpris que j'aie trouvé dans son histoire *exécrable* un moment *où le plus pur patriotisme y régnait*. Vous ne voyez dans son histoire que deux périodes; celle de ses forfaits, quand Charles premier monta sur l'échafaud; celle de son opprobre, quand Cromwel le cassa.

A ce jugement, on le voit, vous n'avez lu l'histoire de ce monstre que dans *Hume*, cet écrivain qui prostitua ses talents au monarchisme, qui si souvent trahit la cause de la liberté. Si vous aviez étudié celle de l'immortelle *Macaulay*, cette histoire si propre à indigner contre la tyrannie, vous n'auriez pas sans doute calomnié si légèrement une des plus brillantes époques, où l'Angleterre enfanta le plus de talents et de vertus.[2]

After setting his opponent straight on that all-important point, Brissot gives the radical view of Stuart history and a litany of answers to Clermont-Tonnerre's accusations:

Vous demandez quand ce parlement fut patriotique; il le fut . . ., quand il *se révolta*.

Il le fut, quand il voulut mettre fin à la tyrannie d'un *Strafford*, d'un prêtre sacrilège, de *Laud*, d'une chambre inquisitoriale, érigée sous le

[1] *Réplique de J.-P. Brissot à Stanislas Clermont*, Paris, 8 octobre 1790, pp. 8–9.
[2] Ibid., pp. 44–45.

nom de *chambre étoilée*; d'un Charles premier, qui ne convoquait des parlements que pour en obtenir des moyens de dissipation et de débauche, qui les cassait, lorsqu'ils se refusaient à ses désirs criminels, qui mettait des impôts sans le consentement du peuple, emprisonnait ceux qui s'y refusaient, &c.

Il fut patriote, quand il se prolongea jusqu'à ce que tous les abus, sous lesquels l'Angleterre gémissait depuis des siècles, fussent réformés.

Il fut patriote quand il ordonna de poursuivre criminellement les ministres qui avaient donné des conseils pernicieux au roi; quand, mettant lui-même la plus grande chaleur dans cette poursuite, il obtint la condamnation des coupables, qui expièrent sur l'échafaud leurs crimes contre la nation.[1]

Il fut patriote, quand il décreta l'éloignement des évêques de la chambre haute, et que le commandement des troupes de terre et de mer ne serait confié qu'à des personnes *choisies par la chambre des communes*: quand il prit des précautions, pour que les ministres et les ambassadeurs fussent choisis dans *le sens de la révolution*; pour que l'éducation de l'héritier présomptif de la couronne ne fût confiée qu'à des mains pures, c'est à dire, *populaires*.

Il fut patriote, quand il fit licensier les troupes étrangères; —quand des conspirateurs, cherchant à s'assurer, pour le roi, d'une place forte, de Hull, pour commencer la guerre; quand, dis-je, il ordonna au gouverneur, de fermer la porte au roi même.

Il fut patriote, quand, voulant éviter la guerre civile, il fit des propositions de paix au roi, qui, le premier, avait levé l'étendard de la guerre contre la nation.

Il fut patriote, quand il arma la nation pour résister à cette violence du roi; quand il arma les gardes nationales de Londres (*trained band*);[2] quand il ne désespéra pas de la chose publique, après trois défaites de

[1] Two weeks after writing this, Brissot in his *Patriote Français* of 25 October 1790 attacked the paragraph (see *supra*, pp. 103–4, n. 4) praising Strafford in Cazalès' speech on the dismissal of the ministers: 'M. Cazalès a souvent rappelé l'histoire de Charles Ier dans ce discours. On sait dans quelle vue les royalistes font ces citations: ils veulent effrayer le chef de notre nation, et comparer l'assemblée nationale au long parlement. . . .' Brissot contradicts Cazalès on the following points: '1° Strafford n'avait point de vertus; 2° Strafford avait peu de talents, et ils furent funestes à la patrie; 3° l'Angleterre se réjouit de sa mort; 4° l'Europe ignore son nom; et le culte pour ce nom n'existe que dans la cervelle de M. Cazalès.' Camille Desmoulins the very same day also attacked Cazalès' Hume-inspired account with a republican appraisal of Charles' minister by Milton. (*Révolutions de France et de Brabant*, IV. 404–7, 25 October 1791.)

[2] 'A cette époque, dit M^{de} Macaulay, tous ne respiraient que la liberté. L'ouvrier quittait son atelier, le marchand sa boutique, les femmes mêmes abandonnaient les soins domestiques, pour s'occuper de politique: on ne parlait que de réforme, que de destruction de la tyrannie. N'est-ce pas là le tableau de notre révolution?'—*Note by Brissot.*

ses troupes; quand, malgré ses défaites, il ordonna de poursuivre, comme criminelle de haute trahison, la reine, qui entraînait le roi dans une guerre aussi coupable.

Il fut patriote, quand, au milieu de cette guerre civile, il prit les mesures les plus vigoureuses pour établir le républicanisme; quand il abolit la chambre haute, n'établit qu'une seule classe parmi les législateurs.[1]

To praise the next accomplishment of the Long Parliament was still a matter of some delicacy in France in October 1790, but Brissot, who at this time was recommending hair-cuts *à la round-head*[2] as superior even to the *coiffure à la Brutus*, does not hesitate in the slightest:

Enfin il fut patriote, quand il abolit la monarchie. —Vous allez crier au scandale, à l'anathème, et me demander, sans doute, s'il fut aussi patriote, quand il condamna son roi à mort? Entendrez-vous ma réponse, vous né d'hier à la liberté! Mais je serai sans doute entendu de ceux qui, convaincus du principe, ne capitulent point lâchement avec les conséquences; de ceux qui ne s'agenouillent point devant les idoles qu'ils ont brisées.

Répondez-moi: un homme coupable du plus grand des crimes, doit-il être puni, ou doit-il être exempt de la peine, par cela même que son crime est plus grand? Si cette dernière opinion est celle de l'ignorance, de l'esclavage, de l'abnégation du bon sens et de la dignité de l'homme; si vous êtes forcé de convenir que nul criminel sur la terre ne peut être exempt de peine, que sa peine doit être en raison de la grandeur de son crime; si vous êtes forcé de convenir que le plus grand des crimes est de plonger une nation dans la servitude, de substituer les fantaisies aux lois constitutionnelles, d'écraser son peuple d'impôts non consentis, d'en dissiper le produit dans des débauches, de se jouer de la justice et de la morale; enfin, si le plus grand des crimes est d'ouvrir une guerre civile, de verser le sang des hommes pour les assujettir; si, dis-je, vous confessez toutes ces vérités, vous avez vous-même jugé Charles Ier; car il n'est pas un de ces forfaits dont il n'ait été coupable.[3]

Before going on to defend the Long Parliament's actions under Cromwell, Brissot adds a note on the supposed inviolability of kings. A king, he maintains, can be judged—as Milton, Sidney, Locke, Mrs. Macaulay, and other patriots have shown.[4] As for

[1] Ibid., pp. 45–47.
[2] *Patriote Français*, 31 October 1790.
[3] *Réplique de J.-P. Brissot*, pp. 48–49.
[4] See also Brissot's speech of 10 July 1791 on this subject in F.-A. Aulard, *La Société des Jacobins. Recueil de documents pour l'histoire du Club des Jacobins*

Cromwell, the French republican maintained that one had to make distinctions between the victor at Naseby and the usurper. To be added to Brissot's current recommendations on hair-styles are his revolutionary toasts. One of these is: 'Aux vrais amis de la liberté et des droits des hommes, qui tentèrent d'établir le gouvernement républicain en Angleterre dans le siècle dernier; à Ludlow, à Ireton, à Saint-John'; it is followed, however, by an equally clear 'Anathème aux Cromwel et à tous les scélérats hypocrites qui couvriraient d'une fausse popularité leurs ambitieux desseins. Puissent-ils tous, comme lui, dévorés par les remords et les terreurs, descendre au Tombeau, au milieu des exécrations du peuple.'[1] In concluding his answer to Clermont-Tonnerre, Brissot feels he can do no better than once more cite Mrs. Macaulay, now to the effect that it was precisely because the Long Parliament had been doing so well in its reform programmes that Cromwell, fearing a possible loss in his military prestige, decided to dissolve that assembly. If Clermont-Tonnerre were to read Mrs. Macaulay instead of Hume, he would no longer be surprised that men exist 'qui citent comme un modèle (non pas en tout) ce long parlement. —Ah! malheur à l'humanité, à la liberté, si ces hommes, brûlant d'un feu dévorant pour elle, ne se multiplient pas; si partout on n'abjure pas les idées dégradantes pour l'homme, outrageantes pour la Divinité, de ces vils courtisans qui élèvent la grandeur d'un seul sur la bassesse de millions. . . .'[2]

Clermont-Tonnerre's reaction which followed in print within only a few days was one of complete horror. The extent to which Brissot's unheard-of views on Stuart history must have seemed politically insane to him is made clear by the fact that he obviously felt it more necessary to reproduce without alteration Brissot's defence of the Long Parliament than he did to attempt a detailed refutation of the republican's 'principes aussi dangereux que coupables':[3]

de Paris, Paris, 1891, II. 608–26; also *Le Patriote Français*, 15 July 1791. In a February 1792 issue of this last work, Brissot rather gratuitously reminded his readers of the anniversary of Charles I's execution. Later, however, his vote in the Convention on Louis' trial was in favour of the *appel au peuple* and the *sursis*.

[1] *Le Patriote Français*, 12 July 1790.

[2] *Réplique de J.-P. Brissot*, p. 51.

[3] *Sur la dernière réplique de J.-P. Brissot*, 14 October 1790, in *Œuvres complètes de Clermont-Tonnerre*, III. 382–92.

—Si J.-P. Brissot les professait seul, je n'en redouterais pas l'effet; mais J.-P. Brissot est l'homme d'un parti qui nous aurait déjà fait maudire la liberté, si elle pouvait se confondre avec la licence à laquelle ils ont prostitué son nom. —J.-P. Brissot est membre du plus accrédité de ces clubs, dont J.-J. Rousseau regardait l'existence et l'influence comme destructives de la véritable volonté générale; il est possible que sa doctrine se soit composée de *oui-dire*, et sans accuser formellement de la partager, tous les prétendus patriotes dont il s'environne, je pense que cette considération suffit pour m'autoriser à appeler l'opinion publique sur cette doctrine abominable.[1]

After citing Brissot's text in full, a text which he obviously feels is enough to destroy any man politically, Clermont-Tonnerre concludes:

La France est une monarchie ou elle n'est rien. Le gouvernement monarchique a dans cet empire deux bases inébranlables; le caractère national et l'étendue du territoire. —Si on altère momentanément la première de ces causes, la seconde agira tôt ou tard d'une manière décisive. —L'Angleterre, après l'assassinat de Charles Ier, fut livrée au despotisme d'un usurpateur, et retourna bientôt après sa mort, sous la domination de Charles II. L'Angleterre n'est devenue libre qu'en adoptant la monarchie tempérée. . . . En vain nous prêchera-t-on le républicanisme; si ce fanatisme politique triomphait, nous serions tourmentés, déchirés pendant vingt ans pour faire la fortune de quelques ambitieux, et redevenir peut-être esclaves. . . .

P.S. Je préviens J.-P. Brissot que je ne lui répondrai plus, quelques injures qu'il me prodigue; je le préviens toutefois qu'il est mal instruit sur les faits: il peut, par exemple, interroger les courtisans patriotes, et il y en a; ils lui diront qu'ils n'ont vu mon visage que dans les premières assemblées de Paris, qui n'étaient pas tout à fait l'œil de bœuf.[2]

For Clermont-Tonnerre the debate ended with the postscript just quoted which Brissot immediately interpreted as a sign of defeat: 'A ceux qui ne se paient pas de mots', he wrote, 'il a dû prouver son impuissance à me répondre.'[3] After ironically thanking his royalist opponent for helping to advertise the merits of the Long Parliament, Brissot concluded with words which forewarned of things to come:

L'Angleterre, libre sous le long parlement, a perdu la plus grande partie de sa liberté à la restauration de Charles second, en a recouvré quelques

[1] Ibid., III. 382–3. [2] Ibid., III. 391–2.

[3] *Le Patriote Français*, 21 October 1790, p. 3.

portions en chassant Jacques second, en 1688, puis les a perdues insensiblement par l'effet de la corruption et de la coalition de la majorité de son parlement avec le roi, sous sa monarchie actuelle, très *intempérante*. . . .

. . . les Français ne peuvent être qu'esclaves avec un roi de l'ancien régime, qu'à moitié libres sous un roi du régime de 1790, et . . . ils ne seront entièrement libres que sans roi.[1]

3. *A Republican antidote: Catherine Macaulay-Graham*

If the debate between Clermont-Tonnerre and Brissot gives proof of the continuing importance of Hume's *Stuarts* in France at this time, it also makes clear the fact that the *History* of his republican rival, Catherine Macaulay-Graham, had begun to play an equally important role in countering its conservative effect.

Five years before the Revolution Brissot had already expressed the hope that Mrs. Macaulay's work would one day be translated into French[2] and in his *Mémoires* he speaks of having discussed at that time the feasibility of such a project with Mirabeau.[3] In fact, although there are some few doubts still remaining on the matter, it seems clear that Mirabeau undertook the initial responsibility for the translation, the first five volumes of which were published in the years 1791 and 1792 after his death.[4]

Even before the appearance of this long-delayed translation

[1] Ibid., p. 4. Brissot on another occasion (see *Le Patriote Français*, 11 February 1790) also complained about Lally-Tollendal's use of Hume's authority in his arguments against Abbé Sieyès' theory on the powers of a *convention* (see *supra*, p. 94). There seems little doubt that Brissot consciously based some of his own political action on the precedents established by the Long Parliament. See, for example, his speech urging sterner measures against the *émigrés*, 20 October 1791; also his various statements of 1792 on war policy for the Republic.

[2] *Supra*, p. 56. [3] *Mémoires de Brissot*, Paris, 1877, pp. 327–8.

[4] Catherine Macaulay-Graham, *Histoire d'Angleterre depuis l'avènement de Jacques I, jusqu'à la révolution. Traduite en français, et augmentée d'un discours préliminaire, contenant un précis de toute l'histoire d'Angleterre, jusqu'à l'avènement de Jacques I: et enrichie de notes. Par Mirabeau.*

Brissot states in his *Mémoires*, but rather unreliably, I think, that Mirabeau knew no English and that others did the work under Mirabeau's supervision. (See preceding reference.) M.-J. Chénier also expressed doubts that Mirabeau translated the first two volumes (the last three were publicly avowed by Guiraudet) since he found the style quite bad: '. . . aucune forme de langage n'y révèle un homme de talent: soit que Mirabeau ait traduit cette partie de l'ouvrage avec une excessive rapidité, soit plutôt qu'il ne l'ait point traduite, et que par un charlatanisme dont les exemples ne sont que trop multipliés, un écrivain médiocre, ou un libraire avide ait spéculé sur un nom célèbre.' (*Tableau historique de l'état et des progrès de la littérature française depuis 1789*, 3eme édition,

other notable revolutionary figures had commented favourably on Mrs. Macaulay's views. Condorcet, in July 1790, for example, contrasts the reactionary activity of Pitt and Burke with the potentially great rôle this republican historian could have played were she herself a member of the British House of Commons: 'Quoique aussi enthousiaste de la liberté que M. Burke peut l'être de la tyrannie, aurait-elle, en défendant la constitution française, approché de l' absurde et dégoûtant galimatias par lequel ce célèbre rhétoricien vient de la combattre? . . .'[1]

Hume rather than Burke, however, soon became the political writer whose villainy was most often opposed to the virtue of this female patriot. The *Journal des Savants*, announcing in 1791 the appearance in translation of her first two volumes, stated quite explicitly that they represented a *correctif* to Hume.[2] The *Moniteur*, giving notice of the *History* in the same month, added the promise to publish a full review of the work which it called 'l'un des plus importants que l'on ait entrepris depuis la révolution'.[3] Mirabeau himself is quoted by the editor of the Macaulay *History* as having stated in the following terms that he considered its translation to be a task of patriotic *civisme*: 'Cette traduction n'est pas, dans nos

Paris, 1818, pp. 186–7.) An undated letter by Mirabeau, probably written in 1784, indicates that he considered the history an important one and that he highly approved, for example, of Catherine Macaulay's portrait of James II; it implies, nevertheless, that J.-B. Durival and Guiraudet were to do the actual work of translation whereas Mirabeau would lend his 'plebeian aristocrat' name to ensure success in the undertaking which is also described as 'an affair of money'. (See *Mirabeau's letters during his residence in England*, London, 1832, II. 230.)

On the other hand, it seems equally clear that Mirabeau was not such a complete stranger to the English language as Brissot implies. In 1778 we find him quoting from Hume's *History* in the original and complaining that the Abbé Prévost had made many alterations in his translation of the *Stuarts* (see *supra*, p. 52). The following quotation from d'Escherny also could suggest that Mirabeau was the actual translator: 'J'ai beaucoup connu le Comte de Mirabeau en Suisse, pendant qu'il y faisait imprimer ses *Lettres de cachet*. Je me le représente échappé des prisons de France, errant en Hollande, sans asile et manquant de pain, se mettant au gage d'un libraire et entreprenant, pour vivre, la traduction d'un ouvrage dont il n'entendait pas la langue; se procurant une grammaire, un dictionnaire, et apprenant l'anglais à mesure qu'il traduisait l'ouvrage en français. (C'est de sa propre bouche que je tiens cette anecdote.)' F.-L. d'Escherny, *Correspondance d'un habitant de Paris*, Paris, 1791, p. 469.

[1] *Sur l'admission des femmes au droit de cité*, 3 July 1790, in *Œuvres de Condorcet*, X. 123–4. Catherine Macaulay was herself attacking Burke at this time in England (see *Letter to the Earl of Stanhope*, 1790).

[2] October 1791, p. 627.

[3] *Gazette Nationale, ou le Moniteur universel*, No. 282, 9 October 1791.

circonstances, un ouvrage ordinaire. Il existe tant de points de contact et de rapport entre ces événements, ces personnages et nous, qu'en se bornant à les indiquer dans de simples notes, on se trouvera faire l'histoire des deux Révolutions.'[1] We see that Republicans were given to making parallels too, but to do this they needed a different historian, one who could avenge the 'outrages' of Hume.[2]

Mirabeau's *Discours préliminaire* underscores some of these. The French parliamentary leader begins by attacking Hume's outrageously conservative premises:

Hume prétend qu'à considérer la distribution du pouvoir parmi les divers membres de la constitution, il y a rarement une autre question à faire que celle-ci: Quel est l'ordre établi?

Mais si l'ordre établi est mauvais, doit-on regarder comme constitutionnel l'usage qui l'empêche d'être bon? Cet ordre fût-il même excellent, quelle autorité humaine peut empêcher une nation de le changer? Cette question de Hume suppose que tout est bien, ce qui est diamétralement opposé aux résultats historiques qu'il a présentés lui-même; elle suppose qu'il suffit d'être le plus fort pour transformer sa force en droit; elle suppose enfin qu'il est des corps peu nombreux, et même de simples individus, à qui des nations entières doivent appartenir.[3]

A passage from Hume, already cited enthusiastically by the royalist de Montjoie[4] and showing very little admiration for political innovators but recommending a warm attitude of understanding toward their opponents, provokes another burst of indignant eloquence from the great French orator:

Quoi! *il ne faut point détester les oppresseurs?* Mais lorsque la plus sévère et la plus exigeante des religions ordonna le pardon des injures privées, elle prescrivit le châtiment public de ces monstres qui vexent et déshonorent des nations entières.

Il faudrait ne louer qu'avec réserves les réparateurs des abus! Quelle confusion d'idées! quel scandale! A qui la gloire décernera-t-elle des couronnes si ce n'est à ceux qui firent tout pour elle? Qu'on respecte les anciennes institutions, quand elles n'ont rien de malfaisant; mais lorsqu'elles sont fatales, pourquoi ne pas les proscrire? Et si c'était un mérite que l'ancienneté, comment l'erreur pourrait-elle disputer cet avantage à l'éternelle vérité? Comment ne pas sentir que le dernier des hommes peut exercer la place de visir, tandis qu'il faut allier tous les

[1] *Histoire d'Angleterre*, Avis de l'éditeur, I. ix.
[2] Ibid., p. vi.
[3] Ibid., *Discours préliminaire*, I. cv.
[4] *Supra*, p. 94.

dons de la nature et de l'art pour préparer, pour mûrir une révolution, pour naturaliser la liberté dans les âmes accoutumées à l'esclavage!

O Hume! il ne suffisait pas d'unir à la profondeur anglaise le goût et les grâces des Français; il ne suffisait pas d'être l'homme de tous les temps et de tous les lieux, l'amant de tous les arts, le peintre fidèle des mœurs, le rapporteur impartial de tous les faits, de toutes les opinions. Il fallait reculer l'enceinte dans laquelle tes compatriotes ont circonscrit la liberté civile et politique; il fallait t'indigner contre le crime, te passionner pour la vertu, tonner contre les oppresseurs; et cette illustre Macaulay, dont les talents, quoique distingués, sont incontestablement inférieurs au tien, ne t'eût ni enlevé ni même disputé la palme de l'histoire.[1]

We see that in this frankly hostile but not entirely unflattering passage Hume's famous impartiality is not questioned; what is impugned is impartiality itself. Revolutions, of course, have little use for impartiality and the French revolution was no exception. Fairness to all sides would have implied a criminal indifference not to truth, for that was a secondary consideration, but to justice. Neutrality as such was scorned. Robespierre was to sum up his chief accusation against the *philosophes* of the eighteenth century with the words *lâche neutralité*. Brissot, attacking Clermont-Tonnerre's professed love of moderation, made the comment that 'la *modération*, l'*impartialité*, dans ces temps de troubles, signifie, en termes d'académie, voir tous les jeux, ou jouer à coup sûr. Ces mots signifient encore', he added, 'protéger les abus anciens contre les innovations utiles.'[2] Mercier too shows his contempt for this once-honoured attribute, the one most often attached in the pre-revolutionary period to Hume's *History* and which had now come to be associated with the monarchist party. His anecdote on the subject is worth quoting:

'Impartiaux.'
C'est ainsi qu'on appelait au commencement de la révolution ces hommes qui n'ayant point d'idées à eux n'osent pas adopter celles des autres, de peur de se compromettre, et finissent par être l'objet de la risée de tous les partis.

Quelques personnes étaient ou feignaient d'être embarrassées (en 1789) pour savoir combien font six et six. Elles s'adressèrent à un député du côté gauche: il répondit: 'Six et six font douze.'

[1] Ibid., I. cvii–cviii.
[2] *J.-P. Brissot à Stanislas Clermont*, Paris, 28 August 1790, pp. 51-52.

'Qui n'entend qu'un parti n'entend rien, s'écria un penseur: écoutons un député du côté droit.'

La question est proposée à cet honorable membre. Celui-ci, après avoir mûrement réfléchi, répond: 'Six et six font quatorze.'

Nouvel embarras. On consulte un membre du milieu de l'Assemblée.

'Combien, demande-t-il, vous a-t-on dit à gauche? —Douze. —Et combien à droite? —Quatorze.'

'En ce cas, six et six font treize: vous voyez que je suis impartial.'[1]

So much for the *impartiaux*, *monarchistes*, *monarchiens*, and *moyennistes*. So much too for Hume's proud claim—recognized as just by so many until now—to being neither Whig nor Tory, neither patriot nor courtier. With Catherine Macaulay there was no room for doubt on these matters and the *Moniteur*, reviewing her *History* at length in February 1792, gratefully elaborates in her defence an intricate dialectic of partiality. The historian must show more than just that imaginative sympathy which makes the past intelligible to the present. Imaginative sympathy must be one of his characteristics but he must also show himself able to preach the good cause:

C'est une vérité déjà triviale pour nous, quoiqu'elle nous soit presque nouvelle, qu'il ne peut y avoir de véritable histoire que chez un peuple libre. Une autre vérité tout aussi incontestable, c'est que même chez un peuple libre la véracité de l'histoire peut être altérée, soit par ambition, par intérêt, par envie de plaire ou de nuire, soit par esprit de parti, soit au contraire, parce que l'historien s'est piqué d'une impassibilité, qui, lui faisant voir de sang froid les attentats du vice contre la vertu, du despotisme contre la liberté, lui fait aussi raconter comme des événements ordinaires et de simples faits, ce qu'il aurait dû peindre comme des crimes. Otez à Tacite cette verve d'indignation qui l'anime contre la tyrannie, et peut-être plus encore contre la servitude, il aurait pu raconter les mêmes atrocités, les mêmes bassesses, et cependant altérer la vérité par cela même qu'il eût semblé impassible.

Il ne faut donc pas se tromper sur cette impartialité si justement recommandée à l'historien. Il ne doit pas sans doute se passionner assez pour mal voir, mais assez pour représenter vivement ce qu'il voit, seul moyen pour qu'il le fasse bien voir à ses lecteurs.

On reconnaît aujourd'hui même en Angleterre, que dans la partie de l'histoire britannique qui contient la querelle du peuple avec ses rois, et dans laquelle le peuple fut le plus fort, comme il l'est toujours quand il

[1] *Paris pendant la révolution (1789–1798) ou le nouveau Paris*, Paris, 1862, I. 268–9.

veut l'être, le célèbre Hume a été pour ainsi dire, partial à force d'impartialité. C'est un reproche qu'on ne peut faire à Madame Macaulay. Ardente amie de la liberté, elle a envisagé sous leur véritable point de vue les attentats des Stuarts contre la constitution anglaise, la connivence de la chambre des pairs, et la fermeté des communes pendant cette époque orageuse, qui s'étend depuis l'avènement de Jacques Ier jusqu'à l'abdication de Jacques II, dans un espace de quatre-vingt-quatre années.[1]

The *Moniteur* concludes by noting that not only was Catherine Macaulay's work important in itself, it had also been transmitted to the French by one of the founding fathers of their liberty; together these two facts formed a sufficient reason for all amateurs of history and all lovers of liberty to read the work carefully.

That the lovers of liberty did read it and that Catherine Macaulay played an important rôle in supporting, against Hume, the ideology of the revolutionaries is beyond any doubt. Let us examine one last example of her revolutionary success which we find to be notably important especially among the Girondins: her influence on Madame Roland.

A letter of November 1790 from Madame Roland to Bancal illustrates again the fact that Catherine Macaulay was being read in English by patriots in France before the appearance of the Mirabeau translation: 'Si je puis cet hiver', she writes, 'donner quelques moments à l'anglais, ce sera pour lire l'*Histoire* de Madame Macaulay. Je ne quitterai les historiens que pour la morale de Rousseau qui convient si parfaitement au civisme. . . .'[2] It is probably fairly safe to assume also that Catherine Macaulay's *History* was being discussed at this time in the influential Roland salon.

Several years later, in 1793, we find Madame Roland in prison, drawing up a list of books she would like to be made available to her:

. . . Je fis une note de ce que j'aurais à me procurer: d'abord les *Vies des hommes illustres* de Plutarque, qu'à l'âge de huit ans je portais à l'église au lieu d'une *Semaine-Sainte*, et que je n'avais pas relues à fond depuis cette époque; l'*Histoire anglaise* de David Hume, avec le *Dictionnaire* de Sheridan, pour me fortifier dans cette langue: j'aurais préféré suivre Macaulay; mais celui qui m'avait prêté les premiers volumes de cet auteur n'était sûrement pas dans sa maison, et je n'aurais su où demander cet ouvrage que déjà je n'avais pu trouver chez les libraires.[3]

[1] *Gazette Nationale, ou le Moniteur universel*, No. 45, 14 February 1792, p. 184.

[2] *Lettres de Madame Roland* (1788–93), 1ère série, Paris, 1902, II. 191.

[3] *Mémoires de Madame Roland*, Paris, 1905, I. 37–38. It was, in fact, Brissot who had lent Madame Roland the first volumes of Mrs. Macaulay's *History*.

With all lovers of liberty presumably following the *Moniteur's* urgent advice to read this work it is perhaps understandable that book dealers were in short supply. The shortage was soon remedied after the Terror, however, for we find the Ministry of the Interior recommending in July 1798 that Catherine Macaulay's *History of England* be included on the list of books distributed as prizes 'à la clôture des Ecoles et dans les fêtes nationales'.[1] Meanwhile, in prison, Madame Roland must do with second best. In her *Mémoires particuliers* we find yet another great tribute paid to the English republican historian who, we remember, had been seen as defamatory, seditious and criminal in France thirty years earlier: 'S'il m'avait été donné de vivre', Madame Roland writes, 'je n'aurais plus eu, je crois, qu'une tentation: c'eût été de faire les *Annales* du siècle, et d'être la *Macaulay* de mon pays; j'allais dire le *Tacite* de la France, mais cela ne serait point modeste. . . .'[2]

Madame Roland wrote these words in prison; soon she would be condemned to die by the hate of the Montagnards and we remember her famous remark as she mounted the revolutionary scaffold: 'O Liberté, que de crimes on commet en ton nom!' It is perhaps worth noting that, thirty years earlier, Hume had already expressed the identical sentiment in a letter to the Englishwoman Madame Roland had most wanted to emulate.[3]

[1] See *La Décade*, lettre du 24 messidor An VI, XVIII. 309.

[2] *Mémoires de Madame Roland*, II. 264.

[3] *Supra*, p. 59, n. 1. Not to be neglected too is the important rôle of Milton's political writings during this period. Also translated by Mirabeau and the honoured recipient of Brissot's revolutionary toasts, Milton is cited enthusiastically along with Catherine Macaulay by Camille Desmoulins as an ardent defender of liberty. (*Révolutions de France et de Brabant*, 12 December 1789, I. 125, 130; 19 December 1789, I. 180–1; 25 October 1790, IV. 404–7.) The *Annales patriotiques* of Mercier and Carra commend him as well (see No. 640, 4 July 1791, p. 1534). Administrators of the Département de la Drôme even ordered the official reprinting (Valence, 1792) of his refutation of Saumaise in anticipation of Louis XVI's execution. It is interesting to note too that Milton figures as a virtuous republican member of Parliament opposed to another M.P., a sinister character named Burke, in M.-L. Tardy's *Cromwel ou le général liberticide* of 1793. It was, of course, especially during Louis' trial that his political writings took on the greatest significance and he is quite frequently cited in the Convention. Royalists, on the other hand, showed a very distinct tendency to reject him as a regicide, despite his Christianity, in favour of the conservative 'atheism' of Hume. Abbé Guillon, for example, points out with horror the rôle of Milton in both the English and the French revolutions. (*Parallèle des Révolutions*, 1792, p. 303.)

IV

THE TRIAL OF 'LE STUART FRANÇAIS'

1. Louis XVI and Charles I: a condemned king's meditations

We remember that during Hume's visit to Versailles in 1763 the historian of the Stuarts had been complimented on his great reputation in France by a nine-year old boy, the future king, Louis XVI. As it turned out, the young prince was to remain an avid and faithful reader of history all his life. No study, everyone agreed, was more suited to form part of the education of a future ruler:

Le second moyen général de connaître les hommes, c'est de les comparer aux hommes des siècles passés, et cette comparaison se fait par la lecture de l'histoire. C'est de toutes les sciences, celle qu'un prince doit le plus étudier.

... Il faut qu'il la lise en prince qui travaille sérieusement à s'instruire des vrais principes du gouvernement et qui veut apprendre à connaître les hommes. Il tirera beaucoup plus de lumières de l'histoire des monarchies, que de celle des républiques, qui se conduisent par des ressorts dont il ne peut faire aucun usage dans un Etat monarchique. ...[1]

The history of the Stuart monarchy, in particular, was of special significance:

Si le prince veut connaître le génie d'un peuple mal gouverné, et savoir à quels excès il est capable de se porter, il n'a qu'à lire la traduction française de l'*Histoire de la rébellion et des guerres civiles d'Angleterre*, par milord Clarendon. Il trouvera que tout prince faible se conduit comme l'infortuné Charles Ier, que tout peuple échauffé et soulevé ressemble au peuple d'Angleterre; que tout homme factieux et entreprenant est de l'humeur de Cromwel, et que, s'il n'en a pas les talents, il en a du moins l'emportement et la malice.[2]

[1] *Réflexions sur mes entretiens avec M. le Duc de La Vauguyon*, par Louis-Auguste, Dauphin, in *Œuvres de Louis XVI*, Paris, 1864, I. 310.

[2] Ibid., I. 314. Louis XVI was not limited to reading English history in translation. His own knowledge of English was apparently excellent and he had even translated Walpole's work on Richard III (published later as *Règne de*

It was not long before Louis XVI was to see his own kingdom in the grip of similar revolutionary upheaval. His former rather scholarly meditations on the lessons of Stuart history were suddenly transformed into something much more urgent. In fact, as the time of his trial approached, one can almost say that his preoccupation with the events of Charles I's reign, Hume's account of which he seems finally to have preferred above all others,[1] had become a veritable obsession.

The obsessive nature of Louis' interest in Stuart history is emphatically pointed out by various contemporary eye-witnesses. Madame Campan, for example, tells how the king consented to wear a *plastron* as protection against assassination during his obligatory attendance at the July 14th ceremonies in 1792. He had agreed to wear the device only to comply with Marie-Antoinette's wishes: '. . . ils ne m'assassineront pas,' Madame Campan quotes the king as saying, 'leur plan est changé; ils me feront mourir autrement.' The queen's reader then continues:

La reine vit que le roi me parlait bas, et quand il fut sorti, elle me demanda ce qu'il avait dit. J'hésitais à répondre; elle insista en disant qu'il fallait ne rien lui cacher, qu'elle était résignée sur tout. Quand elle eut connaissance de la réflexion du roi, elle me dit qu'elle l'avait devinée; que depuis longtemps il lui avait dit que tout ce qui se passait

Richard III, ou Doutes historiques sur les crimes qui lui sont imputés, Paris, 1800), as well as fragments of Gibbon and other English historians. With regard to Louis XVI's reading habits, Necker notes the following in 1792: 'C'est toujours des grands ouvrages d'histoire, de morale et de politique, écrits en français ou en anglais, que j'ai vu le roi s'occuper avec goût et avec assiduité.' (*Réflexions présentées à la nation française sur le procès de Louis XVI* in *Œuvres complètes de M. Necker*, publiées par M. le baron de Staël, Paris, 1820–1, XI. 363.)

[1] The official inventory of Louis XVI's books, made at the Temple after his execution, shows that Hume's was the only work of English history in the imprisoned king's possession. (Archives Nationales, F. 17, 1200, No. 70: see Bapst, op. cit., *La Révolution Française*, XXI. 533.) Delisle de Sales, who had his information from Malesherbe's son-in-law, the *président* Rosanbo, stated in 1803 that Louis XVI 'fit demander au libraire Nyon, par son ancien Ministre (i.e. Malesherbes) *l'Histoire de la Maison des Stuarts*, par David Hume, pour y voir le procès et la mort de Charles premier.' He goes on to add, however, that Louis returned the work to Malesherbes after reading it and that 'cet exemplaire, devenu si précieux par un pareil usage, est resté jusqu'à l'invasion des vandales révolutionnaires, dans la bibliothèque du château de Malesherbes' (see Delisle de Sales, *Malesherbes*, Paris, 1803, p. 268). It thus seems probable that Louis actually had two copies of the *Stuarts*. Cléry, the king's valet during his captivity, explicitly states that Louis read Hume in English during that time. (*Journal de ce qui s'est passé à la tour du Temple pendant la captivité de Louis XVI, Roi de France*, Londres, 1798, p. 96.)

en France était une imitation de la révolution d'Angleterre, sous Charles Ier, et qu'il lisait sans cesse l'histoire de cet infortuné monarque, pour se conduire mieux qu'il ne l'avait fait dans une crise semblable.[1]

Madame Campan refers also to the king's prolonged state of mental depression at this time: '—un découragement qui allait jusqu'à l'abattement physique. Il fut dix jours de suite sans articuler un mot, même au sein de sa famille. . . . La reine le tira de cette position si funeste dans un état de crise où chaque minute amenait la nécessité d'agir. . . . Elle alla jusqu'à lui dire que, s'il fallait périr, ce devait être avec honneur et sans attendre qu'on vînt les étouffer l'un et l'autre sur le parquet de leur appartement.'[2]

It is nevertheless quite possible that the idea of being assassinated was in fact less forbidding to Louis XVI than the fear of being dishonoured by a criminal trial like that imposed on Charles I. Bertrand de Molleville, who as *ministre de la Marine* was in close touch with the king at this time, also suggests that Louis' reading of Stuart history was closely related to his prolonged depression and his generally fatalistic inability to act decisively:

Il ne s'occupait point du tout du soin de sa propre vie; car depuis l'aventure de Varennes, ce malheureux prince était fortement persuadé qu'il serait assassiné; que tous les efforts pour l'en garantir seraient inutiles et pourraient augmenter le danger de sa famille et des amis qui lui restaient fidèles. Livré à ces funestes pressentiments, il attendait la mort avec un calme héroïque, qu'on aurait pu considérer comme un sentiment d'indifférence pour la vie.

Il lisait souvent l'Histoire de Charles Ier d'Angleterre, et mettait sa principale attention à éviter tout ce qui pouvait servir de prétexte pour lui faire criminellement son procès.

Le sacrifice de sa vie semblait ne lui rien coûter. L'honneur de la nation occupait toutes ses pensées. L'idée d'être assassiné publiquement au nom du peuple lui faisait une impression violente. Il aurait préféré de périr par le fer d'un assassin dont le meurtre serait considéré comme le crime de quelques individus, et non comme un acte national.[3]

In a later work Bertrand de Molleville comes back to this point, commenting with surprise on the fact that Louis learned so little

[1] Mme Campan, *Mémoires sur la vie privée de Marie-Antoinette*, Paris, 1822, II. 214–15.

[2] Ibid., II. 205. This would be around June 1792.

[3] *Mémoires secrets pour servir à l'histoire de la dernière année du règne de Louis XVI, Roi de France.* Par Ant.-Fr. Bertrand-de-Molleville, Ministre d'Etat à cette époque, Londres, 1797, II. 259–61.

from his haunted study of Charles I's career: 'Mais ce qu'il y a de plus remarquable, est que l'histoire de Charles Ier, dont Louis XVI fit sa lecture ordinaire, depuis le commencement de la révolution jusqu'à la fin de sa vie, au lieu de l'éclairer sur les mesures qu'il devait adopter ou éviter, devint pour lui la leçon la plus pernicieuse de toutes.'[1] It is Bertrand de Molleville's opinion, for example, that Louis never sought out any opportunity to use the army against the Revolution because he had been so impressed by the fact that such action had served to justify one of the chief accusations against Charles I during the English trial. Remembering the Stuart king's active resistance to Parliament, the former minister maintained, too, that if Charles I had been king of France in 1789 no revolution would have taken place. 'D'un autre côté,' he continues, 'si on considère combien Louis XVI était loin d'être jaloux de sa prérogative, ou d'avoir la moindre idée de l'augmenter par des usurpations sur les privilèges et libertés du peuple, et l'empressement avec lequel il consentit à la réforme de tous les abus dont on se plaignait à cet égard, on pourrait peut-être en conclure avec autant de fondement que si Louis XVI eût été roi d'Angleterre à l'époque où la révolution y éclata, sa condescendance entière et facile sur toutes les demandes qui y donnèrent lieu, n'aurait pas laissé l'ombre d'un prétexte aux mécontents.'[2]

Other contemporary accounts support Bertrand de Molleville's belief that Louis XVI had been harmfully affected by a too vivid appreciation of English revolutionary history. The younger Lacretelle, writing in 1801, tells how the king experienced as a result 'les mortelles angoisses d'un homme qui voit, avec certitude, sa ruine s'avancer, et n'ose rien tenter pour la prévenir. Il relisait sans cesse l'histoire de Charles Ier, et s'étudiait à suivre une conduite entièrement opposée, afin d'éviter, s'il se pouvait, sa fatale

[1] *Histoire d'Angleterre*, Paris, 1815, III. 564.

[2] Ibid., III. 565. In 1816 Mme de Staël expressed certain wise reservations concerning such a view in her *Considérations sur les principaux événements de la Révolution Française:* 'Il me semble curieux', she writes, 'de montrer à ceux qui se persuadent qu'il suffisait en France à cette époque, de tel ou tel homme pour tout prévenir, de telle ou telle résolution pour tout arrêter, il me semble curieux, dis-je, de leur montrer que la conduite de Charles Ier a été, sous tous les rapports, l'opposé de celle de Louis XVI, et que pourtant deux systèmes contraires ont amené la même catastrophe: tant est invincible la force des révolutions dont l'opinion du grand nombre est la cause!' (*Œuvres complètes,* Paris, 1820–1, XIII. 89.)

destinée. Il mettait toujours l'excès de la faiblesse, où celui-ci avait mis l'excès de la confiance et de l'opiniâtreté.'[1] Jacob-Nicolas Moreau, *Historiographe de France* and librarian to Marie-Antoinette, also maintained that these obsessive Stuart readings were the cause of Louis XVI's being 'le premier à désespérer de la chose publique'. He also quotes the French king as saying as early as 1789, just after the march on Versailles: 'Je suis menacé du même sort; . . . s'il existe un moyen de l'éviter, c'est de faire tout le contraire de ce que fit cet infortuné monarque.'[2]

Personal sentiments expressed in various letters by Louis XVI also suggest that the example of Charles I was constantly before his eyes whenever he considered the possible courses of action available to him. 'S'il me faut descendre du Trône,' we read in one of his letters of 1791 to the Prince de Condé, 'monter sur l'échafaud où Charles Ier fut immolé, abandonner ce que j'ai de plus cher au monde, me voilà prêt; *mais point de guerre*! *point de guerre*!'[3] The words 'Je puis éprouver le sort de Charles Ier. . . .' occur also in another letter of 28 April 1792.[4] Interesting to note too is the fact that Louis was, on occasion, given to repeating Charles I's last words. When, for example, it was pointed out to him in 1791 that his use of the veto might have dangerous personal consequences, the king is said to have replied: 'Que me feront-ils? Ils me tueront: eh bien! *j'acquerrai une couronne immortelle pour une périssable*.'[5] It is quite possible even that his close knowledge of Charles I's speeches to the English court guided some of the feelings he expressed concerning the manner in which he wished to have his own defence conducted. The following letter to Malesherbes, written while Louis was a prisoner of the Convention, lends support to this conjecture:

Je ne me fais pas illusion sur mon sort. Les ingrats qui m'ont détrôné ne s'arrêteront pas au milieu de leur carrière, ils auraient trop à rougir de voir sans cesse sous leurs yeux leurs victimes. Je subirai le sort de Charles Ier, et mon sang coulera pour me punir de n'en avoir jamais

[1] Charles-Jean-Dominique de Lacretelle, *Précis historique de la Révolution Française*, Paris, 1801, p. 242.

[2] Jacob-Nicolas Moreau, *Mes Souvenirs*, publiés par Camille Hermelin, Paris, 1898–1901, II. 467–8.

[3] Letter 49, 15 August 1791, in *Œuvres de Louis XVI*, II. 157.

[4] Ibid., II. 182.

[5] See Le Marquis de Beaucourt, *Captivité et derniers moments de Louis XVI; récits originaux et documents officiels*. Paris, 1892, I. 385.

versé. Mais ne serait-il pas possible d'ennoblir mes derniers moments? L'Assemblée nationale renferme dans son sein les dévastateurs de ma monarchie, mes dénonciateurs, mes juges et probablement mes bourreaux. On n'éclaire pas de pareils hommes, on ne les rend pas justes, on peut encore moins les attendrir. Ne vaudrait-il pas mieux mettre quelque nerf dans ma défense, dont la faiblesse ne me sauvera pas? J'imagine qu'il faudra l'adresser, non à la Convention, mais à la France entière, qui jugerait mes juges et me rendrait dans le cœur de mes peuples une place que je n'ai jamais mérité de perdre. Alors mon rôle à moi se bornerait à ne point reconnaître la compétence de ce tribunal où la force me ferait comparaître. Je garderai un silence plein de dignité, et, en me condamnant, les hommes qui se disent mes juges, ne seraient plus que des assassins.[1]

It is not too difficult to find distinct echoes of Charles I's own formal defence in the preceding letter. Whether these are the result of more than the similarity of circumstances in which the two monarchs found themselves is difficult to say. Other questions of an equally idle nature arise: one is permitted to wonder, for example, if Louis was inspired by the English king's actions when he showed an unaccustomed firmness in defending the established church, or, more trivially still, when he too, on hearing his sentence, asked for (but did not receive) three days grace, wore the same colours to the scaffold, and attempted (again unsuccessfully) to address the spectators in the last few minutes before his execution. Such questions cannot of course be answered; indeed, there is some doubt even whether they can be properly asked. Perhaps one can speculate legitimately, however, on how pleased that style-conscious Scot David Hume would have been had he lived long enough to read in Cléry's journal a description of the following rather quiet scene: the setting is the king's prison in the Temple; Louis has just learned that the Convention has voted the death sentence:

Un ancien *Mercure de France* étant tombé sous sa main, il y lut un logogryphe qu'il me donna à deviner; j'en cherchai le mot inutilement. —'Comment, vous ne le trouvez pas? il m'est pourtant bien applicable dans ce moment, me dit-il, le mot est *sacrifice*.'

Le roi m'ordonna de chercher dans la bibliothèque, le volume de

[1] *Œuvres de Louis XVI*, II. 207–8; this letter was, curiously, published as *inédite* in *Episodes de la Terreur extraits des mémoires du comte de Tocqueville*, Compiègne, 1901, pp. 36–37.

l'*Histoire d'Angleterre* où se trouve la mort de Charles Ier: il en fit la lecture les jours suivants. . . .[1]

2. *David Hume and Stuart history for the defence*

Considerations drawn from Stuart history (and chiefly Hume's version of it) form a major part of many unofficial defences of the French king composed during his trial in 1792.

Undoubtedly one of the most important of these was the apology for Louis XVI published by his former minister, Jacques Necker, on 30 October of that year. In an eloquent plea to the Convention, Necker begged its members not to proceed with the trial, promising that they would thus avoid committing a crime even greater than that of the Long Parliament:

[1] Cléry, op. cit., p. 203. In a somewhat cruel forgery of Cléry's journal, published in 1800, an editor's note insists that this part of Louis' final meditations was a salutary *pensum* suggested to the king by members of the Commune: 'Cette histoire ne faisait pas partie de la petite bibliothèque du Temple, quand Louis XVI y arriva; mais elle y fut envoyée par le conseil général de la commune, à qui Chaumette, Hébert et d'autres avaient persuadé qu'il était indécent à Louis XVI de lire des poètes latins auxquels le conseil ne comprenait rien, d'en faire faire de nouveaux achats pour se compléter, et de ne point lire le procès de Charles Ier, qui convenait davantage à sa position.' (*Mémoires de M. Cléry ou Journal de ce qui s'est passé dans la tour du Temple, pendant la détention de Louis XVI; avec des détails sur sa mort, qui ont été ignorés jusqu'à ce jour*. Edition originale seule avouée par l'auteur. Londres, 1800, pp. 127–8.) The same work tells how on the eve of Louis' solemn appearance at the bar of the Convention, Marie-Antoinette spent many gay hours seated before her harpsichord merrily singing a collection of very naughty songs.

Curiously, the account concerning the Commune is a distorted version of an actual report on a meeting of the Conseil général, 23 November 1792, in which we read as follows: 'Au commencement de la séance d'hier soir il a été fait lecture d'une demande des commissaires de service au Temple, qui annonçait que Louis XVI demandait pour son usage et pour celui de son fils différents livres . . . total, trente-trois ouvrages, tant latins que français. . . .

Cette demande de Louis XVI a fait naître les débats les plus vifs.' Several members of the council were in fact strongly opposed to the king's request, one objecting that the prisoner 'avait à peine quinze jours d'existence assurés, et que les livres qu'il demandait suffisaient pour s'occuper pendant la vie la plus longue'. Martin, demanding that at least the works in Latin be suppressed, added: 'Je demande qu'on leur substitue ceux qui ont pour titre: la Révolution d'Amérique, celle d'Angleterre, la vie de Cromwel, la vie de Charles IX et les détails du massacre de la Saint-Barthélemy.' The militantly republican report goes on to say that unfortunately Martin's motion, 'quoique appuyée par quelques membres, n'a pas eu de suite'. The request was finally approved. (See Le Marquis de Beaucourt, op. cit., II. 137–9.) A list of the books requested by Louis XVI may be found in M.-A. de Beauchesne, *Louis XVII; sa vie, son agonie, sa mort; Captivité de la famille royale au Temple*, Paris, 1852, I. 500–2.

C'est à une entreprise unique dans les annales du monde, c'est à un attentat dont les historiens transmettent le récit avec horreur, et que les Anglais expient encore chaque année par un repentir solennel; c'est à ce crime public, dû à l'ambition d'un seul homme, que l'on voudrait préparer par degrés la nation française. Ah! vous qui avez évité soigneusement, et peut-être avec une sorte d'affectation, de prendre en aucun point ces Anglais pour modèles, ne feriez-vous une seule exception qu'en faveur d'une action barbare! Que dis-je? vous croiriez marcher sur les traces des esclaves de Cromwel, de ces juges dévoués à ses passions politiques . . . et vous vous tromperiez encore, car vous n'auriez pas même leur excuse. Oseriez-vous en effet mettre en parallèle avec les reproches trop justes qu'on avait droit de faire au malheureux Stuart . . . les accusations que vous êtes obligés de fonder sur des conjectures, ou que vous tâchez d'extraire de quelques papiers trouvés dans le cabinet du roi . . .? Voici ce qu'avait fait pendant son règne le monarque anglais: une constitution libre, expliquée par les actes les plus solennels, lui indiquait ses obligations et fixait ses prérogatives; cependant, au mépris de cette constitution, il avait levé plusieurs impôts sans le concours des représentants de la nation; il avait exigé des prêts forcés . . .; il avait excédé son pouvoir dans le règlement des affaires écclésiastiques. . . . Enfin, entraîné par les événements, il s'était mis à la tête d'un corps de troupes, et avait commencé la guerre civile dont l'issue lui devint fatale. Quel rapport, quelle ressemblance pourrait-on trouver entre ces divers délits politiques, et la conduite d'un monarque héritier d'un pouvoir dont les limites étaient inconnues, et qui a commencé la liberté par le sacrifice volontaire d'une partie de ses prérogatives dont la couronne était en possession depuis tant de siècles.[1]

Necker's concessions concerning Charles I's real guilt are rarely expressed by members of the Right at this time but represent proof of the Swiss banker's political astuteness. He reveals an awareness, moreover, that in the preceding century of Anglo-French rivalry, the French had often shown pride in the claim that their own annals, at least, had never been defiled by a crime of regicide committed with all the hypocritical trappings of a legal trial. Now, Necker continued, the French would not have even England's excuse that the evil genius of Cromwell had urged on a small fanatic band of usurpers to this hideous crime. The French Convention, claiming as it did to represent openly the justice of the entire French nation, would, if it sentenced Louis XVI to death, make France the guiltiest nation of all.

[1] *Réflexions présentées à la Nation française sur le procès de Louis XVI*, in *Œuvres complètes de M. Necker*, Paris, 1820–1, XI. 376–8.

Necker pursued his defence of Louis XVI by pointing out another consideration which Hume, Adam Smith, and, on different grounds, centuries of theocratic tradition had established in France as something of a dogma: the misfortunes of kings, he observed, have quite extraordinary and awesome effects on the feelings of the people. Kings are not ordinary creatures in this respect. Smith, in his *Theory of Moral Sentiments*, a work which was very well known on the continent at this time and which enjoyed three different French translations, had analysed in detail our feelings for the tragedies of the great. These feelings are often born of our admiration for the advantages of their high position. We like to serve the great in order to share in the completion of a system of happiness which seems so close to perfection. We ask for no other reward. Conversely, when the great suffer adverse fortune, we cannot help feeling that their situation merits a greater compassion on our part than that normally provoked by similar mischance occurring in the lives of lesser men.[1] A like belief underlies the true intent of Burke's rather over-romanticized passage in the *Reflections* bewailing the disappearance of the age of chivalry. Strange things happen when kings and queens are unceremoniously hurled from their thrones; we are as awed by such disasters in the moral world as we would be by a miracle in the physical order of things.

Arguing along such lines and citing Hume's *Stuarts* as proof, Necker addressed the Convention in the following terms:

O Français! au nom de votre gloire passée . . .; mais surtout au nom du ciel, au nom de la pitié, repoussez tous ensemble les projets de ceux qui cherchent à vous entraîner au dernier terme de l'ingratitude, et qui veulent vous associer à leur violentes passions et à leurs sombres pensées. Un roi, vous disent-ils, un roi, n'est qu'un homme, et l'on ne doit à sa destinée aucune sollicitude particulière. Cette assertion n'est point vraie; elle ne l'est point, sous le rapport de nos sentiments. Un roi, dans l'écroulement de sa fortune, un roi lorsqu'il parvient au comble du malheur, nous retrace tous les intérêts qui nous ont unis à lui. Il nous a paru longtemps, par son pouvoir tutélaire, une partie morale de nous-mêmes, et son humiliation semble nous appartenir. . . . Les moments d'enthousiasme ou de passion nous distraient de ces pensées, et semblent déranger, pour un temps, le cours naturel de nos

[1] Adam Smith, *The Theory of Moral Sentiments*, the second edition, London, 1761; see Part I, Section III, Chapter II: 'Of the Origin of Ambition, and of the Distinction of Ranks', pp. 87–90.

sentiments; mais au terme extrême des vengeances, les regards se tournent en arrière, et là commencent les regrets et les repentirs. Je ne présente pas ici les idées spéculatives. Qu'on lise dans l'histoire de la Maison de Stuart, rédigée par un écrivain philosophe, l'impression convulsive que fit sur tous les cœurs la dernière catastrophe de l'infortuné Charles Ier. Qu'on y arrête, si l'on peut, son attention, et que l'on se demande ensuite si, dans le rapport de nos sentiments, un roi n'est qu'un homme; s'il n'est qu'un homme surtout, lorsqu'il fut si longtemps environné de notre amour, lorsqu'il fut si longtemps le signe de nos liens. Ah! qu'on lise le plus affreux des récits, et qu'on essaie ensuite de considérer, sans émotion, les idées funestes auxquelles on voudrait accoutumer la nation française. Oui, qu'on le lise cet affreux récit, et qu'on ose ensuite confier aux passions exaltées du moment présent le jugement d'un prince réduit par la fortune à l'abandon le plus absolu. . . .[1]

If the amount of attention accorded later by the Convention to the task of refuting Necker's points is any true indication, one must conclude that he had chosen arguments which were particularly effective. In another unofficial defence of Louis XVI, Lally-Tollendal also invited that body to meditate on Stuart history:

[1] Necker, op. cit., pp. 400–3. The following is the passage Necker quotes from Prévost's translation of Hume:

'Il est impossible de représenter la douleur, l'indignation et l'étonnement qui succédèrent, non seulement dans les spectateurs qui parurent comme inondés d'un déluge de tristesse, mais dans la nation entière, aussitôt que la nouvelle de cette fatale exécution fut répandue. Jamais un monarque dans le plein triomphe du succès et de la victoire ne fut plus cher à son peuple, que ce malheureux prince l'était devenu au sien par ses infortunes, sa grandeur d'âme, sa patience et sa piété. La violence du retour au respect, à la tendresse, fut proportionnée à la force des illusions qui avaient animé tous ses sujets contre lui. Chacun se reprochait avec amertume, ou des infidélités actives, ou trop d'indolence à défendre sa cause opprimée. Sur les âmes plus faibles, l'effet de ces passions compliquées fut prodigieux. On raconte que plusieurs femmes enceintes se délivrèrent de leur fruit avant terme; d'autres furent saisies de convulsions; d'autres tombèrent dans une mélancolie qui les accompagna jusqu'au tombeau. Quelques-unes, ajoute-t-on, perdant tout soin d'elles-mêmes, comme si la volonté leur eût manqué de survivre à leur prince bien-aimé, quand elles en auraient eu le pouvoir, tombèrent mortes à l'instant. Les chaires même furent arrosées de larmes, non subornées; ces chaires d'où tant de violentes imprécations et d'anathèmes avaient été lancés contre lui. En un mot l'accord fut unanime à détester ces parricides hypocrites qui avaient déguisé si longtemps leurs trahisons sous des prétextes sanctifiés, et qui par ce dernier acte d'une atroce iniquité jetaient une tache ineffaçable sur la nation.' —Those who wish to compare Hume's own words will note that the author of *Manon Lescaut* here does full justice—and no more—to the original.

Français, pensez-y bien, il s'agit de remords sans fin, et d'une tache éternelle. Les Anglais pleurent depuis un siècle, et les siècles suivants les verront pleurer encore, un régicide commis par un bien plus petit nombre de leurs pères, avec bien moins de solennité, et, il faut l'avouer, avec des circonstances bien moins odieuses que celles qui signaleraient aujourd'hui en France le renouvellement du même attentat. On vous a bien outragés Français; on a bien étrangement compté ou sur la prévention, ou sur la légèreté, ou sur l'ignorance, lorsqu'on n'a pas eu honte d'appeler devant vous, du nom d'infâme, ce Charles Ier que toute une nation qui, apparemment, n'a besoin de personne pour connaître ses droits et sentir sa dignité, appelle religieusement du nom de martyr.[1]

Lally-Tollendal continued his plea for the king by assailing what we might now call the Macaulay-Brissot version of the English revolution—a version, moreover, which formed an important part of Mailhe's famous report. Lally preached, on the contrary, the familiar Hume account as he would again in 1797 in his *Défense des émigrés français*.[2]

Cazalès in his *Défense de Louis XVI* also defies the revolutionists to inquire of the English if they now approved of their ancestors' execution of Charles I. Their answer would not, he maintains, be comforting to a nation which seemed perversely decided on taking the same course. Only ask the English, Cazalès warns the Convention, 'et vous ne rappellerez plus une époque de leur histoire qu'ils veulent oublier'.[3] Cazalès in 1792 was not a novice at this sort of thing. Long before the King's arrest he had warned France's revolutionaries that the English still maintained an expiatory cult for the Earl of Strafford; now that even Louis XVI's life was in danger, the 'cult' of Strafford became quite automatically the 'cult' of Charles I.

In yet another defence of the French king, the royalist de Montjoie addressed himself even more directly to the Convention, not more than forty members of which, he believed, sincerely wanted Louis' death. The best advice he could give to the others,

[1] *Plaidoyer pour Louis XVI*, Londres, 1793, pp. 11–12.

[2] A work about which the republican Jean-Jacques Leuliette contemptuously but significantly notes: 'Vous semblez, Monsieur, emprunter le pinceau de Hume, en nous retraçant la catastrophe sanglante du 21 janvier. J'avouerai avec vous que ce fut un triste jour; mais je ne conviendrai point qu'il fût le plus horrible de la révolution; le plus affreux est celui où l'on fit tomber le plus de têtes; il n'en tomba qu'une le 21 janvier. . . .' (*Des Emigrés Français ou Réponse à M. de Lally-Tollendal*, Paris, 1797, pp. 91–92.)

[3] *Discours et opinions de Cazalès*, Paris, 1821, p. 267.

to the vast majority whose opinions would decide the final outcome, was that they should study once more the lessons of Stuart history:

Choisissez; il en est temps encore: quelle renommée voulez-vous que l'histoire porte de vous à la postérité? Optez entre le crime ou la vertu, entre la folie ou la sagesse. . . .

N'allez pas partager la funeste sécurité des collègues de Cromwel. . . . Céderez-vous à la crainte? Laisserez-vous consommer le forfait qui répugne à votre cœur? Qu'y aurez-vous gagné? Il ne sera pas plutôt commis qu'il s'élèvera un homme audacieux qui brisera les instruments du crime dont il n'aura plus que les fruits à recueillir. Ouvrez l'histoire: n'est-ce pas là la marche de tous les usurpateurs? Ils ont besoin de complices pour arriver au suprême pouvoir; mais dès que leur main a saisi le sceptre, ils l'appesantissent sur ceux-là même à qui ils le doivent. . . . Prenez-y garde: l'homme dont je vous parle, vous le connaissez. . . .[1]

The warning about the dangers of a French 'Cromwell' formed, no doubt, the cleverest part of this particular attempt to save Louis XVI's life. De Montjoie was of course quite aware of the fact that the atmosphere in the Convention at this time was heavy with suspicion. Accusations and counter-accusations about hidden Cromwellian ambitions were being made with astonishing frequency. Two dangers seemed especially imminent: that of a Cromwell or that of a Monk. As one reads the Convention speeches from September 1792 to January 1793 one even senses, I think, that the national representatives viewed a Cromwell as not only the more likely threat but as also the more horrifying of the two possibilities. De Montjoie hammered in this point. If, he said, the members of the Convention lacked the courage to be just with Louis XVI, their fate within six weeks would be identical with that of the Cromwellian underlings who had sent Charles I to the scaffold.

A second major warning followed—this, too, taken from Hume's *History*:

Indépendamment de cette considération, votre intérêt de chacun de vous, vous défend un jugement inique. . . . Ce sang n'aurait pas plutôt coulé, que la France si longtemps incorporée avec son chef, jetterait un cri d'effroi et de douleur. Le repentir succéderait à l'injustice. L'amour

[1] *Avis à la Convention Nationale sur le jugement de Louis XVI*, Genève, 1793, pp. 6–7.

et la reconnaissance comprimés depuis trois ans réagiraient avec violence; toutes les consciences vous accuseraient, toutes les voix vous désigneraient, voilà, voilà, entendriez-vous crier à des milliers de Français, les assassins de Louis! On rappellerait ses vertus, ses bienfaits, sa longanimité, sa patience héroïque, sa douceur inaltérable au milieu des outrages dont vous l'avez laissé abreuver, au milieu des fers dont vous l'avez chargé. . . .

Votre assemblée dissoute, que deviendraient ses membres?. . . Permettez que j'ouvre encore à vos yeux les fastes de l'histoire, que je vous rappelle la fin déplorable de tous ceux qui, dans les temps passés, ont contribué à un jugement semblable à celui que sollicitent de vous les trop aveugles ennemis de Louis. . . . En Angleterre, les membres de la cour d'iniquité qui condamnèrent Charles Ier à l'échafaud, périrent dans l'opprobre et dans la misère. . . .

N'allez pas mériter le reproche de ne pas savoir profiter du passé, quand vous voyez renaître les mêmes symptômes, les mêmes crises, les mêmes phénomènes qui précédèrent la lamentable époque que l'Angleterre voudrait pouvoir effacer de ses annales.[1]

De Montjoie thus invoked the traditional lessons of history. He conveniently forgot them, however, when he came to the last piece of advice he had for the members of the Convention. They were not to fear, he said, that they had gone too far to reverse their course; they were not to fear that kings are unforgiving: 'La vengeance', he insisted, 'est une passion dont Louis ne connaît que le nom; . . . *On ne peut lui reprocher*, ainsi que le disait Bossuet de Charles premier, *qu'un excès de clémence*. . . .'[2]

It would be possible to analyse other less important defences of Louis XVI published at this time but the basic pattern of these is not materially different from those of Necker, Lally-Tollendal, Cazalès, or de Montjoie. It is in such pleas for the French king that we find the use of historical parallels attaining a peak of intensity, a note of political urgency, unequalled by the many Stuart parallels drawn before or after Louis' trial. The belief was expressed more and more by royalists in these last few months of the year 1792 that the two revolutions had run along on exactly parallel courses, that Louis XVI would never even have been brought to trial if one hundred and forty-three years earlier, the

[1] Ibid., pp. 9–12.

[2] Ibid., pp. 17–18. See also the *Oraison funèbre de Henriette-Marie de France, Reine de la Grande-Bretagne* (16 November 1669) in *Œuvres complètes de Bossuet*, Tours, 1862, I. 425.

English 'Jacobins' had not executed Charles I. One last eleventh-hour defence of Louis XVI which repeats this sentiment is worth quoting from: 'La marche des factieux d'Angleterre et celle des factieux qui désolent depuis si longtemps notre malheureuse patrie, est absolument la même, et s'il y a quelque différence, c'est que les révolutionnaires actuels ont surpassé en hypocrisie, en scélératesse et en tyrannie les assassins de l'infortuné Stuart.'[1]

3. Cromwell in the Convention: the judgement of posterity

The scores of published opinions emanating from the Convention during Louis XVI's trial and dealing with such questions as whether the King could be judged, how he should be judged and what should be his punishment are all quite heterogeneous in their various tendencies and difficult to group in a significant manner. One common element becomes apparent, however, to anyone who has taken the trouble of going through these opinions: the parallel between the English trial of Charles and the Convention trial of Louis haunted the minds of all but a minority of those who were destined to judge the French king.

Significantly even Mailhe's *Rapport et Projet de Décret*,[2] the Convention's official pre-trial report which formulated so many of the members' reactions in subsequent debates, could not avoid going into the legality of Charles I's parliamentary hearing. Mailhe's report was to conclude that Louis XVI could be judged by the Convention. The troublesome question of what legal forms to follow nevertheless remained. The English condemnation of Charles I was an obvious precedent; obvious too seemed the fact that history reproached the English for having violated legal forms:

Charles Stuart était inviolable comme Louis XVI: mais comme Louis XVI, il avait trahi la nation qui l'avait placé sur le trône. Indépendant de tous les corps établis par la constitution anglaise, il ne pouvait être accusé ni jugé par aucun d'eux; il ne pouvait l'être que par la nation. Lorsqu'il fut arrêté, la chambre des pairs était toute de son parti. Elle ne

[1] A.-J. Dugour, *Mémoire justificatif pour Louis XVI, ci-devant Roi des Français*, Paris, 1793, p. 123. (First published in parts, December 1792–January 1793.)

[2] . . . *présentés à la Convention Nationale, au nom du Comité de Législation*, 7 November 1792.

voulait que sauver le roi et le despotisme royal. La chambre des communes se saisit de l'exercice de toute l'autorité parlementaire; et sans doute elle en avait le droit dans les circonstances où elle se trouvait. Mais le parlement lui-même n'était qu'un corps constitué. Il ne représentait pas la nation dans la plénitude de sa souveraineté; il ne la représentait que pour des fonctions déterminées par la constitution. Il ne pouvait donc ni juger le roi, ni déléguer le droit de le juger.[1]

Although this interpretation of Charles I's trial is far from being Hume's, it is no less certain that Mailhe's inability to avoid dealing with the question altogether is something of a tribute to the successful penetration of the *History of the Stuarts* in France before 1789 and to the use made of Hume's work by the many defenders of the king and of the *ancien régime*, particularly after that date.

Mailhe's report goes on to show that if the English had taken the same precautions as the French, their republic would have survived. The English Commons should have invited the nation to form a convention parliament:

Malheureusement la chambre des communes était dirigée par le génie de Cromwel, et Cromwel, qui voulait devenir roi sous le nom de protecteur, aurait trouvé dans une Convention Nationale le tombeau de son ambition.

Ce n'est donc pas la violation des formes prescrites en Angleterre pour les jugements criminels, mais c'est le défaut d'un pouvoir national, c'est le protectorat de Cromwel, qui ont jeté sur le procès de Charles Stuart cet odieux qu'on trouve retracé dans les écrits les plus philosophiques. Charles Stuart méritait la mort; mais son supplice ne pouvait être ordonné que par la nation, ou par un tribunal choisi par elle.[2]

Many problems remained even though the Convention was seen as representing, in the words of the report, 'entièrement et parfaitement la république française'.[3] Could the Convention, for example, judge alone or should its judgement be ratified by all citizens in an *appel au peuple*? This question and others concerning the form of the king's punishment were to occupy the debates of that body and exasperate the impatient *robespierristes* for many weeks to come.

In examining the Convention speeches during Louis XVI's trial I shall try to classify my sampling of opinions according to three admittedly rather personal headings which relate to the

[1] Jean Mailhe, op. cit., p. 20. [2] Ibid., p. 21. [3] Ibid., p. 22.

speaker's apparent attitude toward history generally and, more particularly, toward Stuart history. My first grouping will include those whose attitudes imply a fundamental belief in the traditional cyclical view of revolution. It will include those who, speaking often of the lessons of history, closely identified the French and English revolutions. This same group emphasized the conservative implications of the parallel and was greatly concerned with the dangerous possibility that the execution of Louis XVI would automatically leave the way open for an ambitious French Cromwell. Those whom I speak of next comprise members of the Convention who, although they seem to believe to some extent in the ideological identity of the two revolutions as well as in the general value of history's lessons, rejected the validity of any parallels drawn between the two trials because the English court had been influenced by Cromwell whereas revolutionary France did not have and could not possibly have any such monster. Lastly, I have found it useful to classify in a third group those who made it quite clear that not only Stuart history but all of history was totally irrelevant to the deliberations, that no historical precedents were necessary, indeed that no trial was necessary, and that the sooner justice (*i.e.* decapitation) was carried out, the better.[1]

Fear of a 'circular' revolution ending inevitably with the usurpation of a Cromwell heads the list of reasons cited by the moderates of the first group and underlies their use of the Stuart parallel. The following opinions represent typical examples: 'Il n'est pas difficile peut-être de prouver, par l'expérience de tous les siècles, que la mort violente ou juridique d'un tyran n'a jamais servi véritablement la cause de la liberté, et n'a fait que placer la tyrannie dans d'autres mains.'—P. Marec. 'Je ne puis voter souverainement pour la mort de Louis XVI, parce que je ne puis transiger ni avec les principes ni avec ma conscience. . .; parce que j'abhorre la royauté beaucoup plus que les rois détrônés, parce que je vois, derrière le rideau, un Cromwel qui prépare à ma patrie le sort

[1] I must point out that I make no claim here to a systematic analysis of the divisions along traditional party lines of opinions expressed in the Convention during the trial. I am concerned only with a sampling of opinions in which the Stuart parallel was actually made whether in a positive or negative sense. I shall also make no distinctions between successive opinions delivered on different but related issues, e.g., on the advisability of judging Louis XVI, on the *appel au peuple*, on the king's guilt or on the form his punishment should take. With a few unavoidable exceptions, the quotations are taken from the original versions printed at the time of the trial by official order of the Convention). (B.N.Le37.2.G).

qu'éprouva l'Angleterre après la mort de Charles Stuart.'—F.-C.-P. Garilhe. 'Et qui nous garantit, citoyens, que quelque ambitieux, profitant de la confiance qu'il s'est acquise par sa popularité, ne saisira pas la conjoncture du jugement de Louis XVI, pour tenter quelque entreprise contre la liberté? Osez jurer qu'il n'existe point de Cromwels dans la République; et s'il en existe un seul, vous tracez la route à son ambition, en suivant celle du parlement d'Angleterre.'—J. Guiter. 'Je ne vois aucun Cromwel derrière la toile; mais il existe encore des hommes qui ont l'âme de Cromwel; et qui me répondra que des circonstances critiques ne sont pas favorables à la conception et au développement de projets liberticides?'—J.-B.-D. Mazade. 'Citoyens, écoutez l'histoire. . . . Considérez le sort du parlement qui fit juger Charles; il se livra à la passion de la vengeance, et oublia l'intérêt général; il ne fit point une constitution, et laissa périr la république. . . . Charles premier devait périr sur un échafaud, non parce qu'il fut très criminel, comme Louis, mais parce qu'il vécut dans un siècle de superstition, et qu'il fut jugé par la faction de l'usurpateur Cromwel, qui voulait régner à sa place.'—H. Bancal. 'Sur les débris fumants du trône de Charles Ier, Cromwel sut asseoir sa puissance; et le même peuple qui avait sollicité la mort de ce roi, s'attendrit sur sa destinée. Représentants du peuple, ne perdez pas de vue cet exemple.'—F. Buzot. 'Républicains trop confiants, prenez-y garde, ce fut une exception bien funeste à la liberté anglaise, que Cromwel! Et je vois trop que pour avoir son audace, on n'a pas besoin d'avoir son génie.'—J.-B. Louvet. 'La politique! ah! c'est dans l'histoire que nous aurions pu en puiser d'utiles leçons: . . . Jamais un peuple n'est plus près du despotisme que lorsqu'il est livré à l'anarchie, parce que, las d'avoir des milliers de maîtres, d'être tyran et tyrannisé, le peuple finit par se mettre sous la protection d'un seul. Lorsque Cromwel, caché derrière les agitateurs, . . .' &c.—J.-P. Rabaut.

There are many other opinions in the same vein. Let us look at one last example, that of Vergniaud:

Lorsque Cromwel, que l'on vous a déjà cité, voulut préparer la dissolution du parlement avec lequel il avait renversé le trône, et fait monter Charles Ier sur l'échafaud, il lui fit des propositions insidieuses. . . . Le parlement céda. Bientôt la fermentation fut générale; et Cromwel brisa sans effort l'instrument dont il s'était servi pour arriver à la suprême puissance.

N'avez-vous pas entendu dans cette enceinte, et ailleurs, des hommes crier avec fureur: si le pain est cher, la cause en est au Temple; si le numéraire est rare, si vos armées sont mal approvisionnées, la cause en est au Temple; si nous avons à souffrir chaque jour du spectacle de l'indigence, la cause en est au Temple.

Ceux qui tiennent ce langage n'ignorent pas cependant que la cherté du pain, le défaut de circulation dans les subsistances, la mauvaise administration dans les armées, et l'indigence dont le spectacle nous afflige, tiennent à d'autres causes que celle du Temple. . . . Qui me garantira . . . que ces mêmes hommes ne crieront pas après la mort de Louis, avec la plus grande violence: si le pain est cher, la cause en est dans la Convention. . . .[1]

Inspired by the Stuart parallel, other moderates added the fear of history's condemnation to their fear of a Cromwell. Mennesson warns of 'l'opinion qui poursuit encore le parlement d'Angleterre de 1648' and adds: 'L'arrêt de la postérité! . . . Législateurs, réfléchissez à ce mot: car un jour aussi vous comparaîtrez devant elle . . .: rappelez-vous, ô mes collègues! rappelez-vous toutes ces voix conjurées qui, pour hâter votre ruine et leur triomphe, vous demandaient par acclamation la tête du tyran sans l'avoir entendu. . . . Ils savent bien que si Brutus, ce modèle des Républicains n'affranchit son pays qu'en expulsant les Tarquins; Cromwel, ce modèle des usurpateurs, réussit à élever un trône sur la tombe des Stuarts.'

P.-F. Louvet too refers to 'une opinion qui, après un siècle et demi, poursuit encore le parlement d'Angleterre de 1648'. It was not, as Mailhe had attempted to prove, because the English parliament had lacked the powers of the Convention that posterity judged it guilty but rather because Charles I's trial had, in every respect, been illegally conducted: 'Jugez maintenant', Louvet continued, 'si vous, à qui on propose d'aller plus loin que le parlement d'Angleterre, puisqu'on vous propose de juger directement vous-mêmes, et de supprimer les témoins, ce que du moins on ne fit pas dans le procès de Charles Stuart; jugez, dis-je, si en admettant la mesure du comité, vous ne devriez pas ensuite vous attendre à une censure plus sévère encore que celle portée sur le parlement d'Angleterre.'

Also objecting that the members of the Convention should not

[1] Vergniaud's final vote despite these high-minded sentiments seemed, in the end, contradictory and disappointing to moderates: although in favour of the *appel au peuple* he later voted for the death-sentence and against the *sursis*.

be Louis' accusers, judges, and executioners, all rolled into one, Antoine Girard expressed the concerned belief that a loss of international esteem was as much to be feared as the judgement of posterity: '. . . les Anglais eurent sans doute raison quant au fond du procès mais le mode illégal et le tribunal monstrueux qui servit de contexture à la cause de ce grand coupable, affaiblirent l'estime des peuples étrangers qui avaient des relations commerciales ou politiques avec l'Angleterre. . . .' Even Brissot, who had evolved somewhat since his debate with Clermont-Tonnerre ('le Brissot de 1791 n'est pas le Brissot de 1793' as J. Pinet *aîné* scornfully informed the Convention), now warned that the European powers would ask for nothing better than Louis' execution 'parce qu'elle leur semble un garant de la résurrection de la royauté; parce que la mort de Charles Ier a valu le cœur de ses sujets et le trône à son fils. . . . Oui, Citoyens, la même comédie qui s'est jouée en Angleterre lors de la mort de Charles Ier, s'est encore jouée de nos jours. Alors le cabinet de France avait l'air d'intercéder, et il payait les Cromwellistes qui le mirent à mort.' Perhaps even, Brissot concluded, the sinister politics of the English cabinet was behind the bloodthirsty cries of the Paris *cannibales*.

Not infrequently mentioned also by those who during the trial debate cited the lessons of Stuart history was the question of a dangerous popular reaction to the King's execution. The Convention was not, of course, excessively concerned with the number of simple women who might, as Hume suggests, cast forth the untimely fruit of their womb or, more simply still, fall down dead on hearing the fatal news. It was, on the other hand, very much concerned with the possible effects of pity which might prepare the way in France for a restoration of the monarchy. To the hearty guffaws of the assembled members, one earnest *conventionnel* even suggested the possible danger that Rome might canonize Louis. The following opinion by A.-G. Kersaint clearly shows that Necker's quotation of Hume on the subject was not lost on all of Louis' judges:

> . . . les vrais républicains redoutent avec raison la réaction des sentiments de la vengeance qu'on voudrait exercer sur des personnes longtemps respectées; ils redoutent cette pitié, qui, par la pente naturelle du cœur humain, s'attache aux malheureux et particulièrement à ceux que leur destinée semblait appeler au faîte du bonheur, et qu'une grande infortune accable. Ce mot profond et cette remarque si judicieuse,

Charles Ier eut des successeurs, les Tarquins n'en eurent point, les ont déterminés dans l'adoption d'un parti modéré. . . .

The same danger seemed equally evident to J.-J. Thomas:

Monk n'eût jamais trouvé tant de bras pour l'aider à faire remonter Charles II sur le trône d'Angleterre, s'il n'eût pas été secondé par le souvenir du supplice de son père. Craignez pour le dehors et le dedans les terribles effets de la commisération et de la pitié. . . . Avez-vous jamais vu le peuple revenir d'une exécution, sans plaindre le coupable? Et cependant l'idée de ses crimes était encore présente. . . . Le mépris, la nullité, l'oubli de l'individu, voilà ce qui peut sauver la patrie. . . .

Agreeing with Kersaint and Thomas, J.-B. Girot added his own corresponding sentiments on the matter: 'La mort de Charles fit une plaie profonde à la liberté; elle fit cesser la haine que ses crimes avaient inspirée. Elle laissa des regrets; elle fit revivre chez cette nation le fanatisme de la royauté qui s'y soutient encore et qui corrompt en elle le sentiment de la liberté.' Thomas Paine's opinion, the reading of which was objected to by Marat on the grounds that a Quaker should not be allowed to vote in a case involving the death penalty, pointed out essentially the same warning: the Stuarts returned to the throne of England after Charles I's *execution* but fell into obscurity after the *banishment* of James II. P.-J. Faure concurred with the American Quaker: 'La mort de Charles premier fut la principale cause de la restauration de la royauté chez un peuple trop éclairé pour aimer les rois. Le supplice du père plaida la cause du fils. Le peuple quelquefois se livre à des mouvements de sensibilité contraires à ses intérêts, et dont on ne peut calculer l'explosion et le délire. A la révolution de Jacques II qui avait aussi un fils, on prit d'autres mesures; on facilita son évasion, et son fils fit de vains efforts pour recouvrer son trône. C'est précisément là votre position. . . .'

Many other *conventionnels* appealed in their opinions to the lessons of the Stuart parallel.[1] Not all drew from it the same conclusions but they nearly all agreed on the similar goals of the two revolutions. Charles-Antoine Chasset, for example, insisted particularly on this last point: 'Et qu'on ne dise pas que les Anglais d'alors manquaient de lumières; ne nous y trompons pas,

[1] See also, for example, the opinions of Bailly, Baudin, Birotteau, Bodin, Bordas, Chasset, Guyomar, Lambert, Marey, Meynard, Morisson, Prunelle, and Riffard St. Martin.

ils connaissaient très bien les principes du gouvernement. On voit dans leur histoire qu'ils renversèrent le trône, et fondèrent une république, éphémère il est vrai, d'après les mêmes maximes que nous.' Like Chasset most of the speakers we have been referring to were, of course, sincere republicans. It is nevertheless important to note that they held at the same time a view of history not too inconsistent with that which had prevailed among traditionalists during the *ancien régime* and which had allowed Hume's account of the reign of Charles I to become an almost integral part of French historical culture. A Hume, republican in practice as well as in principle and viewing the French revolution at this stage of its development, would probably have found little to object to in the following passage drawn from the opinion of J.-F. Barailon:

Il me semble, tout considéré, que la prudence, la prévoyance, la saine politique nous commande de différer, d'éloigner ce fatal jugement, d'amender notre système politique actuel, de corriger, de surseoir, même d'abandonner notre prétendu *pouvoir révolutionnaire*. . . .

Nous ne voulons pas, comme les Anglais, n'avoir fondé une république que pour quelques minutes; à un Charles Stuart, faire succéder un Cromwel; à un despote, substituer un tyran; donner occasion à des proscriptions innombrables, faire ruisseler encore le sang, et favoriser de nouveaux massacres. . . .

La division qui règne et s'accroît, à mesure que l'on approche de l'époque de ce jugement, sollicite vivement notre attention, et nous conseille en outre de grands ménagements. La précipitation des Anglais, leur irréflexion dans l'affaire de Charles Stuart, eurent des suites bien terribles, l'anéantissement de leur république, la perte de leur liberté et le supplice des juges qui avaient été assez lâches pour se prêter à des insinuations perfides, et assez stupides pour seconder l'ambition d'un scélérat.

4. The parallel rejected: Brutus to the rescue

Let us turn now to what we have arbitrarily set aside as a second group and consider those members of the Convention who, although they seem to hold a view of history not altogether incompatible with that of the group whose opinions we have just examined, maintained nevertheless that the much-quoted parallel with the seventeenth-century revolution in England was entirely invalid.

We find a good example of this attitude in the opinion of Sergent, one of the *députés* for Paris. He expresses utter amazement and disbelief at the hesitations of his colleagues who adduced parallels and who warned the Convention of great lessons to be drawn from the English experiment:

Que craignez-vous? l'exemple de l'Angleterre immolant Charles Stuart! Mais on vous l'a dit, Charles fut sacrifié à l'ambition de Cromwel; et Louis sera conduit à la mort par ses perfidies; Charles fut jugé par une commission choisie par l'usurpateur lui-même, et vous, vous êtes choisis par le Peuple qui accuse Louis. Charles n'eut point de défenseurs auprès de ses juges, et Louis en a trouvé même parmi nous. . . . Tant mieux, notre jugement en sera moins suspect, et plus irréprochable. Enfin, la mort de Charles fut la honte du peuple anglais, dit-on. Et qui nous l'a appris? l'Histoire! Mais l'Histoire est-elle donc écrite de la main d'une divinité inaccessible à la crainte. Non, l'histoire de la fin de Charles fut écrite par des HOMMES; à côté d'eux étaient des BASTILLES. Il fallait en imposer aux races futures, ou expirer dans un cachot obscur. Les Rois tourmentaient la pensée jusque sous l'humble toit du philosophe qui croyait être seul avec ce qu'il y a de plus sublime, la Nature et son âme. Les temps ont changé, ce sont des hommes libres, débarrassés du fardeau des Rois, qui ont gravé sur le marbre les événements qui étonneront la postérité.

Philippeaux also questioned the veracity of certain histories of the English revolution which seemed to have impressed too vividly the imagination of 'quelques trembleurs' in the Convention:

. . . la tradition conservée sur cette grande époque, a reçu une teinte odieuse par l'étude constante des rois et de leurs valets à la représenter comme un attentat coupable pour se préserver du même sort. Dans un état monarchique, toutes les affections se dirigent vers l'idolâtrie; l'échafaudage du trône est un composé d'illusions et de prestiges. Tous ceux qui ont intérêt à le maintenir et qui ont en leur pouvoir tous les ressorts de la morale publique, ne pouvaient manquer de faire prendre à la longue un sentiment d'horreur pour l'acte de justice qui leur déplaisait le plus. Mais nous autres républicains, qui avons jugé la tyrannie avant de juger le tyran, notre situation est toute différente: les masques ni les fantômes n'auront plus le droit d'effaroucher notre imagination: il n'y a plus que la laideur du crime et son impunité qui puissent nous contrister l'âme.

Several *conventionnels*, moreover, were not long in pointing out that not all historians of the Stuart reign preached the usual servile principles. The myth of a guilty English nation was nothing more than the *après coup* fabrication of fawning historians since the Restoration, affirmed Michel Azéma:

. . . le déshonneur prétendu de l'Angleterre n'a été que l'effet des préjugés, de l'erreur, de l'aveuglement des peuples, surtout du peuple français, bon, généreux, franc et loyal, idolâtre de ses rois, pour si peu qu'ils le méritassent; . . . la plupart des historiens, des auteurs, des savants contemporains de cet événement, bien loin d'en humilier l'Angleterre, la louent au contraire de son énergie, de son courage, de sa justice, surtout Milton, auteur du *Paradis perdu*, et plusieurs autres.

Depuis que la révolution des bons esprits s'est faite presque partout, que la philosophie et la raison éclairent partout les hommes, les idées premières de préjugé qu'on s'était faites sur la mort tragique de Charles Stuart premier, soigneusement et politiquement nourries et entretenues par tous les despotes, sont totalement changées.[1]

The view that no Cromwell existed or could exist in France formed the basis of most rejections of the Stuart parallel. We find this judgement summed up briefly in the opinion of Nicolas Hentz:

On vous a fait craindre des regrets; on a cité le procès de Charles Stuart pour exemple.

Ecoutez-moi, et je vais bien vous faire voir que notre position est toute différente. Qui est-ce qui a poursuivi la mort de Charles Stuart? C'était un homme qui aspirait au trône, et qui avait tous les moyens d'y parvenir; . . . Il a réussi, et il a usurpé la royauté en Angleterre. Remarquez qu'il y avait toujours une royauté en Angleterre, et qu'il n'y en a plus chez nous.

Dubois-Crancé felt provoked to indignation on the same subject:

Quelle comparaison! Sommes-nous donc des usurpateurs? Le peuple ne connaissait-il pas la mission que nous tenons de lui? N'avons-nous pas juré de le venger et de lui obéir? Avons-nous choisi parmi nous une commission extraordinaire vendue à un conspirateur pour faire tomber la tête de son ennemi? Est-ce enfin la volonté d'un homme qui nous commande, ou le sentiment d'une vengeance légitime et du besoin pressant de 25 millions d'individus opprimés? S'il existait un Cromwel en France, vous l'avez décrété, sa tête appartient au dernier des citoyens; et pour la faire tomber, il ne faut pas être un Brutus. Ne déshonorons

[1] Rühl makes the same point and adds that in Milton's work the Convention would find 'de fortes raisons pour condamner Louis XVI'; see also the opinion of François-Simon Bezard.

donc pas nos augustes fonctions par une comparaison qu'il n'appartient de faire qu'aux Brunswicks et aux Condés.

Directly refuting Vergniaud, Claude-Nicolas Guillermin also could see no rhyme or reason to the parallel:

J'avoue que je suis fort embarrassé pour faire une application de l'exemple. J'ai beau chercher un *Cromwel* dans notre Révolution, je n'en vois pas, c'est à dire je ne vois dans aucun Français ni sa popularité bien établie dans les armées et dans le Peuple entier (car il ne peut s'agir de celui de Paris, qui n'est qu'une Section). Je ne vois dans aucun Français ni cette confiance universelle qu'avait obtenue *Cromwel*, ni ses moyens puissants, ni ses vertus séductrices, ni ses talents militaires, ni ses connaissances politiques, ni son courage, ni son adresse, ni ses vices mêmes, qui ont été autant d'échelons pour monter sur le trône dont il avait renversé Charles.

Mais en revanche je vois beaucoup de *Brutus* pour un *Cromwel* s'il pouvait en exister un ténébreux.

Brutus of course! Here was the answer to all rascally Cromwells! Also claimed, but feebly, by the Right as the patron of all those who defended the ancient constitution against revolutionary usurpers,[1] Brutus was a hero the details of whose career[2] were sufficiently obscured by antiquity to permit his serving as an unassailable example to true republicans when even Sidney, the martyr to Liberty, had to be cast off because he was English.[3] Only his bust and that of Rousseau survived throughout the years of progressive iconoclasm at the Jacobins, and it was his again that dominated the chair of the president of the Convention. No revolutionary hair style, not even that of the Round Heads, ever equalled in fashion the *coiffure à la Brutus*.

Brutus is also Louchet's answer to the threat of a Cromwell: 'Eh! quel homme serait assez insensé pour tenter de se ressaisir de l'autorité royale en France, après qu'il aurait vu tomber sous le glaive de la loi la tête du tyran. Ah! si un tel homme pouvait exister, le faubourg Saint-Antoine est là; il est dans toute la République; la terre de la liberté et de l'égalité . . . n'enfanterait-elle pas aussitôt mille Brutus, qui se disputeraient l'honneur de

[1] See the Comte d'Antraigue's *Adresse à l'ordre de la noblesse de France*, Paris, 1792, pp. 124–35.

[2] Revolutionary orators did not always distinguish between the earlier and the later Brutus.

[3] See *La Décade*, 20 December 1794, III. 543.

porter les premiers coups à ce nouveau Cromwel?' Moïse Bayle was of the same confident opinion: 'N'avez-vous pas décrété', he asked, 'que tout homme qui parlerait d'un roi[1] serait puni de mort? Craindriez-vous que ce décret ne fût pas exécuté, et qu'il n'y eût pas en France un seul Brutus?'

It is in the opinion of Claude-Charles Prost that we find this position most clearly summarized:

Rejetons toute comparaison du jugement de Charles Stuart avec celui de Louis, les données et les résultats ne sont nécessairement pas les mêmes; Charles fut un tyran, mais il fut condamné par des juges qui s'attribuèrent une autorité qu'ils ne tenaient pas de la nation, et votre mission est expresse: Charles fut la victime d'un ambitieux hypocrite; nous n'avons point de Cromwel dans le parlement républicain, et j'y vois plus d'un *Brutus*. La mort de Charles ne fut d'aucune utilité pour la liberté du peuple, la noblesse avait survécu au monarque, et partout où existera cette plante parasite, on doit voir repousser la plante vénéneuse d'un roi ou d'un oppresseur sous un autre nom.[2]

The political image of Cromwell in France during the last three hundred years would provide the basis of a long and interesting study. One fact would emerge certainly from such an investigation with respect to the Convention period, namely, that few revolutionaries[3] found it either in their conscience or in their political interests to express anything but the greatest horror for the leader of the English revolution. The sub-title of M.-L. Tardy's tragedy of 1793, *Cromwel ou le général liberticide*, typically sums up the current attitude although, as we have already noted, the Puritan general had been occasionally viewed as a hero by a few *avant-garde* thinkers before the Revolution. Robespierre frequently defended himself against the accusations of Jean-Baptiste Louvet and others who charged him with harbouring the malign ambitions of a Cromwell. Danton, interrupted in a speech of 1 April 1793 by the cry 'Et Cromwel? . . .', furiously demanded, to the wild applause of his supporters, that the 'vil scélérat qui a eu l'impudeur de dire que je suis un Cromwel soit puni, qu'il soit traduit à

[1] It must be conceded that the modest Bonaparte used only the word *empereur*.

[2] See also the opinions of Baudot, Cledel, Deleyre, Guyton, and Gertoux: the last refers to Louis XVI as 'le Stuart français'.

[3] One might possibly except such men as Deleyre and Jean-Bon Saint-André, perhaps even Saint-Just who, it is worth noting, possessed in his small collection of books a biography of the Protector. (See Bapst, op. cit., *La Révolution Française*, XXI. 535.)

l'Abbaye'.[1] After the Terror, the Convention found it wise to decree a *mention honorable* for Dugour's *Histoire de Cromwel* of 1795 and added the recommendation that the work be referred to the Comité d'Instruction Publique.[2] The *Moniteur* commented with a sigh of relief on 1 May 1795 that Dugour's book could not have been published at a more opportune time: 'C'est dans la conduite de ce tyran', it added, 'que nos derniers oppresseurs avaient puisé les moyens de nous ramener à l'esclavage. En lisant sa vie on retrouvera le même système d'oppression combiné presque de la même manière, on croira parcourir l'histoire du temps présent; les ressemblances sont même si frappantes, qu'on serait tenté de soupçonner la véracité de l'historien, si tout ce qu'il raconte n'était consigné dans les mémoires des auteurs contemporains.'[3] Later still the parallel was frequently applied, perhaps with greater accuracy, to Bonaparte. But no matter which circumstance or which party is involved, the image of the Protector remains constant: Cromwell was as ostensibly *odieux* in 1793 in the Convention as he was in Louis XVI's marginal notes of 1779.[4] A *hero* of any kind was feared and a Cromwell was feared perhaps most of all; for, to transpose a sentiment already expressed by a zealous English republican in 1649, if a king was desired, the last was perhaps as proper as any gentleman in France.

5. *Principles versus precedents*

Finally, let us consider those *conventionnels* whose opinions concerning the relevance of history, expressed during the trial of Louis XVI, permit us to classify them as a third group. These last were, of course, no less politically earnest than the others but they showed a greater amount of impatience to get on with a revolution which had, in their view, vertically outgrown history and which was to lead the French nation to unprecedented heights of virtue and justice. For these true radicals, the Revolution had

[1] *Œuvres de Danton*, ed. Vermorel, Paris, 1866, p. 188.

[2] See *La Décade*, An III, V. 174.

[3] *Gazette Nationale, ou le Moniteur universel*, No. 222, p. 902. See also *Journal de Paris*, No. 202, 11 April 1797.

[4] See also Alexandre Tuetey, *Répertoire général des sources manuscrites de l'histoire de Paris pendant la Révolution française*, IV, Nos. 1,125, 3,342, 3,458, 3,643; VIII, No. 1,403; X, No. 2,102; XI, No. 28.

rendered the old interpretation of history and all of the cyclical parallels meaningless.

Admittedly, some of the Convention parallel-makers had been infuriatingly didactic; Birotteau's triple comparison provides us with a good example: 'Stuart mourut sur l'échafaud, et l'Angleterre eut encore des rois. Rome au contraire, chassa les Tarquins, et Rome fut la république la plus tranquille et la plus florissante; et enfin Denis le Tyran, maître d'école à Corinthe, ne vit plus de nouveaux tyrans lui succéder à Syracuse.'

For our third group this was too much! We are told that as the sober Birotteau prepared to leave the tribune the mocking voice of Jullien was heard to shout: 'Mention honorable!'[1]

To many, such parallels seemed indeed a practice more suited to the pretensions of over-eager schoolboys than to the leaders of the world's greatest revolution. Mont-Gilbert boasts that his opinion will be unusual, that he will quote no obsolete authorities from history:

> Qu'y a-t-il de commun . . . entre les Français libres et les satellites de Cromwel? Cette manie de chercher les comparaisons sonores est indigne de nous.
>
> Je le dis hardiment (que cette dernière réflexion me soit pardonnée) je ne verrai pas cette assemblée dans toute sa majesté, tant que, entre autres réformes, nous n'aurons pas fait celle d'une importune érudition qui, pour nous rendre grands et vertueux, va nous déterrer des modèles jusque dans les ruines d'Athènes et de Sparte. Malheur à nous, si, pour faire de grandes choses, nous avons besoin d'être encouragés par de grands exemples! Et qu'elles sont faibles, ces vertus d'imitation qui n'ont pas leur force dans le caractère moral de ceux qui les professent!

If at all costs Louis' judges wanted to imitate a virtue of the past, let it be, added Mont-Gilbert, the laconism of the Spartans.

The familiar idealist's cry of principles not precedents was heard also from several other members: 'Qu'importe', asked Ichon, 'que l'Angleterre ait jugé Stuart! . . . De pareils rapprochements pour asseoir les droits des peuples contre les rois sont des attentats commis contre la majesté nationale. C'est dans la nature même de l'organisation sociale, c'est dans les principes d'inaltérable justice, c'est dans le code des droits sacrés des peuples, qu'il faut puiser . . . le pouvoir de juger un roi. . . .'

[1] See *Journal des débats et des décrets*, No. 102, 29 December 1792.

Bernard Descamps, attacking Rabaut's Stuart-parallel, made a similar objection: 'J'observerai qu'il est très facile de faire des rapprochements, et que c'est le moyen le plus propre à nous conduire à l'erreur. Mais il s'agit ici moins de ce qui a été, que de ce qui doit être.' What *must be*, he continued, does not depend on the bug-bears of history: 'On est venu montrer la tête sanglante de Charles Ier, et la Convention Nationale de France a été comparée en quelque sorte aux bourreaux de Cromwel; on est venu enfin vous parler, non de justice, mais de politique; non de devoir, mais de responsabilité.'

Moderate appeals to the allegedly prudent lessons of history were nothing more than ill-disguised counter-revolutionary delaying tactics in the opinion of Marc-Antoine Jullien:

Pour justifier les mesures lentes et compliquées que l'on vous propose, on a cité le procès de Charles Stuart, et on vous a dit que c'était faute de les avoir prises, que la nation anglaise avait encouru le blâme des écrivains les plus philosophes. Détrompez-vous, citoyens, et ne prenez pas ce prétexte pour une raison. Si les Anglais, au lieu de tronquer et de raccourcir le sceptre des rois, l'eussent, à votre exemple, brisé et fondu; si le gouvernement qu'ils se donnèrent eût été purement républicain, et si l'histoire de leur révolution n'eût été écrite que par des républicains, croyez qu'il ne serait pas venu dans l'esprit de personne de blâmer la manière dont ils avaient jugé le tyran. Aux yeux d'un vrai républicain, toutes les formes sont bonnes pour détruire les usurpateurs de la souveraineté des nations; mais la meilleure, à leur gré, c'est la plus courte, c'est celle des Scaevola et des Brutus. Ou votre république se maintiendra, et, dans ce cas, l'horreur que doit inspirer la mémoire de votre dernier roi, sera retracée dans tous les écrits; ou la monarchie ressuscitera, et alors, de quelques formalités que vous ayez revêtu le jugement de Louis XVI, de vils esclaves de cours sauront bien flétrir votre gloire, déshonorer vos vertus, et, pour flatter de nouveaux tyrans, vous présenter à la postérité sous les traits odieux des plus sacrilèges régicides. Hâtez-vous donc de trancher avec le glaive une question qui nous a déjà trop longtemps occupés, et, pour fonder une république éternelle, cimentez-la, sans balancer, du sang d'un roi parjure, et ne craignez pas que son supplice vous soit jamais imputé un crime.

Des philosophes qui veulent établir de savantes théories, des orateurs qui veulent composer de sublimes harangues, ont un intérêt d'orgueil à vous persuader que cette cause est difficile et grande. Détournez vos regards de tous ces flambeaux ténébreux et, suivant avec moi la simple et pure lumière de la raison, vous verrez qu'il n'y eut jamais de question plus facile à résoudre.

There are obviously no tiresome schoolboy pretensions in Jullien's opinion, any more than in the following one by Robespierre which probably served as Jullien's model:

L'Assemblée a été entraînée, à son insu, loin de la véritable question. Il n'y a point ici de procès à faire. . . . Proposer de faire le procès à Louis XVI, de quelque manière que ce puisse être, c'est rétrograder vers le despotisme royal et constitutionnel; c'est une idée contre-révolutionnaire, car c'est mettre la révolution elle-même en litige. . . .

Les peuples ne jugent pas comme les cours judiciaires; il ne rendent point de sentences, ils lancent la foudre; ils ne condamnent pas les rois, ils les replongent dans le néant: et cette justice vaut bien celle des tribunaux. . . .

Nous nous sommes laissés induire en erreur par des exemples étrangers qui n'ont rien de commun avec nous. Que Cromwel ait fait juger Charles Ier par une commission judiciaire dont il disposait . . . il est naturel que des tyrans qui immolent leurs pareils, non au peuple, mais à leur ambition, cherchent à tromper l'opinion du vulgaire par des formes illusoires: il n'est question là ni de principes, ni de liberté, mais de fourberie et d'intrigue. Mais le peuple, quelle autre loi peut-il suivre que la justice et la raison appuyées de sa toute-puissance? . . .

Pour moi je rougirais de discuter plus sérieusement ces arguties constitutionnelles; je les relègue sur les bancs de l'école ou du palais, ou plutôt dans les cabinets de Londres, de Vienne et de Berlin. Je ne sais point discuter longuement où je suis convaincu que c'est un scandale de délibérer.

C'est une grande cause, a-t-on dit, et qu'il faut juger avec une sage et lente circonspection. C'est vous qui en faites une grande cause: que dis-je? C'est vous qui en faites une cause. . . .

Louis had to die so that the nation might live—such was Robespierre's conclusion. Saint-Just was equally frank: 'On s'étonnera un jour', he exclaimed, 'qu'au dix-huitième siècle, on ait été moins avancé que du temps de César: là le tyran fut immolé en plein Sénat, sans autres formalités que trente coups de poignard. . . .' One is not obliged to cite legal or historical precedent to prove that kings are guilty. Kings are guilty by definition. All formalities to prove this guilt are vain. Every king is a rebel and a usurper. In Saint-Just's words: '*On ne peut régner innocemment. . . .*'

Quite obviously it would be a fruitless task to search for the influence of Stuart history in these last opinions. One is almost tempted to say that the influence of historical precedent is completely absent for, with these men, the Revolution seemed at last to have outgrown all history.

If, however, one detects no influence, one at least senses in the words of Robespierre and his supporters a quite intense and highly revealing mood of exasperation. The debate over the wisdom of the Long Parliament in judging Charles I had gone on a very long time, far too long in the opinion of these men who wished to make haste. If at worst the question of the Stuart parallel and the closely related issue concerning the *appel au peuple* represented nothing more than a clever device invented by those moderates who wished to save the king's life (and I believe it was much more than that), it clearly was a question on which a high proportion of members felt urged to speak or publish[1] their sentiments.

The seventeenth-century revolution in England had provided the only really significant modern European precedent to the French revolution. How, so many *conventionnels* felt obliged to ask, did this precedent affect the new French Republic? What lessons could be learned from it? Hume, through his long established positive influence on conservative thinking up until the time of the trial and through his specific impact on the writings of the king's chief apologists, had generated an important and not always totally negative reaction among Louis' judges. The Mailhe report and the many 'Stuart' opinions delivered during the trial can be interpreted to a substantial extent as bearing witness to the intensity of this reaction. Many in the Convention were apparently willing to admit that there existed an ideological relationship between the events in England and those in France. But they were obliged to admit also that the English revolution had ended in counter-revolution and, finally, in the restoration of the monarchy. What course of action would best prevent the occurrence of a similar failure a century and a half later?

As it turned out, of course, the bloody spectre of Charles I was not enough to save Louis XVI from the guillotine. It is true, nevertheless, that this spectre remained to haunt even those who pretended to feel only contempt for it. The symbols of Stuart history continued to present a threat of potential counter-revolution to France's revolutionary leaders. The following incident, recorded during the Reign of Terror, though trivial in itself, is

[1] After a time there were so many opinions that they could not all be delivered orally.

sufficient, I think, to illustrate this point. Late in December 1793, a certain Amable-Augustin Clément, clock-maker by profession and living in the rue Montmartre, was condemned to death by the revolutionary tribunal. He had been denounced as an aristocrat and partisan of Lafayette, charged with having wickedly and intentionally fired on the patriots during the day of 17 July 1791, and also with having voiced counter-revolutionary sentiments tending to restore the monarchy. Part of the damning evidence heard by the examining judge Etienne Foucault, two weeks before sentence, was to the effect that the accused had admitted having in his possession several *gravures*: notably a picture of Charlotte Corday and another of the execution of Charles I of England.[1]

[1] See Alexandre Tuetey, op. cit., IX. 293–4.

V

THE AFTERMATH

1. Republican qualms

THE counter-revolutionary use of Hume's *History of the Stuarts* as a bible of unshakeable prophecies, complacently illustrating the irrationalism and ineradicable sins of human nature, the implacable 'force of things', and the inevitable failure of all revolutions, continued with perhaps even greater intensity in the last five years of the century. Disheartening to some revolutionists too was the fact that political events as they progressed seemed to lend a new respectability to the fashionable science of historical analogies as more and more of the royalist predictions were, in appearance at least, fulfilled.

On the whole, however, few republicans showed signs of discouragement. Although leaders of the Right flattered themselves with the hope of restoration and pointed again and again to the failure of the English republican experiment, those on the Left, now publishing parallels of their own, staunchly denied the validity of such royalist hopes.

Much of this republican optimism seems to have been based on the belief that the established church, acknowledged as the throne's chief support, was now gone forever. Such, for example, is the opinion of Jean-Jacques Leuliette writing in 1797: '. . . s'il m'était permis de hasarder mon opinion, je dirais que le retour de la royauté est impossible en France, que ses fondements sont renversés, que si ce colosse pouvait se relever un jour, semblable à la statue de Nabuchodonosor, son trône ne serait appuyé que sur des pieds d'argile. Jacques Stuart dit un mot profond: point d'église, point de monarchie. Qu'on ne pense pas que l'empire de la superstition se rétablisse si facilement. . . .'[1]

Republicans were generally confident on this last point too. Neither the Church nor the Monarchy could ever return to power. Also writing in 1797, the *idéologue* Roederer explained just why

[1] *Des Emigrés Français ou Réponse à M. de Lally-Tollendal*, Paris, 1797, pp. 104–5.

there was no need to fear a religious revival. His reasons, given only a few years before the appearance of the *Génie du Christianisme* and the ratification of the Concordat, are worth noting and invite certain reflections on the advantages held, temporarily at least, by the empirical conservatives of the opposing camp who spoke so lovingly of the inertia in the nature of things and who went on making their hopeful historical parallels:

Savez-vous qu'il y a en France deux millions d'exemplaires d'Helvétius, de Voltaire, de Rousseau, de Montesquieu, et que tous les jours il se lit au moins cent mille pages de philosophie en France? Ne pensez-vous pas qu'il serait difficile de détruire tout à fait la puissance de ces hommes-là, leurs ouvrages n'eussent-ils que l'avantage d'être une partie du mobilier d'une foule de gens? Nul ne veut qu'on dégrade le meuble dont il se sert, ou dont il orne sa chambre. Croyez que le vélin, le maroquin, la dorure de nos Montesquieu et de nos Voltaire, sont un poids dans notre balance. Demandez aux anciens avocats qui ont vu avec tant de regret tomber les plus mauvaises lois, s'ils n'y tenaient pas un peu à cause de leur bibliothèque?[1]

Confidence in the future of the new Republic and the reasoned hope that it would consolidate its forces now that the days of anarchy were over thus seem to have been the prevailing attitude on the Left at this time. Some republicans, however, despite such assurances, did in fact worry about the Stuart parallels. Typically concerned was Antoine Boulay de la Meurthe, a member of the Conseil des Cinq-Cents who in December 1797 became president of the Assembly. Although Boulay had himself narrowly escaped the Terror, he became in this post-Terror period a strong advocate of harsher measures against refractory priests and against members of the nobility who had not emigrated. Such measures are best described as indicative of his own pronounced fears of a counter-revolution. At his suggestion even, a special promise not to aid in attempts to restore the monarchy was added to the oath of civil officers at this time.

[1] *Journal d'économie politique, de morale, et de politique; rédigé par Roederer de l'Institut national de France*, Paris, 1797, II. 370. It is curious to note that Montesquieu's conservatism, although it was often attacked during the Revolution, was also very often 'explained away' as representing nothing more than the exoteric principles of a basically radical but prudent political thinker who was obliged to use the subterfuge of a double doctrine under the oppression of the *ancien régime*. See, for example, Destutt de Tracy, *M. de Tracy à M. Burke*, p. 9; *La Décade*, 1795, V. 468; Brissot, *Le Patriote Français*, No. 915, 11 February 1792, pp. 167–8; Thomas Paine, *The Rights of Man*, 1791, Part I, p. 75.

It can safely be said, I think, that much of Boulay's preoccupation with the dangers of a counter-revolution came to him from his study of Stuart history.

The English republic had not survived because, obviously, the English had made mistakes. But what were those English mistakes? As an answer to this question, Boulay published in 1798 his popular essay showing the causes of failure in the English revolution.[1]

The basic implication of Boulay's work is that the art of revolution is a difficult one—more difficult certainly than was admitted by those who had nursed France's great social experiment through its earliest years. The English had faced the same original problem. They too had overthrown the monarchy in hopes of destroying despotism: 'Une des causes les plus immédiates de cette révolution, fut le despotisme royal, élevé fort haut par les princes de la maison de Tudor, et imprudemment soutenu par ceux de la maison de Stuart qui lui succéda.'[2] They had failed to maintain their republic, however, because of rigorous extremism. The English republic would have survived if patriots had steered a middle course between the servile policies of the royalists—which Hume, Boulay asserts, despite all his airs of impartiality, obviously supports—and the fanatic conduct of the extreme Left wing. Boulay admits, of course, that some harsh measures were necessary at the time:

> De quelque modération qu'on veuille se piquer, il serait difficile de nier que, la révolution faite, les chefs populaires n'eussent le droit de comprimer le parti royaliste, en le réduisant à l'impuissance de nuire. Quand un changement politique est fait dans l'intérêt et avec l'approbation du peuple, il est évident que toutes les mesures nécessaires à son affermissement sont non seulement autorisées, mais commandées par la justice, non cette justice distributive qui a lieu de particulier à particulier, mais cette justice générale qui préside à la conservation et au bonheur des sociétés, et dont les actes, toujours avantageux au grand nombre, paraissent quelquefois ne l'être pas au petit.[3]

Having gone this far, Boulay warns, leaders of revolution must be careful to go no farther. Harsh measures must be restricted to

[1] *Essai sur les causes qui, en 1649, amenèrent en Angleterre l'établissement de la République; sur celles qui devaient l'y consolider; sur celles qui l'y firent périr*. Par Boulay (de la Meurthe), Représentant du Peuple, Paris, An VII.

[2] Ibid., p. 4. [3] Ibid., p. 121.

what is absolutely necessary: 'Le grand art, dans les révolutions, est d'arriver à son but en faisant le moins de mal possible.'[1] The delicate trick of survival rests in giving only a half-turn to the political wheel, which must come to rest at precisely the right point before the necessity of reaction sets in. There are implications in the following passage which make it possible for us to understand how republicans were soon able to reconcile in their minds the Revolution and the arrival of Bonaparte—however much they were to murmur eventually at the title of Emperor:

Un des plus grands besoins de l'homme, et surtout d'un peuple quelconque, est celui du repos. . . . Un des premiers devoirs du gouvernement est donc d'assurer le repos du peuple, non pas ce repos que procure quelquefois le despotisme, et qui ressemble beaucoup à celui des tombeaux, mais ce repos qui se combine avec le mouvement dans la proportion la plus salutaire au corps politique comme au corps humain: repos qui n'est jamais que le fruit d'une liberté sagement et fortement réglée par la constitution et des lois.[2]

Disagreeing with Boulay de la Meurthe on several points but supporting basically his view that extremism could only harm the Revolution, the young republican Benjamin Constant also invoked Stuart history at this time to warn France of the dangers of counter-revolution.

First of all, Constant maintained, it was a mistake to say that the English revolution had failed. Confusion had arisen on this question because it had been assumed that the French and English revolutions had had similar goals:

Ce qui trompe quelquefois sur le succès des révolutions, que produisent les idées, c'est qu'on prend des accessoires pour le but principal. Ainsi, par exemple, on croit que la révolution d'Angleterre, en 1648, a échoué, parce que la royauté a été rétablie. Mais ce n'était pas l'idée de la république qui avait causé la révolution, c'était celle de la liberté religieuse. La république n'était qu'un accessoire, et l'accessoire a été manqué. . . .[3]

Even though an ideological identity did not exist, there were important lessons to be learned from Stuart history by those who wished to maintain the Republic in France:

[1] Ibid., p. 122. [2] Ibid., pp. 126–7.

[3] *De la force du gouvernement actuel de la France et de la nécessité de s'y rallier*, 1796, p. 95, note f.

La révolution d'Angleterre, qui avait été faite contre le papisme, ayant dépassé ce terme en abolissant la royauté, une réaction violente eut lieu, et il fallut, vingt-huit ans après, une révolution nouvelle, pour empêcher le papisme d'être rétabli. La révolution de France, qui a été faite contre les privilèges, ayant de même dépassé son terme, en attaquant la propriété, une réaction terrible se fait sentir, et il faudra, non pas, j'espère, une révolution nouvelle, mais de grandes précautions, et un soin extrême, pour s'opposer à la renaissance des privilèges.[1]

Stuart history shows, according to Constant, that the greatest difficulties are encountered when one attempts to restore to its just and moderate limits a revolution that has gone too far. The political pendulum swings an equal distance in both directions. Repressive reaction equal to former excess is a constant threat. It was to warn against the dangers of such a reaction that Benjamin Constant added his own remarks to Boulay's treatment of the English revolution. Boulay had described the oppressive extremes of the English revolutionaries; he had not, however, sufficiently emphasized the greater horrors perpetrated by those who had restored the monarchy. This was the lesson of Stuart history which, Constant urged, called for France's immediate attention:

L'état actuel de la république m'a paru un motif additionnel d'entreprendre cet ouvrage. Des hommes de tous les partis semblent annoncer, par leurs écrits et par leurs discours, qu'une transition serait désirable, que des conditions seraient possibles. Je veux prouver que des conditions entre la république et la royauté ne sont jamais que des stipulations mensongères pour désarmer ceux qu'on veut punir; que les transactions avec les rois sont toujours sans garantie; que la même impulsion qui porte à relever la puissance monarchique, porte inévitablement à renverser toutes les barrières dont on veut entourer cette puissance; et que la nation qui ne sait pas vivre sans un maître, sait encore moins le contenir.[2]

To prove these points, Constant proposed to quote authorities who could not be suspected of republican bias. He deftly agrees to leave aside Mrs. Macaulay's account and promises to use the royalists Clarendon and Hume. Even these, he implies, had found it impossible to veil the atrocities of the bloody Jefferies and Kirkes. What is more, the force of this English lesson had to be

[1] *Des réactions politiques*, An V, pp. 2–3.

[2] *Des suites de la contre-révolution de 1660 en Angleterre*, Paris, An VII, pp. viii–ix.

multiplied several times over for just application to circumstances in France since conditions in England had been of such a nature as to soften the violence of counter-revolution.

. . . quel lecteur attentif peut n'être pas frappé des différences qui distinguent cette situation de l'Angleterre de notre situation actuelle; différences qui rendraient le rétablissement de la royauté mille fois plus redoutable parmi nous? . . .

Prévenir la contre-révolution, maintenir la république, est donc l'intérêt commun de toutes les classes des Français. D'où viennent néanmoins cette indifférence universelle, ce sommeil profond, dans lequel le peuple paraît plongé, au milieu des dangers qui l'environnent?[1]

As we have already noted, not all republicans were as worried about the Stuart parallels as Constant and Boulay seem to have been. Commenting on Boulay's work, J.-B. Salaville in the same year made the objection that such a show of uneasiness was bad for the morale of republicans generally and politically most unwise. Boulay had no doubt been well-intentioned in his desire to warn the French by citing the failures of the English revolution. But however laudable his motives were, he was guilty in effect of telling his compatriots that much of what they had already accomplished was somehow invalid and that the course of the revolution would have to be changed. Was this not, Salaville asked, the very line preached by French royalists who also liked to talk about the revolutionary failures of the English? Had not Boulay unwittingly played into the hands of the counter-revolutionaries? 'On m'assure', Salaville asserted, 'que votre ouvrage produit un effet bien différent de celui que vous en avez attendu; qu'il décourage les vrais républicains, les sincères amis de la liberté; que d'un autre côté il ranime singulièrement les espérances des royalistes par l'espèce de conformité qu'ils croient apercevoir entre la révolution d'Angleterre et celle qui vient de s'effectuer chez nous et que c'est à leurs yeux une caution suffisante de la contre-révolution, après laquelle ils soupirent.'[2]

France's republicans had to be encouraged, not told that their efforts had been wasted. Royalists, on the other hand, had to be

[1] Ibid., pp. 77–80.

[2] J.-B. Salaville, *De la Révolution Française comparée à celle de l'Angleterre ou Lettre au Représentant du peuple Boulay (de la Meurthe), sur la différence de ces deux révolutions; pour servir de suite à l'ouvrage publié par ce Représentant sur celle de l'Angleterre*, Paris, An VII, p. 2.

stripped of any comforting and politically dangerous illusions. The best way to effect both of these salutary measures was, in Salaville's opinion, to prove that the English and French revolutions, which even republicans now seemed to see as 'parfaitement semblables', were in fact quite dissimilar and that nothing at all could be concluded from the one to the other except perhaps that re-establishment of the monarchy in France, in any form whatever, was henceforth an impossibility.

To begin with, the English would not have had a revolution had it not been for the disagreement over religion. This in itself, Salaville maintained, was enough to show that the French and English revolutions were quite different. England's quarrel over religion could have been resolved without a political revolution. France's revolution, on the other hand, had been a product of the vicious socio-political structure of the *ancien régime*; a political revolution had been absolutely necessary to change that structure.

Salaville repeated also—only a few months before the *Dix-huit brumaire*—the arguments so popular with those members of the Convention who during Louis' trial had rejected the Stuart parallel:

Je crois qu'on pourrait soutenir avec succès que la république n'a jamais existé en Angleterre. Cromwel était déjà roi lorsque Charles monta sur l'échafaud; on ne voit dans cet événement qu'un despote qui fait périr son compétiteur. La même chose est arrivée dans une foule de monarchies. . . . La royauté, cachée sous la dénomination du protectorat, n'en fut que plus absolue, et enfin on lui rendit jusqu'à l'hérédité en permettant à Cromwel de désigner son successeur.

En France la royauté fut abolie de droit et de fait, et aucun individu ne prit, sous une dénomination quelconque, la place de celui qui en était en possession: les généraux restèrent aux armées. . . . C'est un exemple qu'aucune révolution n'avait encore offert. . . .[1]

The Eighteenth Brumaire was, of course, and very soon, to spoil even this splendid example. Once again we are forced to think, with all our advantages of hind-sight, of Roederer and the warm sense of security he felt as he contemplated the two million copies of Voltaire, Helvétius, &c., which existed in France and which were to provide an insurmountable barrier to the religious revival. The makers of parallels frequently showed, it must be admitted, less innocence at least in their empirical prophecies. Innocence too

[1] Ibid., p. 26.

is perhaps the word which best characterizes Salaville's apparent inability to equate more closely the factor of religion in the seventeenth century with that of politics one hundred and fifty years later. It is an inability which he illustrates well in the following criticism of Boulay:

Au reste, citoyen représentant, ces factions ou ces partis qui, surtout dans votre ouvrage, paraissent avoir des traits frappants de conformité avec ceux que la révolution a créés chez nous, pourraient bien, d'après une analyse peu sévère, être trouvés très différents dans leurs principes et dans leur manière d'opérer; tout le monde a cru voir dans vos presbytériens, ceux qu'on a nommés chez nous *fédéralistes* ou *modérés* et dans vos *indépendants*, ceux qu'on a plus particulièrement désignés sous le nom de *jacobins*; mais le fait est que les presbytériens et les indépendants, conformément au génie de la révolution anglaise, étaient des bigots ou des fanatiques dont la grande affaire était la religion; la politique n'entrait que subsidiairement dans leurs vues et simplement comme moyen d'obtenir les changements qu'ils désiraient dans le culte; cela ne ressemble pas beaucoup à l'esprit qui a successivement animé nos divers partis.[1]

With the concluding thought that Salaville, even for his day, was perhaps too exclusive in his application of the terms *bigot* and *fanatic*, let us turn now to those whom he described as sighing for the counter-revolution and as excessively comforted by the belief that what had happened in England was happening even then in France.

2. *Waiting for General Monk*

The Abbé Duvoisin in his *Défense de l'ordre social contre les principes de la Révolution Française* (1798) gives, along with the usual history-inspired theocratic account of the origin of society, perhaps the most precise expression to the royalists' counter-revolutionary hopes at this time. God is the author of society in the sense that he made man a social creature. Hereditary monarchy gives the best demonstration of this natural form of government; the 'force of things' as evidenced in the reassuring example of Stuart history must inevitably return the French to their old *régime*:

[1] Ibid., pp. 29–30. Salaville rather than Mirabeau is sometimes credited with the translation of Milton's *Théorie de la royauté* (see *supra*, p. 119, note 3).

Semblable dans son origine à la république d'Angleterre, la république française lui ressemblera encore dans sa fin. Après la mort de Cromwel, l'Angleterre, également lasse de l'anarchie parlementaire et de la tyrannie protectoriale, n'espéra de repos qu'en plaçant sur le trône le fils de ce roi qu'elle avait vu périr sur un échafaud. Le Directoire qui a subjugué le corps législatif, qui a détruit la représentation nationale, qui a dépouillé le peuple de tous ses droits constitutionnels, le Directoire est le Cromwel de la république française. Il tombera, et avec lui disparaîtra tout ce qui reste de la république, les dénominations et les formes. . . .

Le gouvernement monarchique est un principe restaurateur pour les nations épuisées par les discordes civiles.[1]

Duvoisin then provides hints, drawn from his knowledge of Stuart history, as to how France's government would become legal once more:

Des généraux enthousiastes ou ambitieux, des armées séduites, ont prêté leur force au Directoire contre la nation. Au milieu de ces mêmes armées, une ambition plus noble et plus éclairée peut susciter un Monk, qui se verra le chef et le libérateur de la nation, du moment qu'il aura déployé l'étendard de la royauté. . . .

Si le passé peut nous fournir des conjectures pour l'avenir, l'histoire est pleine de traits qui semblent justifier les espérances des amis de la religion et de la royauté.[2]

That the counter-revolution would be the work of a few men was also the opinion of Joseph de Maistre in his famous *Considérations sur la France* published two years before Duvoisin's work in 1796.

En formant des hypothèses sur la contre-révolution, on commet trop souvent la faute de raisonner comme si cette contre-révolution devait être et ne pouvait être que le résultat d'une délibération populaire. . . . Quelle pitié! le peuple n'est pour rien dans les révolutions, ou du moins il n'y entre que comme un instrument passif. Quatre ou cinq personnes, peut-être, donneront un roi à la France. . . . Le peuple, si la monarchie se rétablit, n'en décrétera pas plus le rétablissement qu'il n'en décréta la destruction ou l'établissement du gouvernement révolutionnaire.[3]

Benjamin Constant had warned republicans that a counter-revolution would be bloody and vengeful and he had cited Hume's *History* to prove this. De Maistre, also writing with the pages of

[1] *Œuvres complètes de Duvoisin*, p. 1,302. [2] Ibid., pp. 1,307–8.
[3] *Œuvres complètes de J. de Maistre*, I. 113.

Hume's *Stuarts* open before him, sees the exact contrary to be the case. He soothingly reassured his republican enemies that the restoration would be forgiving:

C'est un sophisme très ordinaire à cette époque d'insister sur les dangers d'une contre-révolution, pour établir qu'il ne faut pas en revenir à la monarchie. . . .

Se persuaderait-on, par hasard, . . . que la monarchie, renversée par des monstres, doit être rétablie par leurs semblables? Ah! que ceux qui emploient ce sophisme lui rendent bien justice dans le fond de leur cœur! Ils savent assez que les amis de la religion et de la monarchie ne sont capables d'aucun des excès dont leurs ennemis se sont souillés. . . .[1]

The return of the monarchy, far from producing such evils, would put an end to the maladies afflicting France. Only the forces of destruction, he blithely asserted, would be destroyed. Were there foolish sceptics among his readers who still remained unconvinced? For these de Maistre appealed to his weightiest arguments, the evidence of history:

. . . croyons au moins à l'histoire, qui est la politique expérimentale. L'Angleterre donna, dans le siècle dernier, à peu près le même spectacle que la France a donné dans le nôtre. Le fanatisme de la liberté, échauffé par celui de la religion, y pénétra les âmes bien plus profondément qu'il ne l'a fait en France, où le culte de la liberté s'appuie sur le néant. Quelle différence, d'ailleurs, dans le caractère des deux nations, et dans celui des acteurs qui ont joué un rôle sur les deux scènes! Où sont, je ne dis pas les Hampden, mais les Cromwel de la France? Et cependant, malgré le fanatisme brûlant des républicains, malgré la fermeté réfléchie du caractère national, malgré les terreurs trop motivées des nombreux coupables et surtout de l'armée, le rétablissement de la monarchie causa-t-il, en Angleterre, des déchirements semblables à ceux qu'avait enfantés une révolution régicide? Qu'on nous montre les vengeances atroces des royalistes. Quelques régicides périrent par l'autorité des lois; du reste, il n'y eut ni combats, ni vengeances particulières. Le retour du roi ne fut marqué que par un cri de joie, qui retentit dans toute l'Angleterre; tous les ennemis s'embrassèrent. Le roi, surpris de ce qu'il voyait, s'écriait avec attendrissement: *N'est-ce point ma faute, si j'ai été repoussé si longtemps par un si bon peuple!* . . .[2]

After citing that impartial historian David Hume as his authority for the statement just quoted, de Maistre in aphoristic style defines the one great truth he wished the French to make theirs:

[1] Ibid., I. 121–2. [2] Ibid., I. 153–6.

'Le rétablissement de la monarchie, qu'on appelle contre-révolution, ne sera point une révolution contraire, mais le contraire de la révolution.'[1]

Stuart history properly interpreted was thus, according to de Maistre, a marvellous specific against the unfounded fears of even the guiltiest republicans. They had no need to be anxious about a future restoration of the monarchy. That Stuart history could give unique hope and assurance to long-suffering royalists is made equally clear by the last chapter in de Maistre's book, the title of which is self-explanatory and needs no further comment. It is called, quite simply, 'Fragment d'une histoire de la révolution française, par David Hume'.[2]

[1] Ibid., I. 157.

[2] See *supra*, p. 77, n. 1. Royalists were immensely pleased with this clever bit of editing (see, for example, the *Spectateur du Nord*, July-September 1797, pp. 93–94).

The influence of Hume on de Maistre is undeniably profound but defies simple analysis. He quotes the 'orthodox' Hume often, as, for example, in the following attack on *a priori* constitutions: 'Le principe que tout pouvoir légitime part du peuple est noble et spécieux en lui-même, cependant il est démenti par tout le poids de l'histoire et de l'expérience.' (*Œuvres complètes de J. de Maistre*, I. 286–7.) He also quotes Hume's authority on the origins of European government (I. 440–1); against the alleged superiority of English eloquence (I. 194, 527); on the Council of Trent (II. 28–29); against the Reformation: 'Hume qui, ne croyant rien ne se gênait pour rien, avoue sans compliment que le véritable fondement de la réforme fut l'envie de "voler l'argenterie et tous les ornements des autels".' (II. 413, 521); against so-called English tolerance in religion: 'L'Angleterre elle-même, qui prêche si fort la tolérance aux autres nations, comment a-t-elle pris patience lorsqu'elle a cru sa religion attaquée? Hume lui a reproché son Inquisition contre les Catholiques, *plus terrible*, dit-il, que celle d'Espagne, puisqu'elle exerçait la *même tyrannie en se débarrassant des formes*.' (III. 359); against the Enlightenment heroes Bacon and Locke (IV. 272, 375; VI. 44–45, 56–57); on the worthy rôle of the Church in preserving civilization during the Dark Ages (VI. 473–4), &c.

On the other hand, it is also clear that David Hume represented for de Maistre perhaps the most frightening example possible of human wickedness: 'Qui n'a pas entendu parler de David Hume, *cui non notus Hylas*? Je crois qu'à tout prendre, le dix-huitième siècle, si fertile dans ce genre, n'a produit aucun ennemi de la religion qu'on puisse lui comparer. Son venin glacé est bien plus dangereux que la rage écumante de Voltaire. . . . Si jamais parmi les hommes qui ont pu entendre la prédication évangélique, il a existé un véritable athée (ce que je ne m'avise pas de décider), c'est lui. Jamais je n'ai lu ses ouvrages anti-religieux sans une sorte d'effroi, sans me demander à moi-même comment il était possible qu'un homme, à qui rien n'avait manqué pour connaître la vérité, avait pu néanmoins descendre jusqu'à ce point de dégradation. Toujours il m'a semblé que l'endurcissement de Hume, et son calme insolent, ne pouvaient être que la dernière peine d'une certaine révolte de l'intelligence, qui exclut la miséricorde, et que Dieu ne châtie plus qu'en se retirant.' (III. 386–7). The long letter against Hume from which this quotation is taken, along with several other

There was little doubt in the minds of most royalists that the French revolution was going exactly the way of its English predecessor. The only question that remained involved the length of time the whole inevitable process would take. Was it necessary, for example, for the French Republic to pass through the Cromwell phase? Wasn't it possible that the Cromwell era had already occurred? We remember that Duvoisin had seen the Directoire in 1798 as Cromwell although, earlier still, others had maintained that Robespierre was Cromwell and that counter-revolutionary France had to make itself ready to welcome its General Monk.

Charles de Villers expressed the belief in 1798 that this last opinion attributed possibly too much importance to Robespierre

passages in de Maistre's works, indicates a quite extraordinarily ambivalent attitude to the Scottish historian whose political conservatism attracted traditionalists with much the same force as his religious scepticism repelled them. De Maistre nevertheless insisted that the David Hume *Fragment* remain in later editions of his noted counter-revolutionary work.

Also influenced by Hume but in a more straightforward manner is Joseph de Maistre's fellow theoretician of the counter-revolution, Louis de Bonald. De Bonald and de Maistre shared identical views concerning the prophetic significance of English history and similar views on nearly every other subject as well: 'Est-il possible, Monsieur,' de Maistre wrote to his friend in 1818, 'que la nature se soit amusée à tendre deux cordes aussi parfaitement d'accord que votre esprit et le mien! C'est l'unisson le plus rigoureux, c'est un phénomène unique. . . .' (From Turin, 18 July 1818, ibid., XIV. 137.) De Bonald too attacks *a priori* politics and maintains that constitutions are as natural as gravity and can never be 'pocketable'. History is the sole validating principle of all political speculation. Like de Maistre, de Bonald also attacks Hume for his irreligion but cites his authority against Calvinism, English republicanism, &c. (See, for example, *Œuvres complètes de M. de Bonald*, Paris, 1859, II. 224: 'Hume remarque avec raison qu'en Angleterre, depuis sa dernière révolution, l'indépendance et la liberté publiques, d'où naît la sécurité individuelle, sont plus incertaines et plus précaires.') He too applauds Hume's impartiality and fairness to France: 'M. Hume remarque que dans la rivalité des deux nations, les Français haïssent beaucoup moins les Anglais que les Anglais ne les haïssent' (ibid., II. 509). De Bonald even found Hume less 'English' in his prejudices than the historian Lingard, who was not only a Catholic but a member of the Catholic clergy (ibid., III. 917). He also invokes Hume's authority against the physical determinism of Montesquieu (ibid., II. 28–29) and against divorce (ibid., II. 113, 121, 125).

In many ways the use of these orthodox themes taken from Hume by de Maistre, Duvoisin, de Bonald and others, although it represents a fresh reading of the Scottish historian in the counter-revolutionary context, consists of little more than a tiresome repetition of material already exploited to the limit by such historical conservatives and *anti-anglomanes* of the pre-revolutionary period as Gerdil, Bergier, the editors of the *Mémoires de Trévoux*, Lefebvre de Beauvray, &c. It would deserve a more lengthy treatment here were it not for the fact that we have already given a good deal of attention to the writings of these others in our first chapter.

who is described in a dialogue by de Villers as newly arriving in hell and greeting the English Protector as follows:

Robespierre: 'Depuis que je suis arrivé ici, je vous cherche. La grande ressemblance de nos destinées, la conformité de nos projets, de nos moyens, de nos talents, nous porte à nous rapprocher et à nous rappeler ensemble les grands événements dont nous avons été les ressorts.'

Much offended, Cromwell disagrees and states that Robespierre is nothing more than a 'petit populacier, un intrigant des halles':

Robespierre: 'Cependant on me compare hautement à vous sur la terre.'
Cromwell: 'C'est que sur la terre on a toujours la manie des comparaisons; et que la plupart de ceux qui vous assimilent à moi, ne me connaissent que de nom. . . . Si jamais la France a un Cromwel, ce ne sera qu'un général d'armée, grand capitaine, homme d'état, orateur, et heureux par-dessus tout.'
Robespierre: 'Et qui donc sera cet heureux? Car il faut bien que tout cela finisse par un maître, comme on dit.'
Cromwell: 'Le temps nous l'apprendra. . . .'[1]

Time would indeed tell. Mallet du Pan, perhaps the wisest spokesman of the royalists at this time, indicated in December 1798 that the answer to de Viller's question was close: 'Le Directoire', he stated, 'se trouve au période où se trouva Cromwel lorsqu'il chassa le parlement. Il n'y a pas de Cromwel . . . en France, mais l'analogie des situations nécessite celle du dénouement.'[2]

Not long after this, however, he began to express important doubts about the wisdom of counting on such parallels: 'Vouloir porter la lumière dans l'histoire de la révolution par de semblables moyens, c'est prouver qu'on n'en connaît pas réellement le vrai caractère.'[3] Not only were there bad analogies involved; politically speaking, the parallels made the counter-revolution seem just a little too easy: 'Proposez à l'individu qui a sauvé sa vie et son grabat des échafauds de Robespierre, proposez-lui de se confier de nouveau, au hasard des événements! Le ressort des âmes une fois brisé, il faut un concours rare de circonstances pour le retremper.'[4]

[1] 'Dialogue entre Cromwel et Robespierre', *Le Spectateur du Nord; journal politique, littéraire et moral*, Hambourg, July–September 1798, VII. 76–85.

[2] *Mercure Britannique ou notices historiques et critiques sur les affaires du tems*, par J. Mallet du Pan, Londres, 25 December 1798, II. 23.

[3] Ibid., 25 April 1799, III. 31.

[4] Ibid., 10 August 1799, III. 481.

The Stuart parallel was especially harmful if, as seemed to be the case, it encouraged royalists merely to sit back and wait complacently for the English restoration to be duplicated automatically in France. Much active preparation had to be carried out:

Les éléments d'un parti royaliste immense existent; mais sans chefs, sans concert, sans argent, sans armes, sans pouvoir, sans lieux de rassemblement, le parti même est encore à former.

Les quatre cinquièmes des Français détestent leur gouvernement; mais, observe très bien David Hume, l'erreur des royalistes anglais sous la république était de regarder comme des partisans de la monarchie, tous ceux qui se plaignaient du nouveau régime. . . .

Le Roi de France a moins d'ennemis à vaincre que d'indifférents et d'égoïstes à décider; il s'agit moins pour lui de mettre en activité les royalistes que d'*en faire*: sa victoire la plus utile sera celle qui diminuera le nombre des oppositions à son autorité.[1]

Mallet du Pan, himself an active agent of the counter-revolution, is probably one of the few royalists at this time who, for various reasons, felt it was necessary to abandon the fashionable parallel. Speaking of this current 'abus des similitudes', he made the following objection:

Le ciel préserve les cabinets de l'Europe et les conseils de Louis XVIII de se laisser abuser par ces parallèles romanesques. Un écolier apercevra ces rapports grossiers qui semblent identifier les deux révolutions; mais c'est le tableau de leur dissemblances qui doit former l'étude de quiconque travaille à l'anéantissement de la République Française.

Il ne fut pas nécessaire d'armer l'Europe, ni de faire descendre en Angleterre des forces étrangères, pour opérer une restauration, dont les matériaux étaient tous assortis et disposés. Lorsqu'on les confronte avec la poussière où sont réduits les usages et les institutions de l'ancienne France; lorsqu'on voit la noblesse, le clergé, les gentilshommes anglais demeurés presque tous sur leurs foyers, conservant leurs titres, leurs terres, la considération et l'affection publiques; lorsqu'on oppose l'intensité de l'esprit religieux, les mœurs, les coutumes, les lois, l'ordre judiciaire, le caractère national et celui de l'armée en Angleterre, au bouleversement universel sous lequel la France est ensevelie; lorsqu'on entend Cromwel appeler *Milord* le seigneur de la chambre haute qui se présentait devant lui, on jette au feu les parallèles, et l'on découvre que ce pourrait bien être une question toute neuve que celle des mobiles composés auxquels la France devra son retour à sa première existence.[2]

[1] Ibid., III. 482–3. [2] Ibid., III. 483–5.

Mallet du Pan's warning about the potential dangers of the *rapprochements* seems to have done little good. English-French parallels, almost all foretelling the imminent appearance of a French General Monk, became the hackneyed prediction and commonplace hope of much *émigré* literature and threatened even to grow to the proportions of an elegant literary genre. Sometimes the treatment was very light indeed as can be seen in the following passage, judged by its author P.-J.-B. Nougaret as a 'morceau curieux et piquant, digne d'être considéré comme un fragment de notre histoire':

'Lorsque les partis divisaient les îles britanniques, dit Hume; que les citoyens étaient armés les uns contre les autres, que le sang y coulait de toutes parts, deux citoyens se présentèrent devant le roi, avec des visages pâles, maigres et tout à fait effrayants; figures si étranges et si négligées, si singulièrement vêtues et accoûtrées qu'elles excitaient tout à la fois les plus graves contenances à rire, et les cœurs les plus joyeux à s'attrister.'

N'est-ce pas là le portrait de nos hideux jacobins, sales, dégoûtants, vestes courtes, appelées carmagnoles, longues culottes ou pantalons, cheveux noirs, gras, luisants, bonnet de poil ou de laine rouge, comme celui des galériens, ou couleur du sang qu'ils aimaient tant à verser, de larges moustaches, et, encore maigres, hâves de l'abstinence forcée qu'ils avaient faite dans l'état d'abjection et de misère dont ils sortaient?[1]

Admittedly, we are not dealing here with the most ponderous examples of the genre and Nougaret derived few great prophecies from his observation that both Round Heads and Jacobins had the bad taste to be cosmetically below standard. Other parallels pretended, however, to greater things. Chateaubriand in his *Essai sur les Révolutions* (1797) states that the Jacobins in executing Louis XVI had directly imitated the English execution of Charles I: 'J'ose dire plus: si Charles n'avait pas été décapité à Londres, Louis n'eût vraisemblablement pas été guillotiné à Paris.'[2] Supporting such claims, Rivarol complained at the turn of the century that only the leftist leaders had taken the trouble to learn from previous revolutions. He affirmed, even, that he had personally seen members of the Constituent Assembly in 1789 reading Stuart

[1] P.-J.-B. Nougaret, *Parallèle de la Révolution d'Angleterre en 1642, et celle de France*, Metz, p. 13.

[2] *Œuvres complètes*, Paris, 1834, I. 153.

history for the first time 'pour y voir comment se conduisit le long parlement avec Charles Ier'.[1]

The Eighteenth Brumaire, immediately viewed by many royalists as a first step in the long-awaited fulfilment of the great prophecy, rallied immensely the hopes of those who had been carefully tending their parallels: 'Les royalistes pensent à Monk', wrote Rivarol, 'et sont plus partisans de Bonaparte que les démocrates, et en attendant il est adulé comme Necker, Lafayette et Pétion.'[2] Even the head of the counter-revolutionary party, Louis XVIII, at first expressed the hope that Napoleon would be magnanimous enough to play the rôle of Monk. On Bonaparte's refusal to be so generous and after a later counter-proposal from the French *consul à vie* that Louis XVIII renounce his claim to the throne in exchange for certain indemnities, the latter turned to an equally common practice of the day, that of calling Bonaparte a Cromwell. As the French monarch in exile explained to Cardinal Maury in 1803: '. . . si Cromwel, après avoir conquis la Jamaïque, l'avait offerte à Charles II, celui-ci ne pouvait l'accepter: c'eût été reconnaître l'existence légale du Protecteur. Tel est mon cas. . . .'[3]

Bonaparte's own 'republican' admirers felt that all the modern parallels were too confining when it came to describing the greatness of the French Consul. Lacretelle *le jeune*, for example, made this sentiment dramatically clear in 1802:

> Son étonnante destinée l'a fait plus d'une fois comparer à tous les hommes extraordinaires qui ont paru sur la scène du monde. Je n'en vois aucun dans ces derniers siècles qui ait de la ressemblance avec lui.
>
> Quelques observateurs superficiels ou malveillants l'ont, dit-on, rapproché de Cromwel. Quelques insensés espèrent en lui un nouveau Monk. La France et l'Europe lui trouvent une conformité plus frappante avec César.[4]

The truth is, of course, that the epithet Cromwell was still seen as highly insulting by everyone in France at this time. J.-B. Say, writing in *La Décade* in 1801, indignantly took to task Sir Francis

[1] *Pensées inédites de Rivarol*, Paris, 1836, pp. 80–81. [2] Ibid., p. 92.

[3] Letter of 10 August 1803, from Warsaw; in *Correspondance diplomatique et mémoires inédits du Cardinal Maury*, annotés et publiés par Mgr Ricard, Lille, 1891, II. 271.

[4] *Parallèle entre César, Cromwell, Monck et Bonaparte: Fragment traduit de l'Anglais* (published anonymously by Charles-Jean-Dominique de Lacretelle, Paris, 1802), p. 2.

d'Ivernois for having made the 'comparaison si usée et si fausse de notre Bonaparte avec Cromwel. Ce Cromwel', he added, 'est un nom dont on a toujours essayé de flétrir les amis de toute espèce de réforme. Pendant la guerre d'Amérique, il fut donné à Washington; dès avant notre révolution il devint l'apanage de Fox, et il nous semble que pendant l'Assemblée constituante, on en qualifia Lafayette qui le méritait moins encore que les autres.'[1]

Decidedly the tag of Caesar was better. There would be no rest ahead for the French if Bonaparte was a Cromwell. Cromwell inspired fear; Bonaparte inspired admiration and hope. 'L'un a détruit,' wrote Lacretelle *le jeune* in 1802, 'l'autre répare.'

Conclusion

We shall end here our considerations on the influence of Stuart history, and more particularly David Hume's *History of the Stuarts*, in France from the *ancien régime* to the counter-revolution.

Although the high point of critical French interest in the English revolutionary period had passed by the time Napoleon made his dramatic appearance on the scene, the force of Hume's enormous influence over a subject which was so remarkably suited to exploitation by pundits and prophets of the Right was by no means entirely spent. Rivarol before his death in 1801 gave a fair indication of how it would be possible, for some time yet, to continue playing the merry game of parallels. His French projection of Stuart history, well worth quoting here, provided in fact an advance outline of many similar future speculations which events of the following thirty years seemed to justify: 'Il y a une singulière parité entre la Révolution d'Angleterre et celle de France; le long parlement et la mort de Charles Ier; la convention et la mort de Louis XVI; et puis Cromwel et puis Bonaparte. S'il y a une restauration aurons-nous un autre Charles second mourant dans son lit et un autre Jacques second quittant son royaume, et puis une dynastie étrangère? C'est une idée tout comme une autre que cette prévision.'[2]

Whatever the merits of Hume's presentation of the English revolution, it is undeniable that the case he put to the French during the critical years from roughly 1760 to 1800 had had

[1] *La Décade*, XXVIII. 281. [2] Rivarol, op. cit., p. 111.

profound and far-ranging effects. It is no exaggeration to say that his particular interpretation of that revolution, in a sense almost written for France, had become an integral part of the French historical consciousness and had imposed etiological categories which the vast majority of Frenchmen on the political Right and even a fair number on the moderate Left felt obliged to follow when giving explanation to what were seen as similar political processes in their own country. Admittedly, much of the detailed use made of Hume's *History* was purely polemical. That the greater part of it cannot be dismissed as such, however, seems obvious. We have only to look into a work such as *De l'usage et de l'abus de l'esprit philosophique durant le dix-huitième siècle* by J.-E.-M. Portalis to see the permanent importance of Hume's total impact at this time on the thinking of French rightists.

Portalis' book was written between 1798 and 1800. It did not exert the influence or enjoy the reputation of Chateaubriand's more frothy production, the *Génie du Christianisme*, perhaps because its message came too late. It appeared first as a posthumous publication in 1820, thirteen years after its author's death. It nevertheless represents one of the few truly important end-of-the-century French rejections of the Enlightenment and was motivated not by the cramped and brutal spirit of some of Joseph de Maistre's formulas, but rather by a certain wise science of man which Hume himself, on whose writings some of it is based, would probably not have disavowed.

Portalis approved of the eighteenth century's love of philosophical history and Hume, he felt, had surely written his history of England 'en philosophe'. The French *philosophes*, on the other hand, had not produced an equivalent history of France. Voltaire, it is true, had boasted of writing philosophical history but had succeeded, like Gibbon, only in writing history that was anti-ecclesiastical.[1]

The eighteenth century had prided itself on having no religious superstitions. It had nevertheless ended up by being politically superstitious. It was an eighteenth-century superstition, not shared by Hume, to imagine that any political act was good provided it was committed in favour of liberty: 'En politique, on canonise tous les crimes des factions, dans la crainte de blesser les droits des peuples. . . . On a osé faire un reproche à Hume de sa

[1] Portalis, op. cit., seconde édition, Paris, 1827, II. 24–26.

partialité dans les jugements qu'il porte contre les excès commis pendant les révolutions d'Angleterre.'[1]

Thinking no doubt of histories like that of Catherine Macaulay, so highly praised by the Mirabeaus, Condorcets, and Brissots, Portalis pointed out that not only had revolutionary opinion dared to question Hume's impartiality, it had attempted as well to make history over again into an arsenal of political propaganda: 'Quelques philosophes ne regardent plus les faits historiques que comme une base sur laquelle on peut bâtir les systèmes les plus arbitraires.' But history, wrote the man of the Concordat, could not be denied, nor could its true function which was to present 'un immense recueil d'expériences morales faites sur le genre humain'[2] be frustrated.

Such history damns forever all *a priori* political theorists: 'Toutes nos fausses idées, tous nos principes exagérés sur les droits de l'homme et sur son indépendance, toutes nos déclamations contre les institutions civiles et politiques, ont leur première source dans l'idée que nous nous sommes formée d'un prétendu état de nature. . . . Voulons-nous être philosophes? Abdiquons tout système; ne vaguons pas dans la région des chimères. . . .'[3]

History never confronts us with a state of nature; society does not exist by reason of any social pact. It cannot therefore be dissolved at will like a business arrangement simply because of an alleged breach of contract. Society, in short, is not a pact but a fact:

La société est, à la fois, un mélange et une succession continue de personnes de tous les âges et de tous les sexes, que l'intérêt, le hasard, que mille relations diverses rapprochent ou séparent à chaque instant. . . . L'ordre social a pour objet le bien permanent de l'humanité. Il est fondé sur les rapports essentiels et indestructibles qui existent entre les hommes. Il ne dépend pas d'une institution libre et arbitraire: il est commandé par la nature; . . . il a sa source dans la constitution de notre être, et il ne peut finir qu'avec elle.[4]

Men are united in society because such is the wish of nature which made them social creatures. Of course nothing is immutable; time brings the necessity of change and adaptation, but a society, in its transformations, must be very careful that it does not put its

[1] Ibid., II. 28. [2] Ibid., II. 39.
[3] Ibid., II. 299. [4] Ibid., II. 301.

very existence to the test: 'Il faut donc des maux bien grands, bien extrêmes, bien intolérables, pour autoriser l'idée d'un changement toujours funeste, toujours marqué par les plus violents orages, pour légitimer une révolution qui attaque les sources mêmes de toute légitimité.'[1] Politics is not the art of the ideal but of the real: 'N'allons donc pas nous repaître de fausses idées, et gardons-nous de chercher dans les institutions humaines, une perfection dont elles ne sont pas susceptibles.'[2] If man were a totally reasonable creature such perfection would be possible. The sad truth is, however, that he is not so constituted. The human cogitative aspect is probably of less importance in our practical behaviour than the sensitive parts of our nature. Man's sentiment, his irrationalism, is as basic and natural to him as his reason. Politically man is a creature of emotion, habit, opinion, and prejudice. When political reforms prove necessary, these less flexible elements must not be forgotten. Reforms must be approached with circumspection: one does not tolerate everything, nor must one destroy everything:

Comme l'homme ne change point de nature en changeant de mœurs, il faut changer les formes sans abandonner les principes qui naissent de la nature même de l'homme.

Le propre du faux esprit philosophique est de nous faire méconnaître les principes. On imagine que des institutions qui ont pu dégénérer n'ont jamais été utiles. . . . On regarde comme des fraudes politiques tous les établissements religieux ou profanes auxquels on ne croit plus. . . .[3] On ne veut que des vérités et des maximes absolues,

[1] Ibid., II. 334. [2] Ibid., II. 363.

[3] Portalis, though fully aware of Hume's religious scepticism, believed along with a number of other French conservatives that Hume regretfully bore his disbelief as an unwholesome burden. He makes some of the same distinctions we have already encountered in Trublet and opposes religious sceptics to the eighteenth-century atheists: 'A la vérité, ces hommes ne blâment point les institutions religieuses. Ils veulent qu'on les laisse à ceux dont elles remplissent l'âme; ils ont même l'air de se plaindre de leur philosophie, qui les empêche d'y croire. Nous sentons, disent-ils, qu'on est malheureux quand on ne croit pas, et que rien ne peut combler, dans le cœur, le vide qu'une foi vive aux vérités de la religion remplirait. Ainsi J.-J. Rousseau disait à ses amis: *J'aimerais mieux être dévot que philosophe*. Ainsi Hume, après une des scènes touchantes et sublimes, dont la religion seule peut nous offrir le spectacle, s'écriait: "Si je n'avais jamais douté, je serais bien plus heureux!"' (ibid., II. 191–2). Portalis is not the only victim at this time of a purely fictional anecdote concerning Hume, the 'Story of La Roche', contributed by Henry Mackenzie to the Scottish publication *The Mirror* in 1779 but which, perhaps not too strangely, received wide circulation in France after the Revolution. We find it reproduced in *La*

comme s'il y en avait de telles dans la politique et dans la législation. On remplace par de vaines spéculations les leçons de l'expérience. . . . On ne veut pas se dire que nous avons été façonnés par ces institutions et par ces lois qui, aujourd'hui décriées et affaiblies, se survivent à elles-mêmes dans les habitudes qu'elles nous ont fait contracter. . . .

On compromet la civilisation d'un peuple, si, sous prétexte de lui donner une meilleure police, on ne laisse rien subsister de ce qui l'a civilisé; on le replonge dans la barbarie en l'isolant de toutes les choses qui l'en ont fait sortir.[1]

It is not difficult to detect the essentials of Hume's own science of human nature in Portalis' important manifesto of revolt against some of the more transient bursts of illumination emitted by the *siècle des lumières*. One also notes, of course, the influence of Burke; but it should be remembered that Burke himself was probably influenced by Hume to an extent greater than his Christian Whig principles cared to admit. Soon, completing the image, and contributing to the destruction of what were seen as Enlightenment excesses in non-political fields, a new Hume was to enter France via Kant's Germany. Hume the philosopher as opposed to Hume the *philosophe* was destined to make the world almost forget that there had ever been a *Tacite des Anglais*.

But Hume's radically empirical *History*, which some modern scholars have tended to view as entirely unrelated to his radically empirical philosophy, was not yet completely dead in France.

Décade in 1796 (VIII. 554–62); the *Bibliothèque britannique* in 1798 (VII. 199–215); and in the *Spectateur du Nord* (VII. 297–312) also in 1798.

The long sentimental anecdote which shows the sceptic Hume weeping almost religiously at his own incredulity (so different a picture from Joseph de Maistre's icy sketch!) helped to reinforce occasional efforts to rehabilitate the whole Hume in the eyes of those orthodox thinkers who warmly appreciated his 'politics' but who were dismayed by his 'philosophy'. Similarly his 'social' ethics—often opposed to the 'egotistic' moral philosophy of the materialists—had invariably seemed a redeeming feature in the eyes of such men as Gerdil, Bergier, Barruel, de Bonald, and Portalis. Hume's moral views were even adduced on one occasion as sufficient proof that he was not the guilty party in the quarrel with Rousseau! Of course, the essential feature of Hume's image in the eyes of the Right remained his political conservatism. Religious disbelief was not always seen, moreover, as incompatible with royalist sentiments. (See J.-J. Mounier, *De l'influence attribuée aux Philosophes, aux Francs-Maçons et aux Illuminés sur la Révolution de France*, Tübingen, 1801, p. 70.) Hobbes versus Milton was a good case in point and, although Hume might very well be an *incrédule*, he was, in the words of the *Spectateur du Nord*'s translator, *le meilleur des incrédules*.

[1] Portalis, op. cit., II. 503–4, 512.

Quite to the contrary, after the Restoration, during the reign of Louis XVIII, its importance seemed still great enough to ultra-royalists for several of their number to set about editing a completely revised translation preceded by a long study of Hume's life and works by the French academician Vincent Campenon.[1] Needless to say, the *Avertissement* of this new edition begins by reverently calling Hume nothing less than 'l'historien le plus impartial et le plus judicieux qui ait jamais existé'.[2]

Other editions of this work were to follow but as France's political events evolved towards more liberal goals, Hume's great historical reputation and influence fell. A different, although not necessarily a more serious, conception of history was being born. Guizot in 1826 triumphantly proclaimed the new era: 'De nos jours . . . l'histoire de la révolution d'Angleterre a changé de face: Hume était en possession de former sur son compte l'opinion de l'Europe; et, malgré l'appui de Mirabeau, les déclamations de Mistress Macaulay n'avaient pu ébranler son autorité.'[3]

Europe, Guizot was happy to announce, had at last recovered its independence. Two pages farther on, he voiced the judgement that seems to have endured among historians ever since: 'Hume ne suffit plus à personne.'

[1] *Histoire d'Angleterre depuis l'invasion de Jules-César jusqu'à la révolution de 1688 par David Hume et depuis cette époque jusqu'à 1760 par Smollett.* Traduite de l'anglais. Nouvelle édition, revue, corrigée et précédée d'un *Essai sur la vie et les écrits de D. Hume*, par M. Campenon de l'Académie Française, Paris, 1819.

[2] Ibid., I. v.

[3] *Histoire de la Révolution d'Angleterre depuis l'avenèment de Charles Ier jusqu'à la restauration de Charles II*, Première partie, Paris, 1826, I. xvii.

INDEX OF NAMES AND TITLES

Note: Occasionally short title only is given. Modern editions of collected works and Convention *Opinions* of Chapter IV (Bibliothèque Nationale series 8⁰ Le37. 2. G.) are not listed.

Accord de la Révélation et de la Raison contre le divorce (Chapt de Rastignac), 92.
Actes des Apôtres, 90, 96–99.
Adresse à l'ordre de la noblesse de France (D'Antraigues), 103, 143.
Alembert, Jean Le Rond d', 26–27, 30, 40–41, 47.
Algarotti, Count Francesco, 12.
l'Ami du Roi, 40.
'Anagramme-Epigramme sur deux chefs de parti très connus', 90.
Analogies de l'histoire de France et d'Angleterre (de Bonald), 77.
l'An deux mille quatre cent quarante (Mercier), 60, 62.
l'Angleterre instruisant la France, 7, 104.
Annales patriotiques, 119.
Annales politiques, civiles et littéraires (Linguet), 40–41, 104.
Année littéraire, 10, 21–23, 40–41.
Antraigues, Emmanuel de Launay, *comte* d', 95–96, 103, 143.
Aristotle, 4.
Artois, Comte d', 1, 79, 101.
Autobiography (Gibbon), 5.
Avis à la Convention Nationale sur le jugement de Louis XVI (de Montjoie), 130–2.
Azéma, Michel, 142.

Bacon, Sir Francis, 88, 161.
Bailly, E.-L.-B., 139.
Balestrier de Canilhac, Abbé L.-S., 70.
Bancal des Issarts, Jean-Henri, 86, 118, 136.
Barailon, Jean-François, 140.
Barnave, Joseph, 95, 104.
Barruel, Abbé Augustin, 171.
Basset de la Marelle, Louis, 34.
Baudin, Pierre-Charles-Louis, 139.
Baudot, Marc-Antoine, 144.
Bayle, Moïse-Antoine-Pierre-Jean, 144.
Beccaria, C. de, 12.
Belot, Mme Octavie-Guichard Durey de Meynières, 9.
Bergier, Abbé Nicolas-Sylvestre, 28, 41–46, 47, 49, 67, 88, 92, 162, 171.
Berkeley, George, 35.
Bernardin de Saint-Pierre, Jacques-Henri, 64.
Berry, Duc de (*see also* Louis XVI), 1.
Bertrand de Molleville, Antoine-François, 122–3.
Bezard, François-Siméon, 142.
Bibliothèque britannique, 171.
Bibliothèque de l'homme public, 70.
Bibliothèque de Madame la Dauphine (Moreau), 15.
Bibliothèque des Sciences et des Beaux-Arts, 5, 17–18, 20.
Bibliothèque d'un homme de goût (Chaudon), 12.
Birotteau, J.-B.-B.-H., 139, 146.
Blackstone, Sir William, 71.
Bodin, P.-J.-F., 139.
Bolingbroke, Henry St. John, 1st Viscount, 24.
Bonald, Louis de, 3, 36, 44, 77, 162, 171.
Bonaparte, Napoléon, 102, 144, 145, 154, 166–7.
Bordas, Pardoux, 139.
Bossuet, Jacques-Bénigne, 38, 45, 57, 88, 90, 102, 132.
Boswell, James, 59.
Boufflers, Marie, *comtesse* de, 9, 65.
Boulay de la Meurthe, Antoine, 152–4, 155, 156, 158.
Bourlet de Vauxcelles, Abbé Simon-Jacques, 30.
Bradshaw, John, 102.
Brissot de Warville, Jacques-Pierre, 55–56, 59, 62–64, 67, 86, 105–14, 116, 118, 119, 130, 138, 152, 169.

Brosses, Charles de, 10.
Brutus, 112, 137, 142–4, 147.
Brutus (Voltaire), 104.
Buckingham, George Villiers, 1st Duke of, 56.
Buffier, Claude, 33.
Burke, Edmund, vii–viii, 27, 58, 70, 72, 78, 95, 114, 119, 128, 152, 171.
Burnet, Gilbert, 11, 21.
Burney, Fanny, 2.
Buzot, François-Nicolas-Léonard, 136.

Caesar, Julius, 166–7.
Calas, Jean, 60.
Calonne, Charles-Alexandre de, 94.
Cambacérès, Jean-Jacques de, 4.
Campan, Mme Jeanne-Louise Genet, 121–2.
Campenon, François-Nicolas-Vincent, 172.
Captivité et derniers moments de Louis XVI, 124.
Carra, Jean-Louis, 86, 119.
Cartouche, Louis-Dominique Bourguignon, *called*, 57.
Castilhon, J.-L., 17.
Catilina (Crébillon), 57.
Cazalès, Jacques de, 104, 109, 130, 132.
Cecilia (Burney), 2.
Cerutti, J.-A.-J., 15, 71.
Chabroud, Jean-Baptiste-Charles, 102.
Chapt de Rastignac, Abbé Armand-Anne-Auguste-Antonin-Sicaire de, 92.
Charlemagne, 94.
Charles I, King of England, vii, ix-xii, xiv-xvii, 14, 15, 19, 21, 25, 52, 56, 57, 60, 61, 62, 63, 66, 77, 79, 89, 96, 97, 99, 100, 101, 102, 104, 107, 108, 109, 110, 111, 112, 120–50, 157, 165, 166, 167, 172.
Charles II, King of England, 90, 98, 104, 112, 139, 166, 167, 172.
Charles IX, King of France, 126.
Charles IX (M.-J. Chénier), 104.
Chasset, Charles-Antoine, 139–40.
Chastellux, F.-J., *marquis* de, 4, 9, 10, 27.
Chateaubriand, F.-R. de, 79-80, 165, 168.
Chaudon, Dom Louis-Mayeul, 12, 35.
Chaumette, Pierre-Gaspard, 126.
Chénier, Marie-Joseph, 113.
Clarendon, Edward Hyde, 1st Earl of, ix, 120, 155.
Clarissa Harlowe (Richardson), 92.
Cledel, Etienne, 144.
Clément, Amable-Augustin, 150.
Clermont-Tonnerre, Stanislas, *comte* de, 105–13, 116, 138.
Cléry, Jean-Baptiste-Antoine Hanet, *called*, 121, 125, 126.
Collection complète des oeuvres de l'Abbé de Mably, 54.
Common Sense (Paine), 84.
Complete History of England (Smollett), 4, 16, 17.
Comte de Strafford (Lally-Tollendal), 104.
Condé, Louis-Joseph de Bourbon, *prince* de, 124.
Condorcet, Antoine-Nicolas Caritat, *marquis* de, 70, 85, 86, 114, 169.
Congreve, William, 24.
Considérations sur la France (de Maistre), 30, 77, 159–62.
Considérations sur les principaux événements de la Révolution Française (Mme de Staël), 123.
Considérations sur l'esprit et les mœurs (Sénac de Meilhan), 7.
Constant de Rebecque, Benjamin, 154–6, 159.
Constitutions des principaux états de l'Europe et des Etats-Unis de l'Amérique (Delacroix), 95.
Contrat social (Rousseau), 3, 36, 49.
Corday d'Armont, Marie-Charlotte, 150.
Corneille, Pierre, 30.
Correspondance diplomatique du Cardinal Maury, 166.
Correspondance d'un habitant de Paris (d'Escherny), 114.
Correspondance entre quelques hommes honnêtes (Servan), 30, 75–76.
Correspondance littéraire (Grimm), 3, 23–25.
Correspondance politique (Mallet du Pan), 73.
Correspondance universelle (Brissot), 56.
Court de Gébelin, Antoine, 12.
Crébillon, Prosper Jolyot de, 57.
Cromwel (Maillet-Duclairon), 57.

Cromwel ou le général liberticide (Tardy), 119, 144.
Cromwell, Oliver, xiv, xvii, 20, 21, 32, 39, 56–58, 60–62, 96, 98–99, 100, 102, 103, 107, 108, 110, 111, 119, 120, 126, 127, 131, 134–7, 140, 141, 142–5, 146, 147, 148, 157, 159, 160, 162–3, 164, 166, 167.

Damiens de Gomicourt, Auguste-Pierre, 15.
Danton, Georges-Jacques, 102, 144.
Dauphin of France (son of Louis XV), 1.
Décade philosophique, littéraire et politique, 85, 119, 143, 145, 152, 166–7, 170–1.
Defence of the English People (Milton), 119, 158.
Défense de l'ordre social contre les principes de la Révolution Française (Duvoisin), 158–9.
Défense de Louis XVI (Cazalès), 130.
Défense des émigrés français (Lally-Tollendal), 130.
Défense du Siècle de Louis XIV (Voltaire), 17.
De J.-J. Rousseau considéré comme l'un des premiers auteurs de la Révolution (Mercier), 85.
Delacroix, J.-V., 95.
De la félicité publique (Chastellux), 27.
De la force du gouvernement actuel de la France (Constant), 154.
De l'Allemagne (Mme de Staël), 7.
De la manière d'écrire l'histoire (Mably), 55.
De la philosophie de la nature (Delisle de Sales), 28.
De la Révolution Française comparée à celle de l'Angleterre (Salaville), 156–8.
De l'esprit (Helvétius), 24.
De l'Etat de la France, présent et à venir (Calonne), 94.
Deleyre, Alexandre, 144.
De l'homme (Helvétius), 25, 30.
De l'influence attribuée aux Philosophes, aux Francs-Maçons et aux Illuminés sur la Révolution de France (Mounier), 171.
Delisle de Sales, J.-C. Izouard, *called*, 27–28, 60, 121.
De l'origine des principes religieux (Meister), 69–70.
De l'usage et de l'abus de l'esprit philosophique (Portalis), 168–71.
Descamps, Bernard, 147.
Descartes, René, 2.
Des droits et des devoirs du citoyen (Mably), 55.
Des Emigrés Français ou Réponse à Lally-Tollendal (Leuliette), 130, 151.
Des lettres de cachet (Mirabeau), 52–54, 114.
Desmoulins, Camille, 109, 119.
Des premiers principes du système social appliqués à la révolution présente (Meister), 69.
Des principes et des causes de la révolution en France (Sénac de Meilhan), 73–74.
Des prisons d'état (Mirabeau), 52.
Des réactions politiques (Constant), 155.
Des révolutions dans les grandes sociétés civiles (Servan), 75.
Des suites de la contre-révolution de 1660 en Angleterre (Constant), 155–6.
Destutt de Tracy, Antoine-Louis-Claude, *comte*, 152.
'Dialogue entre Cromwel et Robespierre' (de Villers), 163.
Dialogues concerning Natural Religion (Hume), 27.
Dictionary (Sheridan), 118.
Dictionnaire anti-philosophique (Chaudon), 35.
Dictionnaire philosophique (Voltaire), 39.
Dictionnaire philosophique de la religion (Nonnotte), 39.
Dictionnaire social et patriotique (Lefebvre de Beauvray), 31–33.
Diderot, Denis, 26, 27, 47.
Différence du patriotisme national chez les François et chez les Anglois (Basset de la Marelle), 34.
Diogène moderne ou le désapprobateur (Castilhon), 17.
Discours choisis sur divers sujets de religion et de littérature (Maury), 88.
Discours contre la Défense de Louis Capet (Carra), 86.
Discours et opinions de Cazalès, 104.

Discours et projet de décret de Henri Bancal, 86.
Discours philosophique sur l'homme (Gerdil), 36–38.
Discours sur la divinité de la religion chrétienne (Gerdil), 36.
Discours sur la sanction royale (Maury), 90.
'Discours sur la science sociale' (Cambacérès), 4.
Dubois-Crancé, E.-L.-A., 142.
Du Deffand, Marie de Vichy Chamrond, *marquise*, 6, 24.
Dugour, A.-J., 96, 133, 145.
Dumouriez, Charles-François, 102.
Du Pape, (de Maistre), 39.
Durival, J.-B., 114.
Duvoisin, Abbé Jean-Baptiste, 45, 158–9, 162.

Elizabeth I, Queen of England, x, xii, xiv, 39.
Eloge de Milord Maréchal (d'Alembert), 40–41.
Emile (Rousseau), 32, 36, 49.
Encyclopédie Méthodique, 13, 27, 41.
Enquiry concerning Human Understanding (Hume), 4, 23.
Enquiry concerning the Principles of Morals (Hume), 29.
Episodes de la Terreur, 125.
Erreurs de Monsieur de Voltaire (Nonnotte), 39.
Escherny, François-Louis, *comte* d', 114.
Esprit de l'Histoire (Ferrand), 71.
Esprit des Lois (Montesquieu), 5, 27, 52, 65, 67.
Essai polémique sur la religion naturelle (Duvoisin), 45.
Essai sur la manière d'écrire et d'étudier l'histoire (Levesque), 85.
Essai sur la tragédie (Delisle de Sales), 60.
Essai sur la vie et les écrits de D. Hume (Campenon), 172.
Essai sur les causes qui amenèrent en Angleterre l'établissement de la République (Boulay de la Meurthe), 152–4, 156–8.
Essai sur les Mœurs (Voltaire), 22, 27, 39.
Essai sur les Révolutions (Chateaubriand), 80, 165.
Essai sur l'histoire des comices de Rome, &c. (Gudin de la Brenellerie), 65.
Essais pour servir d'introduction à l'histoire de la Révolution française (Sallier-Chaumont de la Roche), 74.
Etude sur la souveraineté (de Maistre), 3.
Etudes de la Nature (Bernardin de Saint-Pierre), 64.

Fairfax, Thomas, 3rd Baron, 102.
Falkland, Lucius Cary, 2nd Viscount, 97, 104.
Faure, Pierre-Joseph-Denis-Guillaume, 139.
Fénelon, François de Salignac de La Mothe, 90, 92.
Ferguson, Adam, 71.
Ferrand, Antoine-François-Claude, *comte*, 36, 71–72.
Formey, Reverend Samuel, 12, 43.
Foucault, Etienne, 150.
Fox, Charles James, 167.
'Fragment d'une histoire de la révolution française par David Hume' (de Maistre), 77, 161–2.
la France plus qu'Angloise (Linguet), 104.
François de Neufchâteau, Nicolas-Louis, 57.
Frederick the Great, King of Prussia, 47.
Fréron, Elie-Catherine, 10, 12, 21–23, 40.

Gaillard, G.-H., 6.
Galilei, Galileo, 88.
Garat, D.-J., 5.
Garilhe, François-Clément Privat de, 135–6.
Gassendi, Pierre, 33.
Gazette littéraire de l'Europe, 4, 11.
Gazette Nationale, ou le Moniteur universel, 114, 117–19, 145.
Génie du Christianisme (Chateaubriand), 152, 168.
Genovesi, Antonio, 12.
Gerdil, Sigismond-Hyacinthe, 36–38, 45, 47, 88, 91, 92, 162, 171.

Gertoux, Brice, 144.
Gibbon, Edward, 3, 5, 121, 168.
Girard, Antoine-Marie-Anne, 138.
Girot-Pouzol, Jean-Baptiste, 139.
Graffigny, Françoise de, 24.
Grégoire, Abbé Henri, 102.
Grimm, F.-M., *baron* de, 3, 23–24, 25.
Grosley, Pierre-Jean, 61.
Gudin de La Brenellerie, Paul-Philippe, 64–65.
Guide de l'histoire (Née de la Rochelle), 12.
Guillaume Tell (Lemierre), 104.
Guillermin, Claude-Nicolas, 143.
Guillon, Abbé Marie-Nicolas-Silvestre, 102–3, 119.
Guiraudet, Charles-Philippe-Toussaint, 113–14.
Guiter, Joseph-Antoine-Sébastien, 136.
Guizot, François, 172.
Gustavus III, King of Sweden, 65.
Guyomar, Pierre-Marie-Augustin, 139.
Guyton-Morveau, Louis-Bernard, 144.

Hampden, John, xiii, 59, 97, 160.
Hébert, Jacques-René, 126.
Helvétius, Claude-Adrien, 10, 13, 24–25, 29–30, 152, 157.
Henri IV, King of France, 6.
Henriette-Marie de France, 110, 132.
Henry VIII, King of England, x, 21.
Hentz, Nicolas-Joseph, 142.
Herodotus, 64.
Herring, Thomas, Archbishop of Canterbury, 14.
Herschel, Sir Frederick William, 5.
Hertford, Francis Seymour Conway, 1st Earl of, 1.
Hippocrates, 4.
Histoire abrégée de la session de 1828, 76–77.
Histoire d'Angleterre (Bertrand de Molleville), 122–3.
Histoire de Cromwel (Dugour), 145.
Histoire de la Révolution d'Angleterre (Guizot), 172.
Histoire de la Révolution de France et de l'Assemblée Nationale (Montjoie), 93–94.
History of England (Hume), viii–xvii, 1–2, 4, 9, 11, 13–14, 18, 22, 24, 28–29, 30, 31, 46, 49, 50, 52, 55, 56, 62, 64–65, 71, 93–94, 111, 114–19, 155, 159, 168, 171–2.
History of England (Macaulay-Graham), 54, 56, 58–60, 62, 86, 108–11, 113–19, 155, 169.
History of the Rebellion and Civil Wars in England (Clarendon), ix, 120, 155.
Hobbes, Thomas, 33, 37, 171.
Holbach, P.-H.-T., *baron* d', 29, 41, 45, 46, 47.
Holland, G.-J., 29, 41.
Hudibras (Butler), 96, 98.

Ichon, Pierre-Louis, 146.
'Idea of a Perfect Commonwealth' (Hume), 30.
Index librorum prohibitorum, 36.
Introduction à la Révolution Française (Barnave), 95.
Ireton, Henry, 102, 111.
Ivernois, Sir Francis d', 167.

Jacquin, *procureur du Roi à Darney*, 45.
James I, King of England, x, xi–xii, 59, 93, 113, 118, 151.
James II, King of England, 17–18, 20, 40–41, 56, 61, 63, 94, 113, 114, 118, 139, 167.
Jean-Bon Saint-André, André Jeanbon, *called*, 144.
Jefferies (*or* Jeffreys), George, 155.
Joannet, Abbé Jean-Baptiste-Claude, 35.
Johnson, Samuel, 24, 59.
Journal Britannique (Maty), 17.
Journal Chrétien, 35–36.
Journal de ce qui s'est passé à la tour du Temple (Cléry), 121, 125–6.
Journal d'économie politique, de morale, et de politique (Roederer), 151–2.
Journal de l'Abbé de Véri, 52, 66.
Journal de M. Suleau, 101–2.
Journal de Paris, 145.
Journal des débats et des décrets, 90, 146.
'Journal des livres suspendus', 64.
Journal des Savants, 114.
Journal du Licée de Londres, 56, 62–64.
Journal Encyclopédique, 7, 10–11, 16–17, 56, 58–60.

Journal Etranger, 14–15.
J.-P. Brissot à Stanislas Clermont, 106–7, 116.
Jullien, Marc-Antoine, 146, 147–48.

Kant, Immanuel, 29, 171.
Keith, George, 10th Earl Marischal, 40.
Kersaint, Armand-Guy-Simon de Coetnempren, *comte* de, 138–9.
Kirke, Colonel Percy, 155.

Laclos, Pierre Choderlos de, 2.
Lacretelle, Charles-Jean-Dominique de, 123–4, 166, 167.
Lafayette, Marie-Joseph Motier, *marquis* de, 102, 150, 166, 167.
La Harpe, Jean-François de, 103.
Lally-Tollendal, Trophime-Gérard, *comte* de, 94, 95, 97, 104, 113, 129–30, 132, 151.
Lambert, Charles, 139.
Laud, William, Archbishop of Canterbury, xii–xiii, 56, 108.
La Vauguyon, Antoine de Quélen, *duc* de, 120.
Le Blanc, Abbé Jean-Bernard, 6, 8, 16, 25.
Le Chapelier, Isaac-René-Guy, 70.
Lefebvre de Beauvray, Claude-Rigobert, 31–33, 47, 162.
Le Long Parlement et ses crimes (Comtesse de Montrond), 99–101.
Le Mercier de La Rivière, Pierre-Paul-François-Joachim-Henri, 3.
Letter to the Earl of Stanhope (Macaulay-Graham), 114.
Lettre à Monsieur Rabaut de Saint-Etienne (Servan), 75.
Lettre de Charles Ier (François de Neufchâteau), 57.
Lettre de M. Cerutti adressée au café de Foix, 71.
Lettres à Sophie Volland (Diderot), 47.
Lettres de Madame Roland 1788–93), 118.
Lettres philosophiques (Voltaire), 2, 5, 24, 30, 33, 88, 104–5.
Lettres sur l'imagination (Meister), 70.
Leuliette, Jean-Jacques, 130, 151.
Levesque, J.-J.-G., 85.
Life of Johnson (Boswell), 59.
Lingard, John, 162.
Linguet, S.-N.-H., 40, 103.
Livy, 7, 74.
Locke, John, ix, 2, 24, 35, 37, 60, 80, 110, 161.
Lolme, J.-L. de, 71.
Londres (Grosley), 61.
Louchet, Louis, 143.
Louis XIV, 6, 12, 17, 20.
Louis XV, 79.
Louis XVI, 52, 61, 68, 78, 79, 86, 95, 96, 98, 100–1, 102, 103, 104, 111, 119, 120–50, 157, 165, 167.
Louis XVII, 126.
Louis XVIII, 71, 164, 166, 172.
Louvet, Pierre-Florent, 137.
Louvet de Couvrai, Jean-Baptiste, 136, 144.
Ludlow, Edmond, 111.
Lycée ou cours de littérature (La Harpe), 103.

Mably, Abbé Gabriel Bonnot de, 54–55, 64, 65.
Macaulay-Graham, Catherine, 54, 56, 58–60, 62, 86, 108, 109, 110, 111, 113–19, 130, 155, 169, 172.
Mackenzie, Henry, 170.
Mailhe, Jean-Baptiste, 78, 130, 133–4, 137, 149.
Maillet-Duclairon, Antoine, 57.
Maistre, Joseph de, 3, 30, 36, 38, 77, 88, 92, 159–62, 168, 171.
Malesherbes, Chrétien-Guillaume de Lamoignon de, 9, 65–67, 121, 124.
Malesherbes (Delisle de Sales), 121.
Mallet du Pan, Jacques, 73, 163–5.
Malouet, Pierre-Victor, 49.
Manon Lescaut (Prévost), 129.
Marat, Jean-Paul, 139.
Marec, Pierre, 135.
Marey, Nicolas-Joseph, 139.
Marie-Antoinette, 15, 101, 121–2, 124, 126.
Martin, Jean-Marie, 126.
Mary Stuart, 15, 61.
Mary Tudor, 39.
Maty, Dr. Matthew, 17.
Maury, Abbé Jean-Siffrein, 36, 37, 88–92, 166.
Mazade-Percin, Julien-Bernard-Dorothée de, 136.
Mazarin, Jules, 89.
M. de Tracy à M. Burke, 152.

Meister, J.-H., 69.
Mélanges de littérature (Suard), 49.
Mélanges de philosophie, de morale et de littérature (Meister), 70.
Mémoire de Lally-Tollendal, ou Seconde Lettre à ses Commettans, 94, 104.
Mémoire justificatif pour Louis XVI (Dugour), 96, 133.
Mémoires de Brissot, 59, 62, 113.
Mémoires de l'Abbé Morellet, 9.
Mémoires de l'Institut National des Sciences et Arts, 4.
Mémoires de Madame Roland, 118–19.
Mémoires de M. Cléry, 126.
Mémoires de Montlosier sur la Révolution française, 90.
Mémoires de Trévoux, 19–21, 24, 27, 49, 162.
Mémoires historiques et politiques du règne de Louis XVI (Soulavie), 52, 79.
Mémoires historiques sur le 18e siècle (Garat), 5.
Mémoires secrets pour servir à l'histoire de la dernière année du règne de Louis XVI (Bertrand de Molleville), 122.
Mémoires sur la librairie et sur la liberté de la presse (Malesherbes), 65–66.
Mémoires sur la vie privée de Marie-Antoinette (Mme Campan), 121–2.
Mennesson, J.-B.-A.-P., 137.
Mercier, Louis-Sébastien, 60, 61, 85, 116, 119.
Mercure Britannique (Mallet du Pan), 163–4.
Mercure de France, 2, 5, 125.
Mes Souvenirs (Moreau), 124.
Meynard, François, 139.
Miller, Andrew, 14.
Milton, John, 24, 54, 109, 110, 119, 142, 158, 171.
Mirabeau, Honoré-Gabriel Riquetti, *comte* de, 15, 38, 52–54, 55, 62, 86, 88, 90–92, 102, 113–16, 118, 119, 158, 169, 172.
Mirabeau's letters during his residence in England, 114.
Mirror, The, 170.
Mohammed, 32.
Monk, General George, 57, 80, 131, 139, 159, 162, 165, 166.
Montague, George, 14.
Montaigne, Michel de, 33.
Montesquieu, Charles de Secondat, *baron* de La Brède et de, 5, 27, 33, 52, 65, 67, 71, 72, 74, 75, 152, 162.
Mont-Gilbert, François-Agnès, 146.
Montjoie, Félix-Louis-Christophe de, 93–94, 115, 130–2.
Montlosier, François-Dominique de Reynaud, *comte* de, 90.
Montrond, Angélique-Marie Darlus du Taillis, *comtesse* de, 99–100, 103.
Montrose, James Graham, 1st Marquis of, 102.
More, Sir Thomas, 36.
Moreau, Jacob-Nicolas, 15, 124.
Morellet, Abbé André, 9.
Morisson, Charles-François-Gabriel, 139.
Mort de César (Voltaire), 104.
Mounier, Jean-Joseph, 94–95, 104, 171.
My Own Life (Hume), 13–14, 18, 50.

Naigeon, J.-A., 27, 46.
Natural History of Religion (Hume), 23, 37, 42.
Necker, Jacques, 79, 89, 102, 121, 126–9, 132, 138, 166.
Necker, Mme Suzanne Curchod, 65.
Née de la Rochelle, Jean-François, 12.
Newton, Sir Isaac, 68.
Nonnotte, Claude-François, 39, 47, 92.
Nougaret, Pierre-Jean-Baptiste, 165.
Nouveaux mélanges de Mme Necker, 65.
Nouveaux Mémoires de l'Académie de Berlin, 13.
Nouvelles Observations sur les comités des recherches (Clermont-Tonnerre), 107.
Nyon, Jean-Luc, 121.

Observateur Français à Londres (de Gomicourt), 15–16.
Œuvres complètes de Stanislas de Clermont-Tonnerre, 107–12.
Œuvres complettes de M. Helvétius, 30.
Œuvres de Louis XVI, 61, 120, 124–5.
Œuvres de M. Linguet, 40.
Œuvres diverses de M. Cerutti, 15.
'Of Miracles' (Hume), 23.
'Of Suicide' (Hume), 46, 62.
'Of the Balance of Power' (Hume), 34.

'Of the Immortality of the Soul' (Hume), 46, 62-63.
'Of the Original Contract' (Hume), 37–38, 50, 91–92.
Opinion de L.-M. Revellière-Lépeaux, 73.
Opinion sur la souveraineté du peuple (Maury), 90–92.
Oraison funèbre de Henriette-Marie de France (Bossuet), 132.
Orléans, Pierre-Joseph d', 11, 12, 62.

Paine, Thomas, 70, 84, 92, 139, 152.
Paradise Lost (Milton), 142.
Parallèle de la Révolution d'Angleterre et celle de France (Nougaret), 165.
Parallèle des Révolutions (Guillon), 102–3, 119.
Parallèle entre César, Cromwell, Monck et Bonaparte (C.-J.-D. de Lacretelle), 166–7.
Paris pendant la révolution ou le nouveau Paris (Mercier), 116–17.
Patriote Français (Brissot), 106, 109, 110–11, 112, 113, 152.
Pensées inédites de Rivarol, 165–7.
Pétion de Villeneuve, Jérôme, 166.
Peuple anglais bouffi d'orgueil, de bière et de thé, 34.
Peysonel (*or* Peyssonnel), Charles de, 70.
Philippeaux, Pierre-Nicolas, 141.
Philosophical Essays (Hume), 2, 12, 23, 27, 34, 63.
Pinet, Jacques, 138.
Pitt, William, 114.
Plaidoyer pour Louis XVI (Lally-Tollendal), 129–30.
Plantagenets (Hume), 9, 18, 22–25, 26, 27, 28.
Plutarch, 118.
Political Discourses (Hume), 2, 8, 23, 64, 89.
Politique tirée de l'Ecriture Sainte (Bossuet), 38.
Polybius, 4.
Portalis, Jean-Etienne-Marie, 168–71.
Précis historique de la Révolution Française (C.-J.-D. de Lacretelle), 123–4.
Prévost, Abbé Antoine-François, 8–9, 25, 114, 129.
Prost, Claude-Charles, 144.
Provence, Comte de (*see also* Louis XVIII), 1.
Prunelle-Lière, Léonard-Joseph, 139.
Pym, John, 59.

Quelle est la situation de l'Assemblée Nationale? (d'Antraigues), 95–96.
Quotidienne, La, 8.

Rabaut Saint-Etienne, Jean-Paul Rabaut, *called*, 75, 136, 147.
Racine, Jean, 30.
Rapin-Thoyras, Paul de, ix, 11, 12, 17, 55, 104.
Rapport et Projet de Décret (Mailhe), 78, 130, 133–4.
Rapport sur les trente-deux membres de la Convention (Saint-Just), 86–87.
Raynal, Abbé Guillaume-Thomas, 65.
Recherches sur les causes qui ont empêché les Français de devenir libres (Mounier), 94–95.
Recueil philosophique, 46.
Reflections on the Revolution in France (Burke), 78, 128.
Réflexions philosophiques sur le Système de la Nature (Holland), 29.
Réflexions politiques sur la Révolution (Barnave), 104.
Réflexions posthumes sur le grand procès de Jean-Jacques avec David, 29.
Réflexions présentées à la nation française sur le procès de Louis XVI (Necker), 121, 126–30.
Réflexions sur mes entretiens avec M. le Duc de La Vauguyon (Louis XVI), 120.
Règne de Richard III (Walpole), 120–1.
Répertoire général des sources manuscrites de l'histoire de Paris (Tuetey), 145, 150.
Réplique de J.-P. Brissot à Stanislas Clermont, 108–11.
Réponse de J.-J. Rousseau au Roi de Pologne, 57.
Rétablissement de la Monarchie Françoise (Ferrand), 71–72.
Revellière-Lépeaux, L.-M., 73.
Révolutions de France et de Brabant (Desmoulins), 109, 119.
Richard III, King of England, 120.
Richardson, Samuel, 14.

Riffard St. Martin (*see* Saint-Martin).
Rights of Man (Paine), 70, 84, 92–93, 152.
Rivarol, Antoine, 165–6, 167.
Robertson, Reverend William, 7, 9, 24, 71.
Robespierre, Maximilien-François-Isidore de, 64, 84–85, 96, 102, 103, 116, 144, 148–9, 162–3.
Rochester, John Wilmot, 2nd Earl of, 24.
Roederer, Pierre-Louis, *comte*, 151–2, 157.
Roland, Mme Jeanne-Manon Phlipon, 86, 118–19.
Rosanbo, Louis Le Peletier de, 121.
Rousseau, J.-J., 3, 6, 10, 12, 26, 29, 32, 37, 45, 48–49, 54, 55, 57, 67, 84, 85, 112, 118, 143, 152, 170, 171.
Royou, Abbé T.-M., 40–41, 47.
Rühl, Philippe-Jacques, 142.

Saint-John, Oliver, 111.
Saint-Just, Louis-Antoine-Léon de, 86–87, 144, 148.
Saint Louis, King of France, 6, 88.
Saint-Martin, François-Jérôme-Riffard, 139.
Salaville, J.-B., 156–58.
Sallier-Chaumont de la Roche, G.-M., 74.
Sallust, 7, 74.
Saumaise, Claude de, 119.
Say, Jean-Baptiste, 166–7.
Séances des écoles normales, 3.
Seconde Lettre de M. de Lally-Tollendal à M. Burke, 95.
Semaine-Sainte, 118.
Sénac de Meilhan, Gabriel, 7, 74.
Sergent, Antoine-François, 141.
Servan, Joseph-Michel-Antoine, 30, 74–76.
Shaftesbury, Anthony Ashley Cooper, 3rd Earl of, 24, 33.
Shakespeare, William, 24, 30.
Sheridan, Thomas, 118.
Sidney, Algernon, ix, 110, 143.
Sieyès, Abbé Emmanuel-Joseph, 81–83, 113.
Smith, Adam, 128.
Smollett, T. G., 4, 16–17, 172.
Société des Jacobins: recueil de documents, 110.
Soulavie, Jean-Louis Giraud, 6, 52, 79.
Spectateur du Nord, 161, 163, 171.
Staël-Holstein, Anne-Louise-Germaine Necker, *baronne* de, 7, 123.
Stanhope, Charles, 3rd Earl, 114.
Stanislas I, King of Poland, 57.
Stone, George, Primate of All Ireland, 14.
'Story of La Roche' (Mackenzie), 170–1.
Strafford, Thomas Wentworth, 1st Earl of, xiii, xiv, 14, 56, 102, 103–4, 108, 109.
Stuarts (*Hume*), vii–xvii, 1, 8–12, 13–21, 22–23, 25, 27, 28, 31–33, 39, 40–41, 50, 64, 66, 71, 76–77, 78, 92, 96–108, 113, 114, 121–2, 125–6, 128–31, 134, 151, 153, 160, 167–9.
Suard, J.-B.-A., 5, 49.
Suleau, François-Louis, 101–102.
Supplément à la manière d'écrire l'histoire (Gudin de La Brenellerie), 65.
Sur la dernière réplique de J.-P. Brissot (Clermont-Tonnerre), 111–12.
Sur la destruction des Jésuites en France (d'Alembert), 26.
Sur l'admission des femmes au droit de cité (Condorcet), 114.
'Sur les rapports des idées religieuses et morales avec les principes républicains' (Robespierre), 84–85.
Sur l'instruction publique (Condorcet), 85.
Système de la Nature (d'Holbach), 29.

Tableau historique de la littérature française (M.-J. Chénier), 113.
Tacitus, 1, 3, 4, 7, 9, 10, 28, 74, 100, 117, 119, 171.
Tardy, M.-L., 119, 144.
Tarquins, 137, 139, 146.
Théorie du pouvoir politique (de Bonald), 3.
Theory of Moral Sentiments (Smith), 128.
Thomas, Jean-Jacques, 139.
Thou, Jacques-Auguste de, 74.
Thucydides, 7.
Tom Jones (Fielding), 92.

Traité de la composition et de l'étude de l'histoire (Soulavie), 6.
Tressan, Louis-Elisabeth de La Vergne, *comte* de, 12.
Trublet, Abbé Nicolas-Charles-Joseph, 35, 41, 47, 170.
Tudors (Hume), 9, 18, 21–23, 28, 43–45.
Turgot, Anne-Robert-Jacques, *baron* de l'Aulne, 9, 29, 47–52, 54.

Vauxcelles (*see* Bourlet de Vauxcelles).
Velly, Abbé Paul-François, 6, 74.
Vergniaud, Pierre-Victurnien, 136–7, 143.
Véri, Abbé Joseph-Alphonse de, 52, 66.
Vertot, Abbé René Aubert de, 74.
Vies des hommes illustres (Plutarch), 118.
Villers, Charles-François-Dominique de, 162–3.
Volland, Sophie, 47.
Volney, C.-F.-C., *comte* de, 3.
Voltaire, François-Marie Arouet de, 2, 3, 5, 6, 10, 11, 12, 15, 17, 21, 22, 23, 24, 25, 27, 28, 30–34, 35, 39, 42, 45, 57, 63, 85, 88, 104–5, 152, 157, 161, 168.
'Vues sur les moyens dont les Représentans pourront disposer' (Sieyès), 81–83.

Walpole, Horace, 14, 24, 120.
Washington, George, 167.
Wedderburn, Alexander, 2.
Wilkes, John, 30, 51.
William of Orange, 11.
Wolsey, Thomas, 21.

Xenophon, 7.

Zaïre (Voltaire), 34.